LaTeX

A Document Preparation System

Leslie Lamport

Digital Equipment Corporation

Illustrations by Duane Bibby

Addison-Wesley Publishing Company

Reading, Massachusetts • Menlo Park, California
Don Mills, Ontario • Wokingham, England • Amsterdam
Sydney • Singapore • Tokyo • Mexico City • Bogotá • Santiago • San Juan

This documentation was prepared with LaTeX and reproduced by Addison-Wesley from camera-ready copy supplied by the author.

TeX is a trademark of the American Mathematical Society

This book describes LaTeX Version 2.09, released 19 April 1986. Any discrepancy between this description and the behavior of this or any later release of Version 2.09 is an error. There are only minor differences between this release and earlier releases of Version 2.09.

Library of Congress Cataloging-in-Publication Data

Lamport, Leslie.
    LaTeX: A Document Preparation System.

    Includes index.
    1. LaTeX (Computer system) 2. Computerized typesetting. I. Title.
Z253.4.L38L35   1985   686.2'2544   85-19994
ISBN 0-201-15790-X

ISBN 0-201-15790-X
181920-AL-94939291

Contents

List of Tables

List of Figures

Preface

The LaTeX document preparation system is a special version of Donald Knuth's TeX program. TeX is a sophisticated program designed to produce high-quality typesetting, especially for mathematical text. LaTeX adds to TeX a collection of commands that simplify typesetting by letting the user concentrate on the structure of the text rather than on formatting commands. In turning TeX into LaTeX, I have tried to convert a highly-tuned racing car into a comfortable family sedan. The family sedan isn't meant to go as fast as a racing car or be as exciting to drive, but it's comfortable and gets you to the grocery store with no fuss. However, the LaTeX sedan has all the power of TeX hidden under its hood, and the more adventurous driver can do everything with it that he can with TeX.

LaTeX represents a balance between functionality and ease of use. Since I implemented most of it myself, there was also a continual compromise between what I wanted to do and what I could do in a reasonable amount of time. The first version of LaTeX was written about three years ago. A gradual evolution has worn away many rough edges, but there have been no radical changes. LaTeX's small group of initial users were pleased with it and suggested many improvements.

I wish to thank the many people whose comments and complaints about LaTeX and about the preliminary versions of this book have been so helpful, including: Todd Allen, Robert Amsler, David Bacon, Stephen Barnard, Barbara Beeton, Per Bothner, David Braunegg, Daniel Brotsky, Chuck Buckley, Pavel Curtis, Michael Fischer, Russell Greiner, Andrew Hanson, Michael Harrison, B. J. Herbison, Calvin W. Jackson, Mark Kent, Kenneth Laws, David Kosower, Tim Morgan, Mark Moriconi, Stuart Reges, Flavio Rose, A. Wayne Slawson, David Smith, Michael Spivak, Mark Stickel, Gary Swanson, Mary-Claire van Leunen, Mike Urban, Mark Wadsworth, Gio Wiederhold, and Rusty Wright.

The following also gave aid and comfort: SRI International's Artificial Intelligence Laboratory provided the computer facilities on which LaTeX was developed. Richard Furuta helped me make the transition to a new computer system. Chris Torek helped with the SLITeX font files. Arthur M. Keller helped create LaTeX's special fonts. Howard Trickey helped with the fonts and the picture-drawing commands, and designed the BIBTEX bibliography styles. Marshall Henrichs, Lynn Ruggles, and Richard Southall taught me what little I know about typography; they are responsible for whatever is right with the document styles. Oren Patashnik implemented BIBTEX. David Fuchs helped in many ways, providing me with the latest versions of TEX and answering many of my questions. Peter Gordon guided the production of this book and helped make LATEX accessible to a wider audience.

Finally, I want to express my special thanks to Donald Knuth. In addition to making LATEX possible by creating TEX, he answered all my questions, even the stupid ones, and was always willing to explain TEX's mysteries.

L. L.

Palo Alto, California
July, 1985

CHAPTER 1
Getting Acquainted

With modern computers, typesetting is not just for books and documents aimed at a wide audience. Reports, proposals, memos, and tonight's dinner menu can all be made more attractive and easier to read with professional-quality typesetting. LaTeX is a computer program that makes it easy for an author or typist to typeset his document.

LaTeX is available for a wide variety of computer systems. The versions that run on these different systems are essentially the same; an input file created according to the directions in this book should produce the same output with any of them. However, how you actually run LaTeX depends upon the computer system, and certain options may be available on some systems and not on others. For each computer system, there is a short companion to this book entitled something like *Local Guide to LaTeX for the Kludge-499 Computer* containing information specific to that system. This companion will be called the *Local Guide*. It is distributed with the LaTeX software.

1.1   How to Avoid Reading This Book

Many people would rather learn about a program at their computer terminal than by reading a book. There is a small sample LaTeX input file named `small.tex` that shows how to prepare your own input files for typesetting simple documents. It also contains the name of another file that tells how to run LaTeX on your input file and print the result. Before reading any further, you might want to examine `small.tex` with a text editor and modify it to make an input file for a document of your own, then run LaTeX on this file and see what it produces. The *Local Guide* will tell you how to find `small.tex` on your computer and may contain information about text editors. Be careful not to destroy the original version of `small.tex`; you'll probably want to look at it again.

The file `small.tex` is quite short, having just one or two screens full of text, and it shows how to produce only very simple documents. There is a longer file named `sample.tex` that contains more information. If `small.tex` doesn't tell you how to do something, you can try looking at `sample.tex`.

If you prefer to learn more about a program before you use it, read on. Everything in the sample input files is explained in the first two chapters of this book.

1.2   How to Read This Book

While `sample.tex` describes many of LaTeX's features, it is still only about 175 lines long, and there is a lot that it doesn't explain. Eventually, you will want to typeset a document that requires more sophisticated formatting than you can obtain by imitating the two sample input files. You will then have to look in this book for the necessary information. You can read the section containing the information you need without having to read everything that precedes it. However, all the later chapters assume that you have read Chapters 1 and 2. For example, suppose you want to set one paragraph of a document in small type. Looking up "type size" in the index or browsing through the table of contents will lead you to Section 5.8.1, which talks about "declarations" and their "scope"—simple concepts that are explained in Chapter 2. It will take just a minute or two to learn what to do if you've already read Chapter 2; it could be quite frustrating if you haven't. So, it's best to read the first two chapters now, before you need them.

LaTeX's input is a file containing the document's text together with commands that describe the document's structure; its output is a file of typesetting instructions. Another program must be run to convert these instructions into printed output. With a high-resolution printer, LaTeX can generate book-quality typesetting.

This book tells you how to prepare a LaTeX input file. The current chapter discusses the philosophy underlying LaTeX; here is a brief sketch of what's in the remaining chapters and appendices:

Chapter 2 explains what you should know to handle most simple documents and to read the rest of the book. Section 2.5 contains a summary of everything in the chapter; it serves as a short reference manual.

Chapter 3 describes logical structures for handling a variety of formatting problems. Section 3.4 explains how to define your own commands, which can save typing when you write the document and retyping when you change it. It's a good idea to read the introduction—up to the beginning of Section 3.1—before reading any other part of the chapter.

Chapter 4 contains features especially useful for large documents, including automatic cross-referencing and commands for splitting a large file into smaller pieces.

Chapter 5 describes the visual formatting of the text. It has information about document styles, explains how to correct bad line and page breaks, and tells how to do your own formatting of structures not explicitly handled by LaTeX.

Chapter 6 explains how to deal with errors. This is where you should look when LaTeX prints an error message that you don't understand.

Appendix A describes SLiTeX, a version of LaTeX for making slides.

Appendix B describes how to make a bibliographic database for use with BibTeX, a separate program that provides an automatic bibliography feature for LaTeX.

Appendix C is a reference manual that compactly describes all LaTeX's features, including many advanced ones not described in the main text. If a command introduced in the earlier chapters seems to lack some necessary capabilities, check its description here to see if it has them. This appendix is a convenient place to refresh your memory of how something works.

Appendix D is for the reader who wants to use TeX commands from the *TeXbook* that are not described in this book.

When faced with a formatting problem, the best place to look for a solution is in the table of contents. Browsing through it will give you a good idea of what LaTeX has to offer. If the table of contents doesn't work, look in the index; I have tried to make it friendly and informative.

Each section of Chapters 3–5 is reasonably self-contained, assuming only that you have read Chapter 2. Where additional knowledge is required, explicit cross-references are given. Appendix C is also self-contained, but a command's description may be hard to understand without first reading the corresponding description in the earlier chapters.

The descriptions of most LaTeX commands include examples of their use. In this book, examples are formatted in two columns, as follows:

The left column shows the printed output; the right column contains the input that produced it.

```
The left column shows the printed output;
the right column contains the input that
produced it.
```

Note the special typewriter type style in the right column. It indicates what you type—either text that you put in the input file or something like a file name that you type as part of a command to the computer.

Since the sample output is printed in a narrower column, and with smaller type, than LaTeX normally uses, it won't look exactly like the output you'd get from that input. The convention of the output appearing to the left of the corresponding input is also used when commands and their output are listed in tables.

1.3   The Game of the Name

The TeX in LaTeX refers to Donald Knuth's TeX typesetting system. The LaTeX program is a special version of TeX that understands LaTeX commands. Think of LaTeX as a house built with the lumber and nails provided by TeX. You don't need lumber and nails to live in a house, but they are handy for adding an extra room. Most LaTeX users never need to know any more about TeX than they can learn from this book. However, you can add new capabilities to LaTeX by using the lower-level TeX commands described in *The TeXbook* [3].

I will use the term "TEX" when describing standard TEX features and "LATEX" when describing features unique to LATEX, but the distinction will be of interest mainly to readers already familiar with TEX. You may ignore it and use the two names interchangeably.

One of the hardest things about using LATEX is deciding how to pronounce it. This is also one of the few things I'm not going to tell you about LATEX, since pronunciation is best determined by usage, not fiat. TEX is usually pronounced *teck*, making *lah*-teck, lah-*teck*, and *lay*-teck the logical choices; but language is not always logical, so *lay*-tecks is also possible.

The written word carries more legal complications than the spoken, and the need to distinguish TEX and LATEX from similarly spelled products restricts how you may write them. The best way to refer to these programs is by their logos, which can be generated with simple LATEX commands. If this is inconvenient, you should write them as "TeX" and "LaTeX", where the unusual capitalization denotes these computer programs.

1.4   Turning Typing into Typography

Traditionally, an author provides a publisher with a typed manuscript. The publisher's typographic designer decides how the manuscript is to be formatted, specifying the length of the printed line, what style of type to use, how much space to leave above and below section headings, and many other things that determine the printed document's appearance. The designer writes a series of instructions to the typesetter, who uses them to decide where on the page to put each of the author's words and symbols. In the old days, the typesetter produced a matrix of metal type for each page; today he is more likely to produce a computer file. In either case, his output is used to control the machine that does the actual typesetting.

LATEX is your typographic designer, and TEX is its typesetter. The LATEX commands that you type are translated into lower-level TEX typesetting commands. Being a modern typesetter, TEX produces a computer file, called the *device-independent* or `dvi` file. The *Local Guide* explains how to use this file to generate a printed document with your computer.

A human typographic designer knows what the manuscript is generally about and uses this knowledge in deciding how to format it. Consider the following typewritten manuscript:

```
The German mathematician Kronecker, sitting
quietly at his desk, wrote:
     God created the whole numbers; all
     the rest is man's work.
Seated in front of the terminal, with Basic
hanging on my every keystroke, I typed:
     for i = 1 to infinity
     let number[i] = i
```

A human designer knows that the first indented paragraph (`God created ...`) is a quotation and the second is a computer program, so the two should be formatted differently. He would probably set the quotation in ordinary roman type and the computer program in a typewriter type style. LaTeX is only a computer program and can't understand English, so it can't figure all this out by itself. It needs more help from you than a human designer would. The following brief discussion of typography will help you to help it.

The function of typographic design is to help the reader understand the author's ideas. For a document to be easy to read, its visual structure must reflect its logical structure. Quotations and computer programs, being logically distinct structural elements, should be distinguished visually from one another. The designer should therefore understand the document's logical structure. Since LaTeX can't understand your prose, you must explicitly indicate the logical structure by typing special commands. The primary function of almost all the LaTeX commands that you type should be to describe the logical structure of your document. As you are writing your document, you should be concerned with its logical structure, not its visual appearance. The LaTeX approach to typesetting can therefore be characterized as *logical design*.

There is a radically different approach to document production that might be called *visual design*. As the user of a visual-design system types his document, he sees on his terminal screen exactly what will appear on the printed page. Such systems are often described as "what you see is what you get".

Why type the commands LaTeX needs to format the document when a visual design system would allow you to format it yourself as you write it? There are several reasons. First of all, logical design encourages sound typography, while visual design discourages it. Most authors mistakenly believe that typographic design is primarily a question of aesthetics—if the document looks good from an artistic viewpoint, then it is well designed. However, documents are meant to be read, not hung in museums, so the primary function of design is to make the document easier to read, not prettier. With a visual design system, authors usually produce aesthetically pleasing, but poorly designed documents.

Typographic design is a craft that takes years to master. Authors with no training in design often make elementary formatting errors. A LaTeX user once presented me with the following typesetting problem.

> The user wanted to produce a numbered equation, formatted essentially like the following one.
>
> For all x: $$f(x) = g(x + 1) \tag{7}$$
>
> However, he could not figure out how to do it with the ordinary LaTeX commands, so he asked me.

He could have done it quite easily with a visual system, producing an aesthetically pleasing typographic mistake. It is a mistake because it is ambiguous;

the typography does not tell us whether or not the "For all x" is part of equation (7). When we later read: "Assume that (7) holds," we can't tell from (7) whether we should assume $f(x) = g(x+1)$ for some particular x or for all x. We would probably figure out quickly from the text which was meant—so quickly that we might not even be aware of the ambiguity. However, the cumulative effect of a lot of little typographic mistakes is to make reading the document more strenuous than it should be.

LaTeX discourages you from making this mistake by requiring you to describe the logical structure of your text. Its standard method of specifying an equation forces you to choose between the two logical possibilities.

You can make the "For all" part of the equation, as in

$$\text{For all } x\colon\ f(x) = g(x+1) \tag{8}$$

or not part of it, by writing that, for all x:

$$f(x) = g(x+1) \tag{9}$$

Although you can format an equation almost any way you want with LaTeX, you have to work harder to do it wrong.

Another reason why logical design is better than visual design is that it encourages better writing. Having to tell LaTeX the logical structure of your text encourages you to give the text a logical structure. A visual system makes it easy to create visual effects instead of logical structure. The coherent visual structure of equation (7), for example, hides the absence of a logical structure. Logical design encourages you to concentrate on your writing and makes it harder to use formatting as a substitute for good writing.

A third advantage of logical design is its flexibility. Visual design systems have been characterized as "what you see is all you've got".[1] Once you have typed the document, changing the format is a laborious process. If you decide that equations should be numbered with roman instead of arabic numerals, you must change each equation number individually; a visual design system regards an equation number as just a number that happens to appear at the right margin, not as a logical structure.

Fundamental to LaTeX is the idea of a *document style* that determines how the document is to be formatted—an idea stolen[2] from Brian Reid's *Scribe* text formatting system [6]. LaTeX generates equation numbers for you, with the document style specifying what kind of numbers to use. One simple change to the document style can change the way every equation is numbered. LaTeX provides standard document styles that describe how standard logical structures, such as equations and enumerated lists, are formatted. You may have to supplement these styles by specifying the formatting of logical structures peculiar to your

---

[1]Brian Reid attributes this phrase to himself and/or Brian Kernighan.

[2]"Lesser artists borrow, great artists steal." Igor Stravinsky

document, such as special mathematical formulas. You can also modify the standard document styles or even create an entirely new one, though you should know the basic principles of typographic design before creating a radically new style. You will appreciate the flexibility of logical design if you ever have to reformat a document, perhaps to include it as part of a larger document.

The purpose of writing is to present ideas to the reader. This should always be your primary concern. It is easy to become so engrossed with form that you neglect content. Formatting skills are no substitute for writing skills. Good ideas couched in good prose will be read and understood, regardless of how badly the document is formatted. LaTeX was designed to free you from formatting concerns, allowing you to concentrate on writing. If, while writing, you spend a lot of time worrying about form, you are probably misusing LaTeX.

1.5   Turning Ideas into Input

To most readers, the printed page conveys a greater sense of authority than the typewritten manuscript. It must be important to be worth printing. With LaTeX, typesetting is almost as easy as typing. There is no publisher or journal editor standing between the author and the reader. LaTeX will not reject ill-formed ideas or correct bad grammar. With the power to print your own document comes the responsibility to make it worth printing.

Even if your ideas are good, you can probably learn to express them better. The classic introduction to writing English prose is Strunk and White's brief *Elements of Style* [5]. A more complete guide to using language properly is Theodore Bernstein's *The Careful Writer* [1]. These two books discuss general writing style. Writers of scholarly or technical prose need additional information. van Leunen's *Handbook for Scholars* [7] is a delightful guide to academic and scholarly writing. The booklet entitled *How to Write Mathematics* [4] can help scientists and engineers as well as mathematicians. It's also useful to have a weightier reference book at hand; *Words into Type* [8] and the *Chicago Manual of Style* [2] are two good ones.

1.6   Trying It Out

You may already have run LaTeX with input based on the sample files. If not, this is a good time to learn how. The section in the *Local Guide* entitled *Running a Sample File* explains how to obtain a copy of the file `sample.tex` and run LaTeX with it as input. Follow the directions and see what LaTeX can do.

After printing the document generated in this way, try changing the document style. Using a text editor, examine the file `sample.tex`. A few lines down from the beginning of the file is a line that reads:

```
\documentstyle{article}
```

Change that line to:

```
\documentstyle[twocolumn]{article}
```

Save the changed file under the name `chgsam.tex`, and use this file to print a new version of the document. To generate the new version, do exactly what you did the last time, except type `chgsam` wherever you had typed `sample`. Comparing the two printed versions shows how radically the appearance of the document can be altered by a simple change to the document style. To try still another document style, change `chgsam.tex` so the above line reads

```
\documentstyle[11pt]{article}
```

and use the changed file to print a third version of the document.

From now on, I will usually ignore the process of going from the LATEX input file to the printed output and will write something like: "Typing `---` produces a long dash." What this really means is that putting the three characters `---` in your input file will, when that file is processed by LATEX and the device-independent file printed, produce a long dash in the printed output.

CHAPTER 2
Getting Started

2.1   Preparing an Input File

The input to LaTeX is a text file. I assume that you know how to use a text editor to create such a file, so I will tell you only what should go into your input file, not how to get it there. Some text editors can be customized to make it easier to prepare LaTeX input files. Consult the *Local Guide* to find out if such an editor is available on your computer.

On most computers, file names have two parts separated by a period, like `sample.tex`. I will call the first part its *first name* and the second part its *extension*, so `sample` is the first name of `sample.tex`, and `tex` is its extension. Your input file's first name can be any name allowed by your computer system, but its extension should be `tex`.

Let's examine the characters that can appear in your input file. First, there are the upper- and lowercase letters and the ten digits `0 ... 9`. Don't confuse the uppercase letter `O` (oh) with the digit `0` (zero), or the letter `l` (the lowercase *el*) with the digit `1` (one). Next, there are the following 16 punctuation characters:

$$. \ : \ ; \ , \ ? \ ! \ ` \ ' \ (\ ) \ [\ ] \ - \ / \ * \ @$$

Note that there are two different quote symbols: `` ` `` and `'`. You may think of `'` as an ordinary "single quote" and `` ` `` as a funny symbol, perhaps displayed like `` ` `` on your screen. The *Local Guide* should tell where to find `` ` `` and `'` on your keyboard. The characters `(` and `)` are ordinary parentheses, while `[` and `]` are called *square brackets*, or simply *brackets*.

The ten special characters

$$\# \ \$ \ \% \ \& \ \~{} \ \_ \ \^{} \ \backslash \ \{ \ \}$$

are used only in LaTeX commands. Check the *Local Guide* for help in finding them on your keyboard. The underscore character `_` may appear on your screen as ←. The character `\` is called *backslash*, and should not be confused with the more familiar `/`, as in `1/2`. Most LaTeX commands begin with a `\` character, so you will soon become very familiar with it. The `{` and `}` characters are called *curly braces* or simply *braces*.

The five characters

$$+ \ = \ | \ < \ >$$

are used mainly in mathematical formulas, although `+` and `=` can be used in ordinary text. The character `"` (double quote) is hardly every used.

Unless your *Local Guide* tells you otherwise, these are the only characters that you should see when you look at a LaTeX input file. However, there are other "invisible" characters in your file: space characters, such as the one you usually enter by pressing the *space* bar, and special characters that indicate the end of a line, usually entered by pressing the *return* key. These invisible characters are all considered the same by TeX, and I will treat them as if they were a single character called *space*, which I will sometimes denote by ␣. Any sequence of space characters is handled the same as a single one, so it doesn't matter if the space between two words is formed by one space character or several of them. However, a blank line—one containing nothing but space characters—is interpreted by TEX as the end of a paragraph. Some text editors organize a file into pages. TEX acts as if there were a blank line between the pages of such a file.

2.2   The Input

Most LATEX commands describe the logical structure of the document. To understand these commands, you must know how LATEX perceives that logical structure. A document contains logical structures of different sizes, from chapters down through individual letters. We start by considering the very familiar intermediate-sized structures: sentences and paragraphs.

2.2.1   Sentences and Paragraphs

Describing simple sentences and paragraphs to LATEX poses no problem; you pretty much type what comes naturally.

> The ends of words and sentences are marked by spaces. It doesn't matter how many spaces you type; one is as good as 100.
> One or more blank lines denote the end of a paragraph.

```
The ends  of words and sentences are marked
   by   spaces. It  doesn't matter how many
spaces    you type; one is as good as 100.

One   or more   blank lines denote the  end
of  a paragraph.
```

TEX ignores the way the input is formatted, paying attention only to the logical concepts end-of-word, end-of-sentence, and end-of-paragraph.

That's all you have to know for typing most of your text. The remainder of this book is about how to type the rest, starting with some other things that occur fairly frequently in ordinary sentences and paragraphs.

Quotation Marks

Typewritten text uses only two quotation-mark symbols: a double quote " and single quote ', the latter serving also as an apostrophe. Printed text, however, uses a left and a right version of each, making four different symbols. TEX interprets the character ' as a single left quote, and the character ' as a single right quote. To get a double quote, just type two single quotes.

> 'Convention' dictates that punctuation go inside quotes, like "this," but I think it's better to do "this".

```
'Convention' dictates that punctuation go
inside quotes, like ''this,'' but I think
it's better to do ''this''.
```

Remember that the right-quote character ' is the one you're used to thinking of as a single quote, and the left-quote character ' is the one you're probably unfamiliar with. An apostrophe is produced with the usual ' character.

Typing a double quote followed by a single quote, or vice-versa, poses a problem because something like ''' would be ambiguous. The solution is to type the command \, (a \ character followed by a comma) between the two quotation marks.

"'Fi' or 'fum?'" he asked.   `''\,'Fi'  or  'fum?'\,''  he asked.`

The \, is a typesetting command that causes TEX to insert a small amount of space. Don't leave any space in the input file before or after the \, command.

Dashes

You can produce three different sizes of dash by typing one, two, or three "-" characters:

An intra-word dash or hyphen, as in X-ray.   `An intra-word dash or hyphen, as in X-ray.`
A medium dash for number ranges, like 1–2.   `A medium dash for number ranges, like 1--2.`
A punctuation dash—like this.   `A punctuation dash---like this.`

There is usually no space before or after a dash. Minus signs are not dashes; they should appear only in mathematical formulas, which are discussed below.

Space After a Period

Typesetters usually put a little extra space after a sentence-ending period. This is easy for a human typesetter, but not for a program like TEX that has trouble deciding which periods end sentences. Instead of trying to be clever, TEX simply assumes that a period ends a sentence unless it follows an upper-case letter. This works most of the time, but not always—abbreviations like "etc." being the most common exception. You tell TEX that a period doesn't end a sentence by typing a \␣ command (a \ character followed by a space or the end of a line) right after the period.

Tinker et al. made the double play.   `Tinker et al.\  made the double play.`

It doesn't matter how many spaces you leave after the \ character, but don't leave any space between the period and the backslash. The \␣ command produces an ordinary interword space, which can also be useful in other situations.

On the rare occasions that a sentence-ending period follows an upper-case letter, you will have to tell TEX that the period ends the sentence. You do this by preceding the period with a \@ command.

The Romans wrote I + I = II. Really!   `The Romans wrote I + I = II\@.  Really!`

If a sentence-ending period is followed by a right parenthesis or a right quote (single or double), then typesetters usually put extra space after the parenthesis or quote. In this case, too, TEX will need a hand if its assumption that a period ends a sentence unless it follows an upper-case letter is wrong.

"Beans (lima, etc.) have vitamin B."   ``Beans (lima, etc.)\ have vitamin B\@.''

Extra space is also added after a question mark (?), exclamation point (!), or colon (:) just as for a period—that is, unless it follows an upper-case letter. The \␣ and \@ commands are used the same way with each of these punctuation characters.

Special Symbols

Remember those ten special characters, mentioned on page 12, that you type only as part of LATEX commands? Some of them, like $, represent symbols that you might very well want in your document. Seven of those symbols can be produced by typing a \ in front of the corresponding character.

$ & % # _ { } are easy to produce.   \$ \& \% \# _ \{ \} are easy to produce.

The other three special characters (˜, ˆ, and \) usually appear only in simulated keyboard input, which is produced with the commands described in Section 3.7.

You can get TEX to produce any symbol that you're likely to want, and many more besides, such as: § $\mathcal{L}$ ψ $\star$ $\otimes$ $\approx$ $\bowtie$ $\Leftarrow$ $\flat$ $\clubsuit$. Sections 3.2 and 3.3.2 tell how.

Simple Text-Generating Commands

Part of a sentence may be produced by a text-generating command. For example, the TEX and LATEX logos are produced by the commands \TeX and \LaTeX, respectively.

Some people use plain TEX, but I prefer LATEX.   Some people use plain \TeX, but I
                                                      prefer \LaTeX.

A useful text-generating command is \today, which produces the current date.

This page was produced on July 22, 1985.   This page was produced on \today.

Another useful text-generating command is \ldots, which produces an *ellipsis*— the sequence of three dots used to denote omitted material. (Simply typing three periods doesn't produce the right spacing between the dots.)

If nominated ..., I will not serve.   If nominated \ldots, I will not serve.

Most of the command names you've seen so far have consisted of a \ (backslash) followed by a single nonletter. From now on, most commands you will encounter have names consisting of a \ followed by one or more letters. In reading the input file, TEX knows it has come to the end of such a command name when it finds a nonletter: a digit like "7", a punctuation character like ";", a special character like "\", a space, or the end of a line. The most common way to end this kind of command name is with a space or end of line, so TEX ignores all spaces following it. If you want a space after the logo produced by the \LaTeX command, you can't just leave a space after the command name; all such spaces are ignored. You must tell TEX to put in the space by typing a \␣ command.

This page of the LATEX manual was produced on July 22, 1985.	`This page of the \LaTeX\ manual was` `produced on \today`

Note how TEX ignored the space after the \today command in the input and did not produce any space after the date in the output.

The case of letters counts in a command name; typing \Today produces an error, because the correct command name is \today. Most command names have only lowercase letters.

Emphasizing Text

Emphasized text is usually <u>underlined</u> in a typewritten manuscript and *italicized* in a printed document. Underlining and italics are visual concepts; when typing your document, you should be concerned only with the logical concept of emphasis. The \em command tells LATEX that text is to be emphasized.

Here is some silly *emphasized text*.	`Here is some silly {\em emphasized text}.`

The format is {\em followed by a space (to end the \em command), followed by the emphasized text, followed by a } character—with no space before the }. Space before the { or after the } produces space in the output.

You can have *emphasized text* within *emphasized text* too.	`You can have  {\em emphasized text` `{\em within}  emphasized text} too.`

If emphasized text appears inside italicized text, then it is set in ordinary roman type.

Emphasis should be used sparingly. Like raising your voice, it is an effective way to get attention, but an annoying distraction if done too often.

A fine point about italic type is illustrated by the following example.

I told you that he *did*n't!	`I told you that he {\em did}n't!`

Notice how the last *d* of *did* bumps into the next letter. When switching from italic to roman type, a typesetter should add a little extra space to cushion this bump. You instruct TEX to add this space by typing a \/ command, so I should have typed {\em did\/}n't. No extra space needs to be added before a comma or period, so the first example illustrating the \em command is all right, but the next example should be typed as:

You can have *emphasized text* within *emphasized text* too.

```
You can have  {\em emphasized
text\/ {\em within} emphasized text\/} too.
```

There are two \/ commands because the text switches from italic to roman twice. Note that space following a \/ command produces space in the output.

To use the \/ command in this way, you must know where TEX changes from italic to roman type. This is usually not a problem, since the main body of the document is normally printed in roman type. However, there are some contexts where the type style depends upon the document style—for example, theorems may be printed in italic in some styles and roman in others. In this case, you should put a \/ command wherever TEX *might* change from italic to roman; a \/ does nothing if it follows a roman letter.

Unlike other commands you've encountered so far, the \em command produces neither text nor space; instead, it affects the way TEX prints the following text. Such a command is called a *declaration*. Most aspects of the way TEX formats a document—the type style, how wide the margins are, etc.—are determined by declarations. The \em declaration instructs TEX to change the type style from roman to italic, or vice versa. The braces delimit the *scope* of the declaration; when TEX encounters the }, it reverts to the type style in effect just before the {. When you type

```
{\em   . . .   }
```

the { means *begin a new scope*, the \em declaration means *start emphasizing*, and the } means *end current scope*.

It is the *declaration*, not the left brace, that changes the type style.

```
It  {is the \em declaration}, not the left
brace, that changes the type style.
```

The braces in your input file must come in matching pairs.[1] In the following example, representing text from which everything but the braces has been removed, matching braces have the same numbers.

$$\{_1 \qquad \{_2 \quad \}_2 \qquad \{_3 \quad \{_4 \quad \}_4 \quad \}_3 \qquad \}_1$$

---

[1] The brace characters in the commands \{ and \} are not scope-delimiting braces; they are ignored in determining brace matching.

When a { begins a new scope, all declarations currently in effect remain in effect until countermanded by new declarations. The matching } that ends the scope ends the effect of all declarations made between the braces.

It can be difficult keeping track of matching braces that enclose a large amount of text. Typing

```
\begin{em}  ...  \end{em}
```

is equivalent to typing {\em ... } and can make your input file easier to read.

Remember: TEX requires that all braces come in matched pairs, and it is hard to keep track of braces that enclose a lot of text.

```
\begin{em}  Remember:
  \TeX\ requires ... a\/ {\em lot} of text.
\end{em}
```

To avoid typing errors and simplify making changes, it's a good idea to keep your input file as easy to read as possible. The use of spacing and indentation can help. TEX doesn't care how the input file is formatted, but you should.

Preventing Line Breaks

In putting text onto paper, a paragraph must be broken into lines of print. Text becomes hard to read if a single logical unit is split across lines in an arbitrary fashion, so typesetters break lines between words when possible and split words only between syllables (inserting a hyphen at the break). Sometimes a line should not be broken between or within certain words. Human typesetters recognize these situations, but TEX must be told about them.

Line breaking should be prevented at certain interword spaces. For example, the expression "Chapter 3" looks strange if the "Chapter" ends one line and the "3" begins the next. Typing ~ (a tilde character) produces an ordinary interword space at which TEX will never break a line. Below are some examples indicating when a ~ should be used.

```
Mr.~Jones        Figure~7         (1)~gnats
U.~S.~Grant      from 1 to~10
```

A word should not be broken across lines if it is really a symbol, such as an identifier in a computer program. The \mbox command tells TEX not to break such a word. In the following example, TEX will never split "*itemnum*" across lines.

Let *itemnum* be the current item number.

```
Let  \mbox{\em itemnum\/}  be the ...
```

Word-like symbols are usually emphasized.

Most line breaks separate logically related units, and it would be nice if they could be avoided. However, unless you print your document on a mile-long strip of paper tape, line breaking is a necessary evil. Using too many ~ and \mbox commands leaves too few places to break lines. Inhibit line breaking only where necessary.

In the \mbox{\em itemnum\/} command, \mbox is the command name and \em itemnum\/ is its *argument*. An argument is enclosed in braces, which delimit the scope of a declaration like \em appearing inside it.[2] Most commands have either no arguments, like \today, or a single argument, like \mbox. However, there are a few with multiple arguments, each of which is enclosed in braces. Spaces between the command name and its argument(s) are ignored, but there should be no space between separate arguments.

Footnotes

Footnotes are produced with a \footnote command having the text of the footnote as its argument.

Gnus[1] can be quite a gnusance.

⋮
_____
[1] A gnu is a big animal.

```
Gnus\footnote{A gnu is a big animal.} can
be quite a gnusance.
```

There is no space between the Gnus and the \footnote in this example; adding space would have put an unwanted space between the text and the footnote marker (the [1]).

A \footnote command cannot be used in the argument of most commands; for example, it can't appear in the argument of an \mbox command. Section C.2.3 explains how to footnote text that appears in a command argument.

Formulas

If you're writing a technical document, it's likely to contain mathematical formulas. A formula appearing in the middle of a sentence is enclosed by \(and \) commands.

The formula $x - 3y = 7$ is easy to type.

```
The formula \( x-3y = 7 \) is easy to type.
```

Any spaces that you type in the formula are ignored.

Does $x + y$ always equal $y + x$?

```
Does \( x + y \) always equal \(y+x\)?
```

TEX regards a formula as a word, which may be broken across lines at certain points, and space before the \(or after the \) is treated as an ordinary interword separation.

_____
[2] As explained in Section 3.4, argument braces do not act as scope delimiters for commands you define yourself.

Subscripts are produced by the _ command and superscripts by the ^ command.

$a_1 > x^{2n}/y^{2n}$ `\( a_{1} > x^{2n} / y^{2n} \)`

These two commands can be used only inside a mathematical formula.

When used in a formula, the right-quote character ' produces a prime ($'$), two in a row produce a double prime, and so on.

This proves that $x' < x'' - y_3' < 10x'''z$.   ... `\( x' < x'' - y'_{3} < 10 x''' z \)`.

Mathematical formulas can get very complex; Section 3.3 describes many additional commands for formatting them. Here, I will consider the use of formulas in the text. A formula is a grammatical unit; it should be treated as such in the sentence structure.

The formula $a < 7$ is a noun in this sentence. It becomes a clause, complete with verb, when I write that $a < 7$.   `The formula \( a<7 \) is a noun in this sentence. It becomes a clause, ...`

Beginning a sentence with a formula makes it hard to find the start of the sentence; don't do it. Similarly, a formula should never appear as a complete sentence in the running text.

A variable like x is a formula. To save typing, LaTeX treats `$...$` the same as `\(...\)`.

Let x be a prime such that $y > 2x$.   `Let $x$ be a prime such that $y>2x$.`

Use `$...$` only for a short formula, such as a single variable. It's easy to forget one of the `$` characters that surrounds a long formula. You can also type

     `\begin{math} ... \end{math}`

instead of `\(...\)`. You might want to use this form for very long formulas.

Ignorable Input

When TeX encounters a `%` character in the input, it ignores it and all other characters on that line—including the space character that ends the line.

Gnus and armadillos are generally tolerant of one another and seldom quarrel.   `Gnus and armadi%    More  @_#!$^{& gnus?`
                                            `llos are generally ...`

The `%` has two uses: ending a line without producing any space in the output[3] and putting a comment (a note to yourself) in the input file.

---

[3]However, you can't split a command name across two lines.

2.2.2 The Document

We now jump from the document's intermediate-sized logical units to its largest one: the entire document itself. The text of every document starts with a `\begin{document}` command and ends with an `\end{document}` command. LaTeX ignores anything that follows the `\end{document}`. The part of the input file preceding the `\begin{document}` command is called the *preamble*.

The Document Style

Since all text must follow the `\begin{document}`, the preamble can contain only declarations. These declarations are used to specify the document style. The preamble begins with a `\documentstyle` command whose argument chooses one of the predefined styles. The file `sample.tex` begins with

> `\documentstyle{article}`   *\document class*

which selects the `article` style. The other standard LaTeX styles for ordinary documents are the `report` and `book` styles. The `article` style is generally used for shorter documents than the `report` style, and the `book` style is meant for actual books. Consult the *Local Guide* to find out if there are any other document styles available on your computer.

In addition to choosing the main style, you can also select from among certain document-style options. The options for the `article` and `report` styles include the following:

11pt Specifies a size of type know as *eleven point*, which is ten percent larger than the ten-point type normally used.

12pt Specifies a twelve-point type size, which is twenty percent larger than ten point.

twoside Formats the output for printing on both sides of the page.

twocolumn Produces two-column output.

Other options are described elsewhere in this book; all the standard ones are listed in Section 5.1.1. Your *Local Guide* tells if there are any others available on your computer.

You specify a document-style option by enclosing it in square brackets immediately after the "`\documentstyle`", as in

> `\documentstyle [twoside]{report}`

Multiple options are separated by commas.

> `\documentstyle [twocolumn,12pt]{article}`

Don't leave any space inside the square brackets.

The \documentstyle command specifies the standard part of the document style. You may also want to make special style declarations for the particular document, either to modify some aspect of the standard style or to handle special logical structures. For example, if you're writing a cookbook you will probably define your own commands for formatting recipes, as explained in Section 3.4. These declarations go in the preamble, after the \documentstyle command. See also Section 5.1.4 for information on defining your own document style.

The \documentstyle command can be used either with or without the option-choosing part. The options, enclosed in square brackets, are an *optional argument* of the command. It is a LaTeX convention that optional arguments are enclosed in square brackets, while mandatory arguments are enclosed in curly braces. Although TeX ignores spaces after a command name like \documentstyle, you should leave no space between arguments.

The Title "Page"

A document usually has a title "page" listing its title, one or more authors, and a date. I write "page" in quotes because, for a short document, this information may be listed on the first page of text rather than on its own page. The title information consists of the title itself, the author(s), and the date; it is specified by the three declarations \title, \author, and \date. The actual title "page" is generated by a \maketitle command.

Gnus of the World

R. Dather   B. Falters   W. Conkright

4 July 1997

```
\title{Gnus of the World}
\author{R. Dather \and B. Falters
    \and W. Conkright}
\date{4 July 1997}
        . . .
\maketitle
```

Note how multiple authors are separated by \and commands.

The \maketitle command comes after the \begin{document}, usually before any other text. The \title, \author, and \date commands can come anywhere before the \maketitle. The \date is optional; LaTeX supplies the current date if the declaration is omitted, but the \title and \author must appear if a \maketitle command is used. Commands for adding other information, such as the author's address and an acknowledgement of support, are described in Section C.4.3.

2.2.3   Sectioning

Sentences are organized into paragraphs, and paragraphs are in turn organized into a hierarchical *section structure*. You are currently reading Subsection 2.2.3, entitled *Sectioning*, which is part of Section 2.2, entitled *The Input*, which in turn is part of Chapter 2, entitled *Getting Started*. I will use the term *sectional units* for things like chapters, sections, and subsections.

A sectional unit is begun by a sectioning command with the unit's title as its argument.

4.7   Sectioning Commands

LaTeX automatically generates the section number. Blank lines before or after a sectioning command have no effect.

```
\subsection{Sectioning Commands}

\LaTeX\ automatically generates the section
number.  Blank lines before or after a ...
```

The document style determines what sectioning commands are provided, the standard styles have the following ones:[4]

\part	\subsection	\paragraph
\chapter	\subsubsection	\subparagraph
\section		

The `article` document style does not contain the `\chapter` command, which makes it easy to include an "article" as a chapter of a "report" or "book". The above example, like all others in this book, assumes the `article` document style, the 4.7 indicating that this is the seventh subsection of Section 4. In the `report` or `book` styles, this subsection might be numbered 5.4.7, with "5" being the chapter number.

The sectional unit denoted by each of these commands must appear as a subunit of the one denoted by the preceding command, except that the use of `\part` is optional. A subsection must be part of a section which, in `report` and `book` styles, must be part of a chapter.

The `\part` command is used for major divisions of long documents; it does not affect the numbering of smaller units—in the `article` style, if the last section of Part 1 is Section 5, then the first section of Part 2 is Section 6.

If there is an appendix, it is begun with an `\appendix` command and uses the same sectioning commands as the main part of the document. The `\appendix` command does not produce any text; it simply causes sectional units to be numbered properly for an appendix.

The document style determines the appearance of the section title, including whether or not it is numbered. Declarations to control section numbering are described in Section C.3, which also tells you how to make a table of contents.

The argument of a sectioning command may be used for more than just producing the section title; it can generate a table of contents entry and a running head at the top of the page. (Running heads are discussed in Section 5.1.2.) When carried from where it appears in the input file to the other places it is used, the argument of a sectioning command is shaken up quite a bit. Some

---

[4]The names `\paragraph` and `\subparagraph` are unfortunate, since they denote units that are usually composed of several paragraphs; they have been retained for historical reasons.

LaTeX commands are *fragile* and can break when they appear in an argument that is shaken in this way. Fragile commands are rarely used in the argument of a sectioning command. Of the commands introduced so far, the only fragile ones are \(, \), \begin, \end, and \footnote—none of which you're likely to need in a section title.[5] On the rare occasions when you have to put a fragile command in a section title, you simply protect it with a \protect command. The \protect command goes right before every fragile command's name, as in:

> \subsection {Is \protect\(x+y \protect\) Prime?}

This is actually a silly example because $ is not a fragile command, so you can instead type

> \subsection {Is $x + y$ Prime?}

but, because the problem is so rare, it's hard to find a good example using the commands described in this chapter.

An argument in which fragile commands need \protect will be called a *moving* argument. Commands that are not fragile will be called *robust*. For any command that one might reasonably expect to use in a moving argument, I will indicate whether it is robust or fragile. Except in special cases mentioned in Chapter 5 and Appendix C, a \protect command can't hurt, so it is almost always safe to use one when you're not sure if it's necessary.

2.2.4 Displayed Material

We return now to the level of the individual sentence. A sentence like

> He turned and said to me: "My answer is no!", and then he left.

contains a complete sentence quoted within it. An entire paragraph can even appear inside a sentence, as in:

> He turned and said to me: "I've done all I'm going to. I refuse to have any further part in it. My answer is no!", and then he left.

It's hard to understand this sentence the way it is written. However, there's no problem if you read it aloud using a different tone of voice for the quotation. The typographic analogue of changing your tone of voice is setting text off by indentation, also called *displaying*. The above sentence is much easier to read when typeset as follows:

> He turned and said to me:
>> I've done all I'm going to. I refuse to have any further part in it. My answer is no!
>
> and then he left.

---

[5]Section C.2.3 tells you how to footnote a section title.

Displayed material functions logically as a lower-level unit than a sentence, though grammatically it may consist of part of a sentence, a whole sentence, or even several paragraphs. To decide whether a portion of text should be a display or a separate sectional unit, you must determine if it is logically subordinate to the surrounding text or functions as an equal unit.

Quotations are often displayed.

The following is an example of a short displayed quotation.

> ... it's a good idea to make your input file as easy to read as possible.

It is indented at both margins.

```
... example of a short displayed quotation.
\begin{quote}
  \ldots\ it's a good idea to make your
  input file as easy to read as possible.
\end{quote}
It is indented at both margins.
```

This illustrates a type of LaTeX construction called an *environment*, which is typed

> \begin{*name*} ... \end{*name*}

where *name* denotes the name of the environment. The `quote` environment produces a display suitable for a short quotation. You've already encountered three other examples of environments: the `em` environment, the `math` environment, and the `document` environment. Just as the `em` environment corresponds to the `\em` command, any declaration has a corresponding environment whose name is obtained by dropping the \ from the command name.

The `\begin` and `\end` commands delimit the scope of a declaration just as { and } do.

Even though

> *this quote is emphasized,*

the following text is not emphasized.

```
Even though
\begin{quote}
  \em this quote is emphasized,
\end{quote}
the following text is not emphasized.
```

Some environments have arguments; they are typed like additional arguments to the `\begin` command.

The standard LaTeX document styles provide environments for producing several different kinds of displays. Blank lines before or after the environment mark a new paragraph. Thus, a blank line after the `\end` command means that the following text starts a new paragraph. Blank lines before and after the environment mean that it is a complete paragraph. It's a bad idea to start a paragraph with displayed material, so you should not have a blank line before a display environment without a blank line after it. Blank lines immediately following a display environment's `\begin` command and immediately preceding its `\end` command are ignored.

Quotations

LaTeX provides two different environments for displaying quotations. The `quote` environment is used for either a short quotation or a sequence of short quotations separated by blank lines.

Our presidents have been known for their pithy remarks.

> The buck stops here. *Harry Truman*
> I am not a crook. *Richard Nixon*

```
Our presidents ... pithy remarks.
\begin{quote}
  The buck stops here.  {\em Harry Truman}

  I am not a crook.     {\em Richard Nixon}
\end{quote}
```

The `quotation` environment is used for quotations of more than one paragraph; as usual, the paragraphs are separated by blank lines.

Here is some advice to remember when you are using LaTeX:

> Environments for making quotations can be used for other things as well.
>
> Many problems can be solved by novel applications of existing environments.

```
Here is some advice to remember when you
are using \LaTeX:
\begin{quotation}
  Environments for making quotations
  ... other things as well.

  Many ... existing environments.
\end{quotation}
```

Lists

LaTeX provides three list-making environments: `itemize`, `enumerate`, and `description`. In all three, each new list item is begun with an `\item` command. Itemized lists are made with the `itemize` environment and enumerated lists with the `enumerate` environment.

- Each list item is marked with a *label*. The labels in this itemized list are bullets.
- Lists can be nested within one another.
  1. The item labels in an enumerated list are numerals or letters.
  2. A list should have at least two items.

  LaTeX permits at least four levels of nested lists, which is more than enough.
- Blank lines before an item have no effect.

```
\begin{itemize}
  \item Each list item is ...  bullets.
  \item Lists can be ... one another.
    \begin{enumerate}
      \item The item labels ... letters.
      \item A list should  ...  two items.
    \end{enumerate}
  \LaTeX\ permits ... more than enough.

  \item  Blank lines ... have no effect.
\end{itemize}
```

In the `description` environment, you specify the item labels with an optional argument to the `\item` command, enclosed in brackets. (Although the argument is optional, the item will look funny if you omit it.)

Three animals you should know about are:

gnat A small animal, found in the North Woods, that causes no end of trouble.

gnu A large animal, found in crossword puzzles, that causes no end of trouble.

armadillo A medium-sized animal, named after a medium-sized Texas city.

```
Three animals you should know about are:
\begin{description}
  \item[gnat] A small animal ...
  \item [gnu] A large animal ....
  \item [armadillo] A medium-sized ...
\end{description}
```

The characters [and] are used both to delimit an optional argument and to produce square brackets in the output. This can cause some confusion if the text of an item begins with a [or if an \item command's optional argument contains a square bracket. Section C.1.1 explains what to do in these uncommon situations. All commands that have an optional argument are fragile.

Poetry

Poetry is displayed with the **verse** environment. A new stanza is begun with one or more blank lines; lines within a stanza are separated by a \\ command.

There is an environment for verse
Whose features some poets will curse.

For instead of making
Them do *all* line breaking,
It allows them to put too many words
   on a line when they'd rather be
   forced to be terse.

```
\begin{verse}
  There is an environment fcr verse \\
  Whose features some poets will curse.

  For instead of making\\
  Them do {\em all\/} line breaking, \\
  It allows them  ...  to be terse.
\end{verse}
```

The * command is the same as \\ except that it prevents LaTeX from starting a new page at that point. It can be used to prevent a poem from being broken across pages in a distracting way. The commands \\ and * are used in all environments in which you tell LaTeX where to break lines; several such environments are described in the next chapter. The * command is called the *-form of the \\ command. Several other commands also have *-forms— versions of the command that are slightly different from the ordinary one—that are obtained by typing * after the command name.

The \\ and * commands have a little-used optional argument described in Section C.1.6, so putting a [after them presents the same problem as for the \item command. Moreover, the * in the * command is somewhat like an optional argument for the \\ command, so following a \\ with a * in the text poses a similar problem. See Section C.1.1 for the solutions to these unlikely problems. Any command that has a *-form is fragile, and its *-form is also fragile.

Displayed Formulas

A mathematical formula is displayed when either it is too long to fit comfortably in the running text, it is so important that you want it to stand out, or it is to be numbered for future reference. LaTeX provides the `displaymath` and `equation` environments for displaying formulas; they are the same except that `equation` numbers the formula and `displaymath` doesn't. Because displayed equations are used so frequently in mathematics, LaTeX allows you to type \[...\] instead of

```
\begin{displaymath}   ...   \end{displaymath}
```

Here is an example of an unnumbered displayed equation:

$$x' + y^2 = z_i^2$$

and here is the same equation numbered:

$$x' + y^2 = z_i^2 \qquad (8)$$

```
Here is an example of an unnumbered
displayed equation:
    \[ x' + y^{2} = z_{i}^{2} \]
and here is the same equation numbered:
    \begin{equation}
        x' + y^{2} = z_{i}^{2}
    \end{equation}
```

The document style determines how equations are numbered. Section 4.2 describes how LaTeX can automatically handle references to equation numbers so you don't have to keep track of the numbers.

A displayed formula, like any displayed text, should not begin a paragraph. Moreover, it should not form a complete paragraph by itself. These two observations are summed up in a simple rule: in the input, never leave a blank line before a displayed formula.

TeX will not break the formula in a `displaymath` or `equation` environment across lines. See Section 3.3.5 for commands to create a single multiple-line formula or a sequence of displayed formulas.

2.3   Running LaTeX

If you followed the directions in Section 1.6, you now know how to run LaTeX on an input file. If not, you should consult the *Local Guide* to find out. When you use your own input file for the first time, things are unlikely to go as smoothly as they did for `sample.tex`. There will probably be a number of errors in your file—most of them simple typing mistakes. Chapter 6 gives detailed help in diagnosing errors. Here I will tell you how to apply first aid from your terminal while LaTeX is still running.

With your text editor, produce a new file named `errsam.tex` by making the following two changes to `sample.tex`.

- About three-quarters of the way through the file is a line with a `\begin{itemize}` command. Delete the `z` from this command, producing `\begin{itemie}`. This simulates a typical typing error.

- A few lines from the end of the file is a line beginning with the word
  `one-line`. Insert the word `gnomonly`, followed by a space, at the beginning
  of that line. TeX does not know how to hyphenate *gnomonly*; this will
  prevent it from finding a good place for a line break.

Now run LaTeX with `errsam.tex` as input and see what error messages it produces. You needn't write down the messages because everything TeX writes
on your terminal is also written in a file called the *log* file.[6] For the input file
`errsam.tex`, the log file is named `errsam.log` on most computers, but it may
have a different extension on yours; check your *Local Guide*.

LaTeX begins by typing pretty much what it did when you ran it on the
`sample.tex` file, but then writes the following message on your terminal and
stops:

```
LaTeX error.  See LaTeX manual for explanation.
              Type  H <return>  for immediate help.
! Environment itemie undefined.
\@latexerr ...for immediate help.}\errmessage {#1}
                                                   \endgroup
l.140 \begin{itemie}

?
```

LaTeX translates a command like `\begin{itemize}`, which describes the document's logical structure, into TeX's typesetting commands. Some errors are
caught by LaTeX; others cause it to generate typesetting commands containing
errors that TeX finds. The first two lines of this message tell us that the error
was found by LaTeX rather than TeX.

The third line of the message—the one beginning with an exclamation point—
is the *error indicator*. It tells what the problem is. Chapter 6 explains the
meaning of the error indicators for all LaTeX-detected errors and for the most
common errors that TeX finds. Here, LaTeX is complaining that it has never
heard of an environment named `itemie`.

The next two lines are generated by TeX to describe what's happening in
terms of its low-level typesetting commands; they are irrelevant and can be
ignored. Following them comes the *error locator*, telling you where in your
input file the error was discovered. In this case, it was on line 140, after TeX
read the `\begin{itemie}` command.

The `?` that ends the message indicates that LaTeX has stopped and is waiting for you to type something. The description of this error message in Chapter 6 explains how you could fix the error right now by typing in the correct
`\begin{itemize}` command. However, we'll just pass over it by pressing the
return key, which instructs LaTeX to continue processing the input. LaTeX immediately writes the following error message:

---

[6]The log file also has some things that don't appear on your terminal, including blank lines
inserted in strange places.

```
! Undefined control sequence.
\@item ...fi \setbox \@tempboxa \hbox {\makelabel
                                                   {#1}}\global \setbox \@lab...
<to be read again>
                        T
l.141    \item  T
                        his is the first item of an itemized list.  Each item
?
```

The absence of the "LaTeX Error" at the beginning of the message tells us that this error was detected by TEX rather than LATEX. TEX knows nothing about LATEX commands, so you can't expect much help from the error indicator. The error locator indicates that the error was detected on line 141 of the input file, right after TEX had read "\item T", by breaking the input line at that point; the part that TEX hasn't read yet appears on the lower line.

This error is caused by the \item command. This command should occur only inside a list environment, but it doesn't because we replaced the \begin{itemize} with a meaningless \begin{itemie} command. TEX can pass the point where the real error is—here, the \item command—before discovering that something is wrong, but it usually doesn't go very far.

To continue past this error, you press *return*. TEX immediately writes an error message almost identical to the preceding one, with the same error locator. It has discovered a second error in the typesetting commands that the \item command generated. Keep typing *return* and you will find two more errors produced by this \item command, after which you will find a similar error generated by the next \item command—the one on line 145. You must type four *returns* to skip over the four errors it generates, plus four more to skip over the errors generated by the third \item command. LATEX then writes the following message:

```
LaTeX error.  See LaTeX manual for explanation.
            Type  H <return>  for immediate help.
! \begin{document} ended by \end{itemize}.
\@latexerr ...for immediate help.}\errmessage {#1}
                                                  \endgroup
\@checkend ...empa \@currenvir \else \@badend {#1}
                                                  \fi \def \@currenvir {docu...
\end ... end#1\endcsname \endgroup \@checkend {#1}
                                                  \if@ignore \global \@ignor...
l.158 \end{itemize}

?
```

It is caused by the \end{itemize} on line 158, which is incorrect because there was no matching \begin{itemize} command. Typing *return* gets LATEX past the incorrect list, and it will run to the end without stopping again.

One missing z generated fourteen separate errors. However, there was no harm done. Although you might have gotten tired of typing *return*, LATEX provided plenty of information to help you find the error. If this had been a real mistake, you might have been tempted to stop the program, correct it, and start over again. Resist that temptation. If you've made one error, you've probably made more. It's much more efficient to find them all at once than to keep running LaTeX over and over on the same input file, finding one mistake at a time. Keep typing *return* and try to get as far as you can.

Sometimes you will reach an impasse. A single mistake can cause TeX to produce hundreds of error messages, or to keep generating the same message over and over again forever. If you must stop LaTeX before it's finished, the best way is to type I\stop (that's the letter I before a \stop command) followed by a *return* in response to its question mark. Try that a few times. If TeX just keeps producing more error messages, then type X followed by *return*; this always works. However, if you stop TeX by typing X, it won't generate the last page of output—the one it was working on when it encountered the error. Since this output page could help you figure out what went wrong, you should first try stopping TeX with I\stop.

TeX may write a * and stop without any error message. This is probably due to a missing \end{document} command, but other errors can also cause it. If it happens, type \stop (with no I before it) followed by *return*. If that doesn't work, you'll have to use your computer's standard method for halting recalcitrant programs, which is described in the *Local Guide*.

Instead of sitting at your terminal waiting for errors, you can let LaTeX run unattended and find out what happened later by reading the log file. A \batchmode command at the very beginning of the input file causes TeX to process the file without stopping—much as if you were to type *return* in response to every error message, except the messages are not actually printed on your terminal. This is a convenient way to run LaTeX while you go out to lunch, but you could return to find that a small error resulted in a very long list of error messages on the log file.

Meanwhile, remember that besides deleting the z, we added the "gnomonly" to mess up the line breaking. After the last error message, LaTeX writes:

```
Overfull \hbox (10.58649pt too wide) in paragraph at lines 172--175
[]\tenrm Mathematical for-mu-las may also be dis-played. A dis-played for-mula
is gnomonly
```

This is a *warning* message; LaTeX does not stop (it did not print a "?"), but continues to the end of the input file without further incident. This warning was generated because TeX could not find a good place to break the indicated line. If you print the output, you'll find the word "gnomonly" extending beyond the right margin. This is not a serious problem; Section 5.2.1 describes how to correct it.

When you process your input file for the first time, LaTeX is likely to produce lots of error messages and warnings that you may not understand right away. The most important thing to remember is not to panic. Instead, turn to Chapter 6 to find out what to do.

2.4   Helpful Hints

The descriptions of individual LaTeX features include suggestions about their use. Here are a few general recommendations that can make using LaTeX easier.

If your documents contain mathematical formulas, as soon as you have acquired some experience using LaTeX you should read Section 3.4 to learn how to define your own commands and environments. When I write a paper, I find myself changing the notation much more than the concepts. Defining commands to express the concepts allows me to change notation by simply modifying the command definitions, without having to change every occurrence in the text. This saves a lot of work.

Unless your document is very short, you will want to see printed versions while you're writing it. If you print ten versions before completing it, then the first page will have been run through LaTeX and printed ten times before the last page is written. If page one isn't changed, you'll have printed nine unnecessary copies of it. Moreover, new input is seldom free of errors, especially if it contains complicated mathematical formulas. If you have to correct errors and rerun LaTeX each time, page one will have been processed twenty times rather than ten.

The easiest way to avoid all this extra processing is to write new input in a separate file and run LaTeX on that file. After correcting all the errors, you can move the new text to your main input file. The output generated by processing each new bit of text by itself won't have the right page or section numbers, but it will serve as a first draft while you are writing the rest of the document. You can run LaTeX on the main text file once in a while to get a good copy of the partially written document. With this procedure, you might wind up printing page one only three times instead of twenty. For a long document, in which you will frequently be changing parts that have already been written, you should use the commands of Section 4.4 to distribute your input over several files.

Perhaps the most annoying aspect of a computer program is the way it reacts to your errors. As with most programs, LaTeX's train of thought is derailed by simple errors that any person would easily correct. The best way to avoid this problem is to avoid those simple errors. Here are some common ones that are easy to eliminate by being careful.

- A misspelled command or environment name.

- Improperly matching braces.

- Trying to use one of the ten special characters # $ % & _ { } ~ ^ \ as an ordinary printing symbol.

- Improperly matching formula delimiters—for example, a \(command without the matching \).

- The use in ordinary text of a command like ^ that can appear only in a mathematical formula.

- A missing \end command.

- A missing command argument.

A good text editor can detect or help prevent some of these errors. Consult your *Local Guide* to see if such an editor is available on your computer.

2.5 Summary

This chapter has explained everything you have to know to prepare a simple document, which is quite a bit to remember. Here is a summary to refresh your memory.

Input Characters

The input file may contain the following characters: upper- and lowercase letters, the ten digits, the 16 punctuation characters

. : ; , ? ! ' ' ( ) [ ] - / * @

the ten special characters

$ % & _ { } ~ ^ \

(the first seven are printed by the commands \#, \$, etc.), and the five characters + = | < > used mainly in mathematical formulas. There are also invisible characters, which are all denoted by ␣, that produce spaces in the input file.

Commands and Environments

Command names consist of either a single special character like ~, a \ followed by a single nonletter (as in \@), or a \ followed by a string of letters. Spaces and a single end-of-line following the latter kind of command name are ignored; use a \␣ command to put an interword space after such a command. The case of letters in command names counts; most LaTeX command names contain only lowercase letters. A few commands have a *-form, a variant obtained by typing * after the command name.

Command arguments are enclosed in curly braces { and }, except optional arguments are enclosed in square brackets [and]. See Section C.1.1 if an optional argument has a square bracket or if a [in the text could be confused with the start of an optional argument. Do not leave any space between arguments, or any extra space within an argument; use a % to end a line without introducing space.

Some commands have *moving arguments*. The name of a fragile command must be preceded by a \protect command when it appears in a moving argument. Fragile commands include \(, \), \[, \], \begin, \end, \\, \item, and \footnote. A \protect command seldom hurts; when in doubt use one.

A declaration is a command that directs LaTeX to change the way it is formatting the document. The scope of a declation is delimited by enclosing it within curly braces or within an environment.

An environment has the form:

$$\begin\{name\} \ \ldots \ \end\{name\}$$

To every declaration corresponds an environment whose name is the same as the declaration's name without the \.

Sentences and Paragraphs

Sentences and paragraphs are typed pretty much as expected. TeX ignores the formatting of the input file. A blank line indicates a new paragraph.

Quotes are typed with the ' and ' characters, used in pairs for double quotes. The \, command separates multiple quotation marks, as in ''\,'Fum'\,''.

Dashes of various sizes are produced with one, two or three "-" characters.

A period, question mark, or exclamation point is considered to end a sentence unless it follows an uppercase letter. A \@ command before the punctuation character forces TeX to treat it as the end of a sentence, while a \␣ command placed after it produces an interword space.

The TeX and LaTeX logos are produced by the \TeX and \LaTeX commands. The \today command produces the current date, and \ldots produces an ellipsis (...).

Text is emphasized with the \em declaration. Emphasized text is usually set in italic type. A \/ command should appear immediately after an italic letter that is followed by roman text, unless the roman text begins with a period or comma.

The ~ command produces an interword space at which TeX will not start a new line. The \mbox command prevents TeX from breaking its argument across lines.

Footnotes are typed with the \footnote command, whose argument is the text of the footnote.

In-line mathematical formulas are enclosed by \(... \) or $ ... $. Subscripts and superscripts are made with the _ and ^ commands. The ' character produces a prime symbol (').

Larger Structures

The document begins with a \documentstyle command. This is followed by the preamble containing any special style declarations for the particular document. The actual text is contained in a document environment.

A title is produced by using the \title, \author, and \date commands to declare the necessary information, and the \maketitle command to generate the title. Multiple authors are separated by \and commands in the argument of \author.

A sectional unit is begun with one of the following sectioning commands

\part	\subsection	\paragraph
\chapter	\subsubsection	\subparagraph
\section		

whose argument produces the unit's heading and is a moving argument.

Displayed Material

Short quotations are displayed with the quote environment and long quotations with the quotation environment.

LaTeX provides three list-making environments: itemize for itemized lists, enumerate for enumerated lists, and description for lists with user-specified labels. Each item is begun with an \item command whose optional argument provides the item labels in the description environment.

The verse environment is used for poetry. A blank line begins a new stanza, and a line that does not end a stanza is followed by a \\ command—use * instead of \\ to prevent a page break after the line. (See Section C.1.1 if a * follows an ordinary \\ command.)

Displayed mathematical formulas are produced with the displaymath environment or the equivalent \[... \] construction. The equation environment produces numbered displayed formulas.

CHAPTER 3
Carrying On

Chapter 2 described commands for simple documents. Sooner or later, you'll write something that requires more sophisticated formatting. The commands and environments described in this chapter will handle most of those situations. Before getting to them, you should know a little more about how TeX operates.

As TeX processes your input text, it is always in one of three *modes*: paragraph mode, math mode, or left-to-right mode (called LR mode for short).[1] Paragraph mode is TeX's normal mode—the one it's in when processing ordinary text. In paragraph mode, TeX regards your input as a sequence of words and sentences to be broken into lines, paragraphs, and pages.

TeX is in math mode when it's generating a mathematical formula. More precisely, it enters math mode upon encountering a command like `$` or `\(` or `\[` or `\begin{equation}` that begins a mathematical formula, and it leaves math mode after finding the corresponding command like `\)` that ends the formula. When TeX is in math mode, it regards letters in the input file to be mathematical symbols, treating "`is`" as the product of i and s, and ignores any space characters between them.

In LR mode, as in paragraph mode, TeX considers your input to be a string of words with spaces between them. However, unlike paragraph mode, TeX produces output that keeps going from left to right; it never starts a new line in LR mode. The `\mbox` command (Section 2.2.1) causes TeX to process its argument in LR mode, which is what prevents the argument from being broken across lines.

Different modes can be nested within one another. If you put an `\mbox` command inside a mathematical formula, TeX is in LR mode when processing that command's argument, not in math mode. In processing

$y > z$ if x^2 real.

$$\texttt{\textbackslash(y > z \textbackslash mbox\{ if \$x\^{}\{2\}\$ real\} \textbackslash)} .$$

TeX is in math mode when processing `␣y␣>␣z␣`, in LR mode when processing `␣if␣` and `␣real`, and in math mode when processing `x^{2}`. The space between "z" and "if" is produced by the first `␣` in the `\mbox` command's argument, since space characters in the input produce space in the output when TeX is in LR mode. The `␣` in `real}␣\)` is processed in math mode, so it produces no space between "real" and "." in the output.

3.1 Changing the Type Style

Most of this book, including this sentence, is printed in a type style called "roman". It is the style that LaTeX uses unless you instruct it to select a different one. The `\em` declaration described in Section 2.2.1 tells LaTeX to start using

---

[1]Paragraph mode corresponds to the vertical and ordinary horizontal modes in *The TeXbook*, and LR mode is called restricted horizontal mode there. LaTeX also has a restricted form of LR mode called *picture* mode that is described in Section 5.5.

an *italic* type style—unless it already is using italics, in which case it chooses roman style. LATEX also provides five other type styles, shown below with the declarations that select them.

This is a bold type style.	`{\bf This is a bold type style.}`
This is a sans serif type style.	`{\sf This is a sans serif type style.}`
This is a slanted type style.	`{\sl This is a slanted type style.}`
THIS IS A SMALL CAPS TYPE STYLE.	`{\sc This is a Small Caps type style.}`
`This is a typewriter type style.`	`{\tt This is a typewriter type style.}`

The `\rm` declaration chooses roman type and `\it` chooses italic. Since roman is the default and italic is mainly for emphasis, produced by the `\em` command, these two declarations are seldom needed. All these type style declarations are robust.

Slanted and italic are both "leaning" type styles.

Compare closely *slanted* and *slanted.*	`... {\sl slanted\/} and {\it slanted}.`

The `\/` command described in Section 2.2.1 should be used to keep any leaning character from bumping against one that doesn't lean, not just between italic and roman characters. For example, it is used when switching from slanted to sans serif type.

The type style is a visual property of the printed output; it is not part of the document's logical structure. Therefore, these type style declarations should appear not in the text but in the definitions of the commands that describe the logical structure. (See Section 3.4.) However, some disciplines have special type style conventions—in computer science, for example, a programming language's reserved words are usually printed in bold type. In such a case, you might as well put the type style declaration in the text.

3.2 Symbols from Other Languages

Foreign languages have a variety of accents and special symbols; TEX can generate the ones used in most Western languages. The accents and symbols described in this section are not available in the typewriter (`\tt`) type style.

The commands in this section allow you to handle small pieces of foreign text in an English document. They are not adequate for typesetting a complete foreign-language document. Among other problems, foreign languages have different hyphenation rules than English, so an English-language version of LATEX may incorrectly hyphenate foreign words. Consult your *Local Guide* to find out if versions of LATEX designed specifically for other languages are available.

All the commands described in this section are robust.

ò \`{o}	õ \~{o}	ǒ \v{o}	ǫ \c{o}
ó \'{o}	ō \={o}	ő \H{o}	o̧ \d{o}
ô \^{o}	ȯ \.{o}	o͡o \t{oo}	o̲ \b{o}
ö \"{o}	ŏ \u{o}		

Table 3.1: Accents.

3.2.1 Accents

Table 3.1 shows how to make a wide variety of accents. In this and all similar tables, the TeX output is followed by the input that produces it, the first entry in Table 3.1 showing that you produce ó by typing \'{o}. The letter o appears in this table, but the commands can accent any letter.

El señor está bien, garçon.   `El se\~{n}or est\'{a} bien, gar\c{c}on.`

The letters *i* and *j* need special treatment because they should lose their dots when accented. The commands \i and \j produce a dotless *i* and *j*, respectively.

Él está aquí.   `\'{E}l est\'{a} aqu\'{\i}.`

The commands in Table 3.1 can be used only in paragraph and LR modes. Accents in math mode, which produce accented symbols in mathematical formulas, are made with commands described in Section 3.3.6.

3.2.2 Symbols

Table 3.2 shows how to make some foreign-language symbols. Note that the symbols ¿ and ¡ are produced by typing a pair of punctuation characters, in much the same way that a medium-length dash is produced by typing two - characters. The commands in Table 3.2 can appear only in paragraph and LR modes; use an \mbox command to put one inside a mathematical formula.

The following six special punctuation symbols can be used in any mode:

| † \dag | § \S | © \copyright |
| ‡ \ddag | ¶ \P | £ \pounds |

œ \oe	å \aa	ł \l	¿ ?`
Œ \OE	Å \AA	L \L	¡ !`
æ \ae	ø \o	ß \ss	
Æ \AE	Ø \O		

Table 3.2: Foreign Symbols

Remember also that the seven symbols # $ % & _ { } are produced by the seven commands \# \$ \% \& _ \{ \}.

In addition to the symbol-making commands described here, there are many others that can be used only in math mode. They are described in Section 3.3.2.

3.3   Mathematical Formulas

A formula that appears in the running text, called an *in-text* formula, is produced by the math environment. This environment can be invoked with either of the two short forms \(...\) or $...$, as well as by the usual \begin ... \end construction. The displaymath environment, which has the short form \[...\], produces an unnumbered displayed formula. The short forms $...$, \(...\), and \[...\] act as full-fledged environments, delimiting the scope of declarations contained within them. A numbered displayed formula is produced by the equation environment. Section 4.2 describes commands for assigning names to equation numbers and referring to the numbers by name, so you don't have to keep track of the actual numbers.

The math, displaymath, and equation environments put TeX in math mode. TeX ignores spaces in the input when it's in math mode (but space characters may still be needed to mark the end of a command name). Section 3.3.7 describes how to add and remove space in formulas. Remember that TeX is in LR mode, where spaces in the input generate space in the output, when it begins processing the argument of an \mbox command—even one that appears inside a formula.

All the commands introduced in this section can be used only in math mode, unless it is explicitly stated that they can be used elsewhere. Except as noted, they are all robust. However, remember that \begin, \end, \(, \), \[, and \] are fragile commands.

3.3.1   Some Common Structures

Subscripts and Superscripts

Subscripts and superscripts are made with the _ and ^ commands. These commands can be combined to make complicated subscript and superscript expressions.

$$x^{2y} \quad \texttt{x\^\{2y\}} \qquad x^{y^2} \quad \texttt{x\^\{y\^\{2\}\}} \qquad x_1^y \quad \texttt{x\^\{y\}\_\{1\}}$$
$$x_{2y} \quad \texttt{x\_\{2y\}} \qquad x^{y_1} \quad \texttt{x\^\{y\_\{1\}\}} \qquad x_1^y \quad \texttt{x\_\{1\}\^\{y\}}$$

Fractions

Fractions denoted by the / symbol are made in the obvious way.

Multiplying by $n/2$ gives $(m + n)/n$.   `Multiplying by $n/2$ gives \( (m+n)/n \).`

Most fractions in the running text are written this way. The `\frac` command is used for large fractions in displayed formulas; it has two arguments: the numerator and denominator.

$$x = \frac{y + z/2}{y^2 + 1}$$ `\[ x = \frac{y+z/2}{y^{2}+1} \]`

$$\frac{x + y}{1 + \frac{y}{z+1}}$$ `\[\frac{x+y}{1 + \frac{y}{z+1}}\]`

The `\frac` command can be used in an in-text formula to produce a fraction like $\frac{1}{2}$ (by typing `$\frac{1}{2}$`), but this is seldom done.

Roots

The `\sqrt` command produces the square root of its argument; it has an optional first argument for other roots.

A square root $\sqrt{x + y}$ and an nth root $\sqrt[n]{2}$.   `... \( \sqrt{x+y} \) ... \( \sqrt[n]{2} \).`

Ellipsis

The commands `\ldots` and `\cdots` produce two different kinds of ellipsis ($\ldots$).

A low ellipsis: $x_1, \ldots, x_n$.   `A low ellipsis: $x_{1}, \ldots ,x_{n}$.`
A centered ellipsis: $a + \cdots + z$.   `A centered ellipsis: $a + \cdots + z$.`

Use `\ldots` between commas and between juxtaposed symbols like $a \ldots z$; use `\cdots` between symbols like $+$, $-$, and $=$. TEX can also produce vertical and diagonal ellipses, which are used mainly in arrays.

$\vdots$ `\vdots` $\ddots$ `\ddots`

The `\ldots` command works in any mode, but `\cdots`, `\vdots`, and `\ddots` can be used only in math mode.

3.3.2   Mathematical Symbols

There are TEX commands to make almost any mathematical symbol you're likely to need. Remember that they can be used only in math mode.

Lowercase

α	\alpha	θ	\theta	o	o	τ	\tau
β	\beta	ϑ	\vartheta	π	\pi	υ	\upsilon
γ	\gamma	ι	\iota	ϖ	\varpi	ϕ	\phi
δ	\delta	κ	\kappa	ρ	\rho	φ	\varphi
ϵ	\epsilon	λ	\lambda	ϱ	\varrho	χ	\chi
ε	\varepsilon	μ	\mu	σ	\sigma	ψ	\psi
ζ	\zeta	ν	\nu	ς	\varsigma	ω	\omega
η	\eta	ξ	\xi				

Uppercase

Γ	\Gamma	Λ	\Lambda	Σ	\Sigma	Ψ	\Psi
Δ	\Delta	Ξ	\Xi	Υ	\Upsilon	Ω	\Omega
Θ	\Theta	Π	\Pi	Φ	\Phi		

Table 3.3: Greek Letters

Greek Letters

The command to produce a lowercase Greek letter is obtained by adding a \ to the name of the letter. For an uppercase Greek letter, just capitalize the first letter of the command name.

Making Greek letters is as easy as π (or Π).   `... is as easy as $\pi$ (or $\Pi$).`

(The $'s are needed because these commands can be used only in math mode.) If the uppercase Greek letter is the same as its roman equivalent, as in uppercase alpha, then there is no command to generate it. A complete list of the commands for making Greek letters appears in Table 3.3. Note that some of the lowercase letters have variant forms, made by commands beginning with `\var`. Also, observe that there's no special command for an omicron; you just use an `o`.

Calligraphic Letters

TeX provides twenty-six uppercase calligraphic letters $\mathcal{A}$, $\mathcal{B}$, ... , $\mathcal{Z}$, also called script letters. They are produced by a special type style invoked with the `\cal` declaration.

Choose a function $\mathcal{F}$ with $\mathcal{F}(x) > 0$.   `... $\cal F$ with \( {\cal F} (x) > 0 \).`

In this example, no brackets are needed in the first use of `\cal` because the $'s delimit the scope of the declaration. Only the twenty-six uppercase letters are available in the calligraphic type style.

±	\pm	∩	\cap	⋄	\diamond	⊕	\oplus
∓	\mp	∪	\cup	△	\bigtriangleup	⊖	\ominus
×	\times	⊎	\uplus	▽	\bigtriangledown	⊗	\otimes
÷	\div	⊓	\sqcap	◁	\triangleleft	⊘	\oslash
*	\ast	⊔	\sqcup	▷	\triangleright	⊙	\odot
⋆	\star	∨	\vee	◁	\lhd	○	\bigcirc
∘	\circ	∧	\wedge	▷	\rhd	†	\dagger
•	\bullet	\	\setminus	⊴	\unlhd	‡	\ddagger
·	\cdot	≀	\wr	⊵	\unrhd	⨿	\amalg

Table 3.4: Binary Operation Symbols.

A Menagerie of Mathematical Symbols

TeX can make dozens of special mathematical symbols. A few of them, such as $+$ and $>$, are produced by typing the corresponding keyboard character. Others are obtained with the commands in Tables 3.4 through 3.7. Additional symbols can be made by stacking one symbol on top of another with the \stackrel command of Section 3.3.6 or the array environment of Section 3.3.3. You can also put a slash through a symbol by typing \not before it.

If $x \not< y$ then $x \not\leq y - 1$.   If `$x \not< y$` then `\( x \not\leq y-1 \)`.

If the slash doesn't come out in exactly the right spot, put one of the math-mode spacing commands described in Section 3.3.7 between the \not command and the symbol.

There are some mathematical symbols whose size depends upon what kind of math environment they appear in; they are bigger in the displaymath and equation environments than in the ordinary math environment. These symbols are listed in Table 3.8, where both the large and small versions are shown.

≤	\leq	≥	\geq	≡	\equiv	⊨	\models
≺	\prec	≻	\succ	∼	\sim	⊥	\perp
⪯	\preceq	⪰	\succeq	≃	\simeq	∣	\mid
≪	\ll	≫	\gg	≍	\asymp	∥	\parallel
⊂	\subset	⊃	\supset	≈	\approx	⋈	\bowtie
⊆	\subseteq	⊇	\supseteq	≅	\cong	⋈	\Join
⊏	\sqsubset	⊐	\sqsupset	≠	\neq	⌣	\smile
⊑	\sqsubseteq	⊒	\sqsupseteq	≐	\doteq	⌢	\frown
∈	\in	∋	\ni	∝	\propto		
⊢	\vdash	⊣	\dashv				

Table 3.5: Relation Symbols

←	\leftarrow	⟵	\longleftarrow	↑	\uparrow
⇐	\Leftarrow	⟸	\Longleftarrow	⇑	\Uparrow
→	\rightarrow	⟶	\longrightarrow	↓	\downarrow
⇒	\Rightarrow	⟹	\Longrightarrow	⇓	\Downarrow
↔	\leftrightarrow	⟷	\longleftrightarrow	↕	\updownarrow
⇔	\Leftrightarrow	⟺	\Longleftrightarrow	⇕	\Updownarrow
↦	\mapsto	⟼	\longmapsto	↗	\nearrow
↩	\hookleftarrow	↪	\hookrightarrow	↘	\searrow
↼	\leftharpoonup	⇀	\rightharpoonup	↙	\swarrow
↽	\leftharpoondown	⇁	\rightharpoondown	↖	\nwarrow
⇌	\rightleftharpoons	↝	\leadsto		

Table 3.6: Arrow Symbols

ℵ	\aleph	′	\prime	∀	\forall	∞	\infty
ℏ	\hbar	∅	\emptyset	∃	\exists	□	\Box
ı	\imath	∇	\nabla	¬	\neg	◇	\Diamond
ȷ	\jmath	√	\surd	♭	\flat	△	\triangle
ℓ	\ell	⊤	\top	♮	\natural	♣	\clubsuit
℘	\wp	⊥	\bot	♯	\sharp	♢	\diamondsuit
ℜ	\Re	‖	|	\	\backslash	♡	\heartsuit
ℑ	\Im	∠	\angle	∂	\partial	♠	\spadesuit
℧	\mho						

Table 3.7: Miscellaneous Symbols

∑	\sum	∩	\bigcap	⊙	\bigodot
∏	\prod	∪	\bigcup	⊗	\bigotimes
∐	\coprod	⊔	\bigsqcup	⊕	\bigoplus
∫	\int	∨	\bigvee	⊎	\biguplus
∮	\oint	∧	\bigwedge		

Table 3.8: Variable-sized Symbols.

\arccos	\cos	\csc	\exp	\ker	\limsup	\min	\sinh
\arcsin	\cosh	\deg	\gcd	\lg	\ln	\Pr	\sup
\arctan	\cot	\det	\hom	\lim	\log	\sec	\tan
\arg	\coth	\dim	\inf	\liminf	\max	\sin	\tanh

Table 3.9: Log-like Functions.

Subscript-sized expressions that appear above and below them are typed as ordinary subscripts and superscripts.

Here's how they look when displayed:

$$\sum_{i=1}^{n} x_i = \int_{0}^{1} f$$

and in the text: $\sum_{i=1}^{n} x_i = \int_{0}^{1} f$.

Here's how they look when displayed:
```
\[\sum_{i=1}^{n} x_{i} = \int_{0}^{1} f \]
```
and in the text:
```
\(\sum_{i=1}^{n} x_{i} = \int_{0}^{1} f \).
```

Section 3.3.8 tells how how to coerce TEX into producing $\sum_{i=1}^{n}$ in a displayed formula and $\sum\limits_{i=1}^{n}$ in an in-text formula.

Log-like Functions

In a formula like "$\log(x+y)$", the "log", which represents the logarithm function, is a single word that is usually set in roman type. However, typing log in a formula denotes the product of the three quantities l, o, and g, which is printed as "log". The logarithm function is denoted by the \log command.

Logarithms obey the law: $\log xy = \log x + \log y$.   ... `\( \log xy = \log x + \log y \)`.

Other commands like \log for generating function names are listed in Table 3.9. Two additional commands produce the "mod" (modulo) function: \bmod for a binary relation and \pmod for a parenthesized expression. (Remember **b** as in *binary* and **p** as in *parenthesized*.)

$\gcd(m,n) = a \bmod b$ `\( \gcd(m,n)  =  a \bmod b \)`
$x \equiv y \pmod{a+b}$ `\( x  \equiv  y \pmod{a+b} \)`

Note that \pmod has an argument and produces parentheses, while \bmod produces only the "mod".

Some log-like functions act the same as the variable-sized symbols of Table 3.8 with respect to subscripts.

As a displayed formula:

$$\lim_{n \to \infty} x = 0$$

but in text: $\lim_{n \to \infty} x = 0$.

```
As a displayed formula:
  \[ \lim_{n \rightarrow \infty} x = 0 \]
but in text:
  \( \lim_{ ... } x = 0 \).
```

3.3.3   Arrays

The `array` Environment

Arrays are produced with the **array** environment. It has a single argument that specifies the number of columns and the alignment of items within the columns. For each column in the array, there is a single letter in the argument that specifies how items in the column should be positioned: `c` for centered, `l` for flush left, or `r` for flush right. Within the body of the environment, adjacent rows are separated by a \\ command and adjacent items within a row are separated by an & character.

$$
\begin{array}{clcr}
a+b+c & uv & x-y & 27 \\
a+b & u+v & z & 134 \\
a & 3u+vw & xyz & 2,978
\end{array}
$$

```
\begin{array}{clcr}
  a+b+c & uv    & x-y & 27    \\
  a+b   & u+v   & z   & 134   \\
  a     & 3u+vw & xyz & 2,978
\end{array}
```

There must be no **&** after the last item in a row and no \\ after the last row. TeX is in math mode when processing each array element, so it ignores spaces. Don't put any extra space in the argument.

In mathematical formulas, array columns are usually centered. However, a column of numbers often looks best flush right. Section 3.3.4 describes how to put large parentheses or vertical lines around an array to make a matrix or determinant.

A declaration that appears in an array item is local to that item; its scope is ended by the **&**, \\, or **\end{array}** that ends the item. The \\ command is fragile.

Vertical Alignment

TeX draws an imaginary horizontal center line through every formula, at the height where a minus sign at the beginning of the formula would go. An individual array item is itself a formula with a center line. The items in a row of an array are positioned vertically so their center lines are all at the same height.

Normally, the center line of an array lies where you would expect it, half way between the top and bottom. You can change the position of an array's center line by giving an optional one-letter argument to the **array** environment: the argument **t** makes it line up with the top row's center line, while **b** makes it line up with the bottom row's center line.

```
(  (                        )  )                        ↑  \uparrow
[  [                        ]  ]                        ↓  \downarrow
{  \{                       }  \}                       ↕  \updownarrow
⌊  \lfloor                  ⌋  \rfloor                  ⇑  \Uparrow
⌈  \lceil                   ⌉  \rceil                   ⇓  \Downarrow
⟨  \langle                  ⟩  \rangle                  ⇕  \Updownarrow
/  /                        \  \backslash
|  |                        ‖  \|
```

Table 3.10: Delimiters.

The box around each array in the following formula
is for clarity; it is not produced by the input:

$$
x - \begin{bmatrix} a_1 \\ \vdots \\ a_n \end{bmatrix} - \begin{array}{cc} u-v & 13 \\ & \boxed{\begin{array}{r} 12 \\ -345 \end{array}} \\ u+v & \end{array}
$$

```
...\[ x - \begin{array}{c}
         a_{1} \\ \vdots \\ a_{n}
      \end{array}
    - \begin{array}[t]{cl}
         u-v & 13 \\
         u+v & \begin{array}[b]{r}
                 12 \\ -345
              \end{array}
      \end{array}                       \]
```

More Complex Arrays

Visual formatting is sometimes necessary to get an array to look right. Section C.1.6 explains how to change the vertical space between two rows; Sections 3.3.7 and 5.4.1 describe commands for adding horizontal space within an item; and Section C.9.2 tells how to add horizontal space between columns. The **array** environment has a number of additional features for making more complex arrays; they are described in Section C.9.2.

The **array** environment can be used only in math mode and is meant for arrays of formulas; Section 3.6.2 describes an analogous **tabular** environment for making arrays of ordinary text items. The **array** environment is almost always used in a displayed formula, but it can appear in an in-text formula as well.

3.3.4 Delimiters

A *delimiter* is a symbol that acts logically like a parenthesis, with a pair of delimiters enclosing an expression. Table 3.10 lists every symbol that TeX regards as a delimiter, together with the command or input character that produces it. These commands and characters produce delimiters of the indicated size. However, delimiters in formulas should be big enough to "fit around" the expressions that they delimit. To make a delimiter the right size, type a **\left** or **\right** command before it.

Big delimiters are most often used with arrays.

$$\left(\left| \begin{array}{cc} x_{11} & x_{12} \\ x_{21} & x_{22} \\ & y \\ & z \end{array} \right. \right)$$

```
...\[ \left( \begin{array}{c}
              \left| \begin{array}{cc}
                     ... \end{array}
              \right|  \\
              y \\ z
       \end{array}     \right) \]
```

The \left and \right commands must come in matching pairs, but the matching delimiters need not be the same.

$$\vec{x} + \vec{y} + \vec{z} = \left(\begin{array}{c} a \\ b \end{array} \right[$$

```
\[  ... = \left( \begin{array}{c}
                 a \\ b
          \end{array}     \right[ \]
```

Some formulas require a big left delimiter with no matching right one, or vice versa. The \left and \right commands must match, but you can make an invisible delimiter by typing a "." after the \left or \right command.

$$x = \left\{ \begin{array}{ll} y & \mbox{if } y > 0 \\ z + y & \mbox{otherwise} \end{array} \right.$$

```
\[ x = \left\{ \begin{array}{ll}
               y    & \mbox{if $y>0$} \\
               z+y & \mbox{otherwise}
               \end{array}
   \right. \]
```

3.3.5   Multiline Formulas

The displaymath and equation environments make one-line formulas. A formula is displayed across multiple lines if it is a sequence of separate formulas or is too long to fit on a single line. A sequence of equations or inequalities is displayed with the eqnarray environment. It is very much like a three-column array environment, with consecutive rows separated by \\ and consecutive items within a row separated by & (Section 3.3.3). However, an equation number is put on every line unless that line has a \nonumber command.

The middle column can be anything, not just a '='.

$$x = 17y \tag{2}$$
$$y > a+b+c+d+e+f+g+h+i+j+ $$
$$k+l+m+n+o+p \tag{3}$$

```
...\begin{eqnarray}
   x & = & 17y \\
   y & > & a + ... + j +  \nonumber  \\
     &   & k + l + m + n + o + p
\end{eqnarray}
```

Section 4.2 describes how to let LaTeX handle references to equations so you don't have to remember equation numbers.

The eqnarray* environment is the same as eqnarray except it does not generate equation numbers.

$$x \quad \ll \quad y_1 + \cdots + y_n$$
$$\leq \quad z$$

```
\begin{eqnarray*}
 x  & \ll & y_{1} + \cdots + y_{n} \\
    & \leq & z
\end{eqnarray*}
```

A + or - that begins a formula is assumed to be a unary operator, so typing `$+x$` produces $+x$, with no space between the "+" and the "x". If the formula is part of a larger one that is being split across lines, TEX must be told that the + or − is a binary operator. This is done by starting the formula with an invisible first term, produced by an `\mbox` command with a null argument.

$$y \quad = \quad a + b + c + d + e + f + g + h + i + j$$
$$+ k + l + m + n + o + p$$

```
\begin{eqnarray*}
 y & = & a + b + c + ... + h + i + j \\
   &   & \mbox{} + k + ...
\end{eqnarray*}
```

A formula can often be split across lines using a `\lefteqn` command in an `eqnarray` or `eqnarray*` environment, as indicated by the following example:

$$w + x + y + z =$$
$$a + b + c + d + e + f + g + h + i + j +$$
$$k + l + m + n + o + p$$

```
\begin{eqnarray*}
\lefteqn{w+x+y+z = }  \\
 & &  a + ... + j +  \\
 & &  k + ... + o + p
\end{eqnarray*}
```

The `\lefteqn` command works by making TEX think that the formula it produces has zero width, so the left-most column of the `eqnarray` or `eqnarray*` environment is made suitably narrow. The indentation of the following lines can be increased by adding space (with the commands of Section 5.4.2) between the `\lefteqn` command and the `\\`.

Breaking a single formula across lines in this way is visual formatting, and I wish LATEX could do it for you. However, doing it well requires more intelligence than LATEX has, and doing it poorly can make the formula hard to understand, so you must do it yourself. This means that the formula may have to be reformatted if you change notation (changing the formula's length) or if you change document style (changing the line length).

3.3.6   Putting One Thing Above Another

Symbols in a formula are sometimes placed one above another. The `array` environment is good for vertically stacking subformulas, but not smaller pieces— you wouldn't use it to put a bar over an x to form $\bar{x}$. TEX provides special commands for doing this and some other common kinds of symbol stacking.

$\hat{a}$ \hat{a}	$\acute{a}$ \acute{a}	$\bar{a}$ \bar{a}	$\dot{a}$ \dot{a}
$\check{a}$ \check{a}	$\grave{a}$ \grave{a}	$\vec{a}$ \vec{a}	$\ddot{a}$ \ddot{a}
$\breve{a}$ \breve{a}	$\tilde{a}$ \tilde{a}		

Table 3.11: Math Mode Accents.

Over- and Underlining

The \overline command puts a horizontal line above its argument.

You can have nested overlining: $\overline{\overline{x}^2 + 1}$.   ... \(\overline{\overline{x}^{2} + 1} \).

There's an analogous \underline command for underlining that works in paragraph and LR mode as well as math mode, but it's seldom used in formulas.

The value is $\underline{3x}$.   \underline{The} value is $\underline{3x}$.

The \underline command is fragile.

   Horizontal braces are put above or below an expression with the \overbrace and \underbrace commands.

$$\overbrace{a + b + c + d}$$ \overbrace{a+ \underbrace{b + c} + d}

In a displayed formula, a subscript or superscript puts a label on the brace.

$$\underbrace{a + \overbrace{b + \cdots + y}^{24} + z}_{26}$$ \[\underbrace{a + \overbrace{b
                    + \cdots + y}^{24} + z }_{26} \]

Accents

The accent commands described in Section 3.2.1 are for ordinary text and cannot be used in math mode. Accents in formulas are produced with the commands shown in Table 3.11. The letter a is used as an illustration; the accents work with any letter.

   Wide versions of the \hat and \tilde accent are produced by the \widehat and \widetilde commands. These commands try to choose the appropriate-sized accent to fit over their argument, but they can't produce very wide accents.

Here are two sizes of wide hat: $\widehat{1-x} = \widehat{-y}$.   ... \(\widehat{1-x} = \widehat{-y} \).

The letters i and j should lose their dots when accented. The commands \imath and \jmath produce a dotless i and j, respectively.

There are no dots in $\vec{\imath} + \tilde{\jmath}$.   ... \(\vec{\imath} + \tilde{\jmath} \).

Stacking Symbols

The \stackrel command stacks one symbol above another.

$$A \xrightarrow{a'} B \xrightarrow{b'} C$$
$$\vec{x} \stackrel{\text{def}}{=} (x_1, \ldots, x_n)$$

```
\( A \stackrel{a'}{\rightarrow} B ... \)
\( \vec{x} \stackrel{\rm def}{=}  ... \)
```

See Section 3.3.8 for an explanation of the \rm command. The \stackrel command's first argument is printed in small type, like a superscript; use the \textstyle declaration of Section 3.3.8 to print it in regular-size type.

3.3.7   Spacing in Math Mode

In math mode, TEX ignores the spaces you type and formats the formula the way it thinks is best. Some authors feel that TEX cramps formulas, and they want to add more space. TEX knows more about typesetting formulas than many authors do. Adding extra space usually makes a formula prettier but harder to read, because it visually "fractures" the formula into separate units. Study how formulas look in ordinary mathematics texts before trying to improve TEX's formatting.

Although fiddling with the spacing is dangerous, you sometimes have to do it to make a formula look just right. One reason is that TEX may not understand the formula's logical structure. For example, it interprets y dx as the product of three quantities rather than as y times the differential dx, so it doesn't add the little extra space after the y that appears in $y\,dx$. Section 3.4 explains how to define your own commands for expressing this kind of logical structure, so you need worry about the proper spacing only when defining the commands, not when writing the formulas.

Like any computer program that makes aesthetic decisions, TEX sometimes needs human assistance. You'll have to examine the output to see if the spacing needs adjustment. Pay special attention to square root signs, integral signs, and quotient symbols (/).

The following four commands add the amount of horizontal space shown between the vertical lines:

‖	\,	thin space	‖	\:	medium space
‖	\!	negative thin space	‖	\;	thick space

The \! acts like a backspace, removing the same amount of space that \, adds. The \, command can be used in any mode, the others can appear only in math mode. Here are some examples of their use, where the result of omitting the spacing commands is also shown.

$\sqrt{2}\,x$	`\sqrt{2} \, x`	instead of	$\sqrt{2}x$
$n/\log n$	`n / \! \log n`	instead of	$n/\log n$
$\iint z\,dx\,dy$	`\int\!\!\int z\,dx\,dy`	instead of	$\int\int zdxdy$

As with all such fine tuning, you should not correct the spacing in formulas until you've finished writing the document and are preparing the final output.

3.3.8   Changing Style in Math Mode

Type Style

TeX's default type style for letters in math mode is *math italic*, which is somewhat different from ordinary italic.

Is *different* any *different* from dif^2e^2rnt?   `Is $different$ any {\em different\/} ...`

As is evident from this example, you should not use `$...$` as a shorthand for `{\em...}`.

The commands described in Section 3.1 for changing the type style work in math mode too, but they change the style only of letters and numbers, not of other symbols.

Note the nonbold $\sqrt{}$ and $\div$ in: $\mathbf{2}\sqrt{\mathbf{x}}\div\mathbf{y}=z$.   `... \( {\bf 2\sqrt{x} \div y} = z \).`

There are also two style-changing declarations that can be used only in math mode: `\cal` for producing calligraphic letters, described in Section 3.3.2, and `\mit` for math italic. Since math italic is the default in math mode, you'll seldom use the `\mit` command.

TeX regards uppercase Greek letters as letters, but lowercase Greek ones as symbols.

Note the nonbold π in $\mathbf{\Pi}\sim\pi\times\mathbf{x}$.   `... in $\bf \Pi \sim \pi \times x$.`

The `\boldmath` declaration causes TeX to make boldface the default for both letters and symbols in formulas. However, this declaration cannot be used in math mode, so you must use an `\mbox` command if you don't want all the symbols in a formula to be bold.

Only the x and π are bold here: $a+\boldsymbol{x\pi}-\rho$.   `...\(a + \mbox{\boldmath $x \pi$} - \rho\).`

The `\boldmath` and type style declarations do not change the style of everything one would expect them to. For example, subscripts and superscripts are not made bold by `\boldmath`. See Section C.14.4 for a list of all such anomalies.

Math Style

TEX uses the following four math styles when typesetting formulas:

> **display** For normal symbols in a displayed formula.
>
> **text** For normal symbols in an in-text formula.
>
> **script** For subscripts and superscripts.
>
> **scriptscript** For further levels of sub- and superscripting, such as subscripts of superscripts.

Display and text math styles are the same except for the size of the variable-sized symbols in Table 3.8 on page 45 and the placement of subscripts and superscripts on these symbols, on some of the log-like functions in Table 3.9 on page 46, and on horizontal braces. TEX uses small type in script style and even smaller type in scriptscript style. The declarations `\displaystyle`, `\textstyle`, `\scriptstyle`, and `\scriptscriptstyle` force TEX to use the indicated style.

Compare the small superscript in $e^{x(i)}$ with the large one in $e^{y(i)}$.

```
... small superscript in \( e^{x(i)} \)
... large one in \( e^{\textstyle y(i)} \).
```

3.3.9   When All Else Fails

If you write a lot of complicated formulas, sooner or later you'll encounter one that can't be handled with the commands described so far. When this happens, the first thing to do is look at the advanced LATEX features described in Sections C.6 and C.9.2. Commutative diagrams are easy to make with LATEX's `picture` environment, described in Section 5.5, which allows you to draw lines and arrows and to specify exactly where to put each part of the formula. Some formatting problems can be solved by using the commands in Section 5.4.3 to change how big TEX thinks a subformula is.

There are some formulas that can't be handled easily with LATEX commands. If you run into one, you have two choices: reading *The TEXbook* [3] to learn TEX's advanced commands for mathematics, or visually formatting the formula with the `picture` environment. Since this environment allows complete control over where each symbol is placed, it can be used to format any formula exactly the way you want it. However, this is a tedious way to make a formula and should be used only for solving rare problems. If you often encounter formulas that LATEX can't handle easily, then you're probably writing very heavy mathematics; learning more about TEX may ultimately save you time.

3.4   Defining Commands and Environments

The input file should display as clearly as possible the document's logical structure. Any structure, such as a mathematical notation, that is repeated should be expressed in a form that makes the structure apparent. This usually requires defining your own special command or environment. The following two sections explain how to do this. Section 3.4.3 describes how to handle theorems and similar structures.

3.4.1 Defining Commands $\quad$ p 172

The simplest type of repeated structure occurs when the same text appears in different places. The `\newcommand` declaration defines a new command to generate such text; its first argument is the command name and its second argument is the text.

Let Γ_i be the number of gnats per cubic meter, where Γ_i is normalized with respect to $\nu(s)$.

```
\newcommand{\gn}{$\Gamma_{i}$}
 ...
Let \gn\ be the  ...  where \gn\ is  ...
```

The `\␣` commands are needed because TEX ignores space characters following the command name `\gn`.

This example illustrates a common problem in defining commands to produce mathematical formulas. The `\Gamma` command can be used only in math mode, which is why the `$`'s are needed in the `\newcommand` argument. However, the command `\gn` cannot be used in math mode because the first `$` would cause TEX to leave math mode. The command

```
\newcommand{\gnat}{\mbox{$\Gamma_{i}$}}
```

defines `\gnat` to have the same effect as `\gn` when used in paragraph or LR mode, but `\gnat` can also be used in math mode. This is a trick worth remembering.

In addition to making the input more readable, defining your own commands can save typing. LATEX's command and environment names have generally been chosen to be descriptive rather than brief. You can use `\newcommand` to define abbreviations for frequently-used commands. For example, the declarations

```
\newcommand{\be}{\begin{enumerate}}
\newcommand{\ee}{\end{enumerate}}
```

define `\be` ... `\ee` to be equivalent to

```
\begin{enumerate} ... \end{enumerate}
```

For repetitive structures having components that vary, you can define commands with arguments by giving `\newcommand` an optional argument.

Since $gnu(5x; y)$ and $gnu(5x-1; y+1)$ represent adjacent populations, they are approximately equal.

```
\newcommand{\gnaw}[2]{{\em gnu\/}$(#1;#2)$}
 ...
Since \gnaw{5x}{y} and \gnaw{5x-1}{y+1} ...
```

The optional argument 2 (in square brackets) specifies that `\gnaw` has two arguments. The `#1` and `#2` in the last argument of `\newcommand` are called *parameters*; they are replaced by the first and second arguments, respectively, of `\gnaw` when that command is used. A command may have up to nine arguments.

When you define a command like `\gnaw`, the definition is saved exactly as it appears in the `\newcommand` declaration. When TEX encounters a use of `\gnaw`, it replaces `\gnaw` and its arguments by the definition, with the arguments substituted for the corresponding *parameters*—the `#1` replaced by the first argument and the `#2` replaced by the second. TEX then processes this text pretty much as if you had typed it instead of typing the `\gnaw` command. However, defining a command to have space at the end is usually a bad idea, since it can lead to extra space in the output when the command is used.

One command can be defined in terms of another.

The above definition of *gnu*(0; 1) gives *gnu*(5*x*; *y*) the expected value.

```
\newcommand{\usegnaw}{\gnaw{5x}{y}}
... of \gnaw{0}{1} gives \usegnaw\ the ...
```

It doesn't matter whether the `\newcommand` declaration defining `\usegnaw` comes before or after the one defining `\gnaw`, so long as they both come before any use of `\usegnaw`. However, a command cannot be defined in terms of itself, since TEX would chase its tail forever trying to figure out what such a definition meant.[2]

When TEX encounters a command, it looks for that command's arguments before interpreting it or any subsequent commands. Thus, you can't type

```
\newcommand{\gnawargs}{{5x}{y}} \gnaw\gnawargs is wrong
```

because TEX expects the `\gnaw` command to be followed by two arguments enclosed in braces, not by another command.

The braces surrounding the last argument of the `\newcommand` declaration do not become part of the command's definition, and the braces surrounding an argument are thrown away before substituting the argument for the corresponding parameter. This means that the braces delimiting an argument do not delimit the scope of declarations in the argument. To limit the scope of declarations contained within an argument, you must add explicit braces in the command definition.

gnus(*x*; 54) is fine, but in *gnus*(*x*; 54) *the scope of the emphasis declaration extends into the following text.*

```
\newcommand{\good}[3]{{#1}$({#2};{#3})$}
\newcommand{\bad}[3]{#1$(#2;#3)$}
...
\good{\em gnus\/}{x}{54} is fine, but in
\bad{\em gnus\/}{x}{54}, the scope ...
```

---

[2]This kind of recursive definition is possible using more advanced TEX commands, but it cannot be done with the LATEX commands described in this book.

Using `\newcommand` to define a command that already exists produces an error. The `\renewcommand` declaration redefines an already-defined command; it has the same arguments as `\newcommand`. Don't redefine an existing command unless you know what you're doing. Even if you don't explictly use a command, redefining it can produce strange and unpleasant results. Also, never define or redefine any command whose name begins with "`\end`".

The `\newcommand` and `\renewcommand` commands are declarations, their scopes determined by the rules given in Section 2.2.1. It's a good idea to put all command definitions together in the preamble; that way you won't have to search through the input file to find them.

3.4.2 Defining Environments

The `\newenvironment` command is used to define a new environment. A command of the form

> `\newenvironment{cozy}{`*begin text*`}{`*end text*`}`

defines a `cozy` environment for which TeX replaces a `\begin{cozy}` command by the *begin text* and an `\end{cozy}` command by the *end text*. A new environment is usually defined in terms of an existing environment such as `itemize`, with the *begin text* beginning the `itemize` environment and the *end text* ending it.

Here is an example of a user-defined environment:

- *This environment produces emphasized items.*
- *It is defined in terms of* LaTeX*'s* `itemize` *environment and* `\em` *command.*

```
\newenvironment{emphit}{\begin{itemize}
      \em}{\end{itemize}}
... example of a user-defined environment:
\begin{emphit}
 \item This environment produces ...
\end{emphit}
```

An optional argument of the `\newenvironment` command allows you to define an environment that has arguments; it works the same as described above for `\newcommand`.

Observe how a new logical structure—in this example, a labeled description of a single item—can be defined in terms of existing environments.

> *Armadillos*: This witty description of the armadillo was produced by the `descit` environment.

```
\newenvironment{descit}[1]{\begin{quote}
  {\em #1\/}:}{\end{quote}}
  ...
defined in terms of existing environments.
\begin{descit}{Armadillos}
This witty description of the armadillo ...
\end{descit}
```

The parameters (the `#1`, `#2`, etc.) can appear only in the *begin text*. The comments made above about the scope of declarations that appear inside arguments of a command defined with `\newcommand` apply to the arguments of environments defined with `\newenvironment`.

The \newenvironment command produces an error if the environment is already defined. Use \renewenvironment to redefine an existing environment. If \newenvironment complains that an environment you've never heard of already exists, choose a different environment name. Use \renewenvironment only when you know what you're doing; don't try redefining an environment that you don't know about.

3.4.3   Theorems and Such

Mathematical text usually includes theorems and/or theorem-like structures such as lemmas, propositions, axioms, conjectures, and so on. Nonmathematical text may contain similar structures: rules, laws, assumptions, principles, etc. Having a built-in environment for each possibility is out of the question, so LaTeX provides a \newtheorem declaration to define environments for the particular theorem-like structures in your document.

The \newtheorem command has two arguments: the first is the name of the environment, the second is the text used to label it.

Conjectures are numbered consecutively from the beginning of the document; this is the fourth one:

Conjecture 4 *All conjectures are interesting, but some conjectures are more interesting than others.*

```
\newtheorem{guess}{Conjecture}
...
document; this is the fourth one:
\begin{guess}
  All conjectures ... than others.
\end{guess}
```

The \newtheorem declaration is best put in the preamble, but it can go anywhere in the document.

A final optional argument to \newtheorem causes the theorem-like environment to be numbered within the specified sectional unit.

This is the first Axiom of Chapter 3:

Axiom 3.1 *All axioms are very dull.*

```
\newtheorem{axiom}{Axiom}[chapter]
...
\begin{axiom}
  All axioms are very dull.
\end{axiom}
```

Theorem-like environments can be numbered within any sectional unit; using section instead of chapter in the above example causes axioms to be numbered within sections.

Sometimes one wants different theorem-like structures to share the same numbering sequence—so, for example, the hunch immediately following Conjecture 5 should be Hunch 6.

Conjecture 5 *Some good conjectures are numbered.*

```
\newtheorem{guess}{Conjecture}
\newtheorem{hunch}[guess]{Hunch}
. . .
```

Hunch 6 *There are no sure-fire hunches.*

```
\begin{guess} Some good ... \end{guess}
\begin{hunch} There are ... \end{hunch}
```

The optional argument `guess` in the second `\newtheorem` command specifies that the `hunch` environment should be numbered in the same sequence as the `guess` environment.

A theorem-like environment defined with `\newtheorem` has an optional argument that is often used for the inventor or common name of a theorem, definition, or axiom.

Conjecture 7 (Fermat) *There do not exist integers $n > 2$, x, y, and z such that $x^n + y^n = z^n$.*

```
\begin{guess}[Fermat]
   There do not exist integers $n>2$, $x$,
   $y$, and $z$ such that ...
\end{guess}
```

See Section C.1.1 if the body of a theorem-like environment begins with a [.

3.5   Figures and Other Floating Bodies

3.5.1   Figures and Tables

Though documents would be easier to read if no sentence were ever split across two pages, typesetters must break sentences to avoid partially filled pages. Some things, like pictures and tables, cannot be split; they must be "floated" to convenient places, such as the top of the following page, to prevent half-empty pages. The standard LaTeX document styles provide two environments that cause their contents to float in this way: `figure` and `table`. The `figure` environment is generally used for pictures and the `table` environment for tabular information. Special document styles might also have environments for floating other kinds of objects, such as computer programs. However, LaTeX doesn't care what you use these environments for; so far as it's concerned, the only difference between them is how they are captioned.

The caption on a figure or table is made with a `\caption` command having the caption's text as its argument. This is a moving argument, so fragile commands must be `\protect`'ed (see Section 2.2.3). The `figure` or `table` environment is placed in with the text, usually just past the point where it is first mentioned.

The body of the figure goes here. This figure happened to float to the top of the current page.

Figure 7: The caption goes here.

⋮

This is place in the running text that mentions Figure 7 for the first time. The figure will not be put on an earlier page than the text preceding the `figure` environment.

```
This is place in the running text that
mentions Figure~7 for the first time.
  \begin{figure}
    The body of the figure goes here.
    This figure ... the current page.
    \caption{The caption goes here.}
  \end{figure}
The figure will not be put on an ...
```

TEX processes the body of a figure or table in paragraph mode. Figures are usually made with the `picture` environment of Section 5.5 and tables with the `tabular` environment of Section 3.6.2. Section 5.6 tells how to center the figure or table.

The `\vspace` command instructs LaTeX to leave room for material to be pasted in later, its argument specifying how much vertical space to allow. To leave room for a picture that's 3.5 inches high, you type:

```
\begin{figure}
    \vspace{3.5in}
    \caption{Isn't this a pretty picture?}
\end{figure}
```

If you prefer to think in centimeters, you can type `8.89cm` instead of `3.5in`. Section 5.4.1 gives other units for describing vertical space.

The `article` document style numbers figures and tables consecutively throughout the paper; the `report` and `book` document styles number them within chapters. Tables are numbered separately from figures, using the same numbering scheme. Section 4.2 explains how to number cross-references automatically, so you never have to type the actual figure numbers.

The body of a figure or table is typeset as a paragraph the same width as in the ordinary running text. Section 5.4.3 explains how to make paragraphs of different widths, position two half-width figures side by side, and do other sophisticated formatting within a `figure` or `table` environment. More than one `\caption` command can appear in the same `figure` or `table` environment, producing a single floating object with multiple numbered captions. The `\caption` command can be used only in a `figure` or `table` environment.

The standard document styles may place figures and tables above the text at the top of a page, below the text at the bottom of a page, or on a separate page containing nothing but figures and tables. Section C.8.1 describes the rules by which LaTeX decides where a floating object should float and how you can influence its decision; read that section if you don't understand why LaTeX put a figure or table where it did.

3.5.2   Marginal Notes

A marginal note is made with the \marginpar command, having the text as its
argument. The note is placed in the margin, its first line even with the line of   *This is a mar-*
text containing the command. TEX is in paragraph mode when processing the   *ginal note.*
marginal note. The following example shows how I typed this paragraph.

and, having the text as its
line even with the line of   *This is a mar-*
mode when processing the   *ginal note.*
yped this paragraph.

```
... placed in the margin,
\marginpar{\em This is a marginal note.}
its first line even with the line of
... how I typed this paragraph.
```

The standard document styles put notes in the right margin for one-sided
printing (the default), in the outside margin for two-sided printing (the twoside
style option), and in the nearest margin for two-column formatting (the
twocolumn style option). Section C.8.2 describes commands for getting LATEX
to put them in the opposite margin.

You may want a marginal note to vary depending upon which margin it's in.
For example, to make an arrow pointing to the text, you need a left-pointing
arrow in the right margin and a right-pointing one in the left margin. If the
\marginpar command is given an optional first argument, it uses that argument
if the note goes in the left margin and uses the second (mandatory) argument
if it goes in the right margin. The command

```
\marginpar [$\Rightarrow$]{$\Leftarrow$}
```

makes an arrow that points towards the text, whichever margin the note appears
in.[3]

A marginal note is never broken across pages; a note that's too long will
extend below the page's bottom margin. LATEX moves a marginal note down on
the page to keep it from bumping into a previous one, warning you when it does
so. When using notes more than two or three lines long, you may have to adjust
their placement according to where they happen to fall on the page. The vertical
position of a note is changed by beginning it with a vertical spacing command
(Section 5.4.2). You may also have to use the commands of Section 5.2.2 to
control where LATEX starts a new page. This is visual design, which means
reformatting if you make changes to the document. Save this job until the very
end, after you've finished all the writing.

Marginal notes are not handled efficiently by LATEX; it may run out of space if
you use too many of them. How many you can use before this happens depends
upon what computer you're running LATEX on and how many figures and tables
you have, but more than five marginal notes on any one page is dangerous.

---

[3]The arrows won't be symmetrically placed, since both will be at the left of the space
reserved for marginal notes. The \hfill command of Section 5.4.2 can be used to adjust their
horizontal position.

3.6   Lining It Up in Columns

The tabbing and tabular environments both can align text in columns. The tabbing environment allows you to set tab stops similar to the ones on a typewriter, while the tabular environment is similar to the array environment described in Section 3.3.3, except that it is for ordinary text rather than formulas. The tabbing and tabular environments differ in the following ways:

- The tabbing environment can be used only in paragraph mode and makes a separate paragraph; the tabular environment can be used in any mode and can put a table in the middle of a formula or line of text.

- TEX can start a new page in the middle of a tabbing environment, but not in the middle of a tabular environment. Thus, a long tabbing environment can appear in the running text, but a long tabular environment should go in a figure or table (Section 3.5.1).

- TEX automatically determines the widths of columns in the tabular environment; you have to do that yourself in the tabbing environment by setting tab stops.

- A change of format in the middle of the environment is easier in the tabbing than in the tabular environment. This makes the tabbing environment better at formatting computer programs.

3.6.1   The tabbing Environment   ᖯ 179

In the tabbing environment, you align text in columns by setting tab stops and tabbing to them, somewhat as you would with an ordinary typewriter. Tab stops are set with the \= command, and \> moves to the next tab stop. Lines are separated by the \\ command.

The tabbing environment starts a new line.

If it's raining
    then put on boots,
            take hat;
    else smile.
Leave house.

The text that follows starts on a new line, beginning a new paragraph if you leave a blank line after the \end{tabbing} command.

```
... environment starts a new line.
\begin{tabbing}
If \= it's raining          \\
    \> then \= put on boots,\\
    \>         \> take hat;    \\
    \> else \> smile.          \\
Leave house.
\end{tabbing}
The text that follows starts on a new ...
```

Unlike a typewriter's tabbing key, the \> command tabs to the logically next tab stop, even if that means tabbing to the left.

```
                                          \begin{tabbing}
A short column                               A short          \= column.      \\
This is t̸o̸o̸ l̸o̸n̸g̸ / / /                        This is too long. \> / / / / / / /
                                          \end{tabbing}
                                          \mbox{}
```

Remember that the input file's format doesn't matter; one space is the same as a hundred.

The \= command resets the logically next tab stop.

```
                                          \begin{tabbing}
Old Column 1 Old Col 2 Old Col 3          Old Column 1 \= Old Col 2  \= Old Col 3  \\
Col 1        Col 2                         Col 1          \> Col 2                  \\
New Col 1 New 2      Same Col 3           New Col 1  \= New 2       \> Same Col 3 \\
Col 1     Col 2      Col 3                 Col 1      \> Col 2       \> Col 3
                                          \end{tabbing}
```

Spaces are ignored after a \= or \> command, but not before it.

A line that ends with a \kill command instead of a \\ produces no output, but can be used for setting tabs.

```
                                          \begin{tabbing}
                                          Armadillo \= Armament \=        \kill
Gnat     Gnu      Gnome                   Gnat      \> Gnu       \> Gnome \\
Armadillo Armament Armorer                Armadillo \> Armament \> Armorer
                                          \end{tabbing}
```

A declaration made in a **tabbing** environment is local to the current item; its scope is ended by the next \=, \>, \\, \kill, or \end{tabbing} command.

```
A lively gnat     A dull gnu              A lively \em gnat  \> A dull gnu \\
```

The **tabbing** environment has a number of additional features that are described in Section C.9.1.

3.6.2 The **tabular** Environment   ⌐182

The **tabular** environment is similar to the **array** environment, so you should read Section 3.3.3 before reading any further here. It differs from the **array** environment in two ways: it may be used in any mode, not just in math mode, and its items are processed in LR mode instead of in math mode. This makes **tabular** better for tabular lists and **array** better for mathematical formulas. This section describes some features used mainly with the **tabular** environment, although they apply to **array** as well.

A | in the **tabular** environment's argument puts a vertical line extending the full height of the environment in the specified place. An \hline command after a \\ or at the beginning of the environment draws a horizontal line across the full width of the environment. The \cline{i-j} command draws a horizontal line across columns i through j, inclusive.

gnats	gram	$13.65
	each	.01
gnu	stuffed	92.50
emur		33.33
armadillo	frozen	8.99

```
\begin{tabular}{|||l|lr||}          \hline
gnats        & gram     &\$13.65 \\ \cline{2-3}
             & each     &     .01 \\ \hline
gnu          & stuffed &  92.50
                       \\  \cline{1-1} \cline{3-3}
emur         &         &   33.33 \\ \hline
armadillo & frozen   &    8.99 \\ \hline
\end{tabular}
```

This is the only situation in which a \\ goes after the last row of the environment.

A single item that spans multiple columns is made with a \multicolumn command, having the form

$$\multicolumn\{n\}\{pos\}\{item\}$$

where n is the number of columns to be spanned, *pos* specifies the horizontal positioning of the item—just as in the environment's argument—and *item* is the item's text. The *pos* argument replaces the portion of the environment's argument corresponding to the n spanned columns; it must contain a single l, r, or c character and may contain | characters.

Note the placement of "Item" and "Price":

	Item	Price
gnat	(dozen)	3.24
gnu	(each)	24,985.47

```
...\begin{tabular}{llr}
\multicolumn{2}{c}{Item} &
   \multicolumn{1}{c}{Price} \\
gnat & (dozen) &   3.24        \\
gnu  & (each)  & 24,985.47
\end{tabular}
```

A \multicolumn command spanning a single column serves to override the item positioning specified by the environment argument.

When the environment argument has | characters, it's not obvious which of them get replaced by a \multicolumn's positioning argument. The rule is: *the part of the environment argument corresponding to a single column begins with an* l, r, *or* c *character.*

type	*style*	
smart	red	short
rather silly	puce	tall

```
\begin{tabular}{|l|l|r|}      \hline\hline
{\em type} &
   \multicolumn{2}{c|}{\em style} \\ \hline
smart          & red & short \\
rather silly & puce & tall \\ \hline\hline
\end{tabular}
```

The `tabular` environment produces an object that TeX treats exactly like a single, big letter. You could put it in the middle of a paragraph—or in the middle of a word—but that would look rather strange. A `tabular` environment is usually put in a figure or table (Section 3.5.1), or else displayed on a line by itself, using the `center` environment of Section 5.6.

3.7 Simulating Typed Text

A printed document may contain simulated typed text—for example, the instruction manual for a computer program usually shows what the user types. The `\tt` declaration produces a typewriter type style (Section 3.1), but it doesn't stop TeX from breaking the text into lines as it sees fit. The `verbatim` environment allows you to type the text exactly the way you want it to appear in the document.

The `verbatim` environment is the one place where LaTeX pays attention to how the input file is formatted.

```
What the    #%|&$_\^~ is  ``going'' {on}
   here \today \\\\????
```

```
... to how the input file is formatted.
\begin{verbatim}
What the    #%|&$_\^~ is  ``going'' {on}
   here \today \\\\????
\end{verbatim}
```

Each space you type produces a space in the output, and new lines are begun just where you type them. Special characters such as \ and { are treated like ordinary characters in a `verbatim` environment. In fact, you can type anything in the body of a `verbatim` environment except for the fourteen-character sequence "`\end{verbatim}`".

The `verbatim` environment begins on a new line of output, as does the text following it. A blank line after the `\end{verbatim}` starts a new paragraph as usual.

The `\verb` command simulates a short piece of typed text inside an ordinary paragraph. Its argument is not enclosed in braces, but by a pair of identical characters.

The `%\ }{@&` gnat and `--#$` gnus are silly.

```
The \verb+%\ }{@&+ gnat and \verb2--#$2 ...
```

The argument of the first `\verb` command is contained between the two + characters, the argument of the second between two 2 characters. Instead of + or 2, you can use any character that does not appear in the argument except a space, a letter, or a *. The argument of `\verb` may contain spaces, but it should all be on a single line of the input file.

There are also a `verbatim*` environment and a `\verb*` command. They are exactly like `verbatim` and `\verb` except that a space produces a ⊔ symbol instead of a blank space.

You can type $x\_=\_y$ or $\_$x=y$\_$.   ... \verb*|$x = y$| or \verb*/ $x=y$ /.

The verbatim environment and \verb command are inherently anomalous, since characters like $ and } don't have their usual meanings. This results in the following restrictions on their use:

- A verbatim environment or \verb command may not appear within an argument of any other command. (However, they may appear inside another environment.)

- There may be no space between a \verb or \verb* command and its argument.

- There may be no space between "\end" and "{" in \end{verbatim}.

The verbatim environment is for simulating typed text; it is not intended to turn LATEX into a typewriter. If you're tempted to use it for visual formatting, don't; use the tabbing environment of Section 3.6.1 instead.

3.8   Letters

The letter document style is for making letters—the kind that are put in an envelope and mailed. You can make any number of letters with a single input file. Your name and address, which are likely to be the same for all letters, are specified by declarations. The return address is declared by an \address command, with multiple output lines separated by \\ commands.

```
\address{1234 Ave.\ of the Armadillos\\
        Gnu York, G.Y. 56789}
```

The \signature command declares your name, as it appears at the end of the letter, with the usual \\ commands separating multiple lines.

```
\signature{R. (Ma) Dillo  \\  Director of Cuisine}
```

These declarations are usually put in the preamble, but they are ordinary declarations with the customary scoping rules and can appear anywhere in the document.

Each letter is produced by a separate letter environment, having the name and address of the recipient as its argument. The argument of the letter environment is a moving argument. The letter itself begins with an \opening command that generates the salutation.

1234 Ave. of the Armadillos
Gnu York, G.Y. 56789

July 4, 1996

Dr. G. Nathaniel Picking
Acme Exterminators
33 Swat Street
Hometown, Illinois 62301

Dear Nat,

I'm afraid that the armadillo problem is still with us. I did everything ...

```
\begin{letter}{Dr.\ G. Nathaniel Picking \\
   Acme Exterminators\\ 33 Swat Street \\
   Hometown, Illinois 62301}

\opening{Dear Nat,}

I'm afraid that the armadillo problem
is still with us.  I did everything
...
```

The return address is determined by the \address declaration; LaTeX supplies the date. An \address and/or \signature command that applies just to this letter can be put between the \begin{letter} and the \opening command.

The main body of the letter is ordinary LaTeX input, but commands like \section that make no sense in a letter should not be used. The letter closes with a \closing command.

... and I hope you can get rid of the nasty beasts this time.

Best regards,

R. (Ma) Dillo
Director of Cuisine

```
... and I hope you can get rid of the nasty
beasts this time.

\closing{Best regards,}
```

The name comes from the \signature declaration.

The \cc command can be used after the closing to list the names of people to whom you are sending copies.

cc: Jimmy Carter
    Richard M. Nixon

```
\cc {Jimmy Carter \\ Richard M. Nixon}
```

There's a similar \encl command for a list of enclosures.

Additional text after the closing must be preceded by a \ps command. This command generates no text—you'll have to type the "P.S." yourself—but is needed to format the additional text correctly.

A \makelabels command in the preamble will cause LaTeX to print a list of mailing labels, one for each letter environment, in a format suitable for xerographic copying onto "peel-off" labels. A mailing label without a corresponding letter is produced by an empty letter environment—one with nothing between the argument and the \end{letter} command.

The letter document style may have other special features—especially if you are using LaTeX at a company or university. For example, leaving out the

\address declaration may cause the letter to be formatted for copying onto the company letterhead. Consult the *Local Guide* for more information.

CHAPTER 4
Moving Information Around

The commands described in this chapter all enable you to move information from one place to another. For example, when you make a table of contents, the information it contains comes from the sectioning commands that are scattered throughout the input file. Similarly, the LaTeX command that generates a cross reference to an equation must get the equation number from the `equation` environment, which may occur several chapters later.

Moving information in this way requires two passes over the input: one pass to find the information and a second pass to put it into the text. To compile a table of contents, one pass determines the titles and starting pages of all the sections and a second pass puts this information into the table of contents. Instead of making two passes every time it is run, LaTeX reads your input file only once and saves the cross-referencing information in special files for use the next time. For example, if `sample.tex` had a command to produce a table of contents, then LaTeX would write the necessary information into the file `sample.toc`. It would use the information in the current version of `sample.toc` to produce the table of contents, and would write a new version of that file to produce the table of contents the next time LaTeX is run with `sample.tex` as input.

LaTeX's cross-referencing information is therefore always "old", since it was gathered on a previous execution. This will be noticeable mainly when you are first writing the document—for example, a newly added section won't be listed in the table of contents. However, the last changes you make to your document will normally be minor ones that polish the prose rather than add new sections or equations. The cross-referencing information is unlikely to change the last few times you run LaTeX on your file, so all the cross-references will almost always be correct in the final version. In any case, if the cross-referencing is incorrect, LaTeX will type a warning message when it has finished. Running it again on the same input will correct any errors.[1]

4.1 The Table of Contents

A `\tableofcontents` command produces a table of contents. More precisely, it does two things:

- It causes LaTeX to write a new `toc` file—that is, a file with the same first name as the input file and the extension `toc`—with the information needed to generate a table of contents.

- It reads the information from the previous version of the `toc` file to produce a table of contents, complete with heading.

---

[1]If you're a computer wizard or are very good at mathematical puzzles, you may be able to create a file in which a reference to a page number always remains incorrect. The chance of that happening by accident is infinitesimal.

The commands \listoffigures and \listoftables produce a list of figures and a list of tables, respectively. They work just like the \tableofcontents command, except that LaTeX writes a file with extension lof when making a list of figures and a file with extension lot when making a list of tables.

You can edit the toc, lof, and lot files yourself if you don't like what LaTeX does. This allows you to perform such fine tuning as changing the page breaks in a long table of contents. Do this only when preparing the final version of your document, and use a \nofiles command (described in Section C.10.1) to suppress the writing of new versions of the files.

4.2   Cross-References

One reason for numbering things like figures and equations is to refer the reader to them, as in: "See Figure 3 for more details." You don't want the "3" to appear in the input file because adding another a figure might make this one become Figure 4. Instead, you can assign a *key* of your choice to this figure and refer to it by that key, letting LaTeX translate the reference into the figure number. The key is assigned by the \label command, and is referred to by the \ref command. A \label command appearing in ordinary text assigns to the key the number of the current sectional unit; one appearing inside a numbered environment assigns that number to the key. In the following example, the \label{eq:euler} command assigns the key eq:euler to the equation number, and the command \ref{eq:euler} generates that equation number.

Equation 12 in Section 2.3 below is Euler's famous result.

⋮

2.3 Early Results

Euler's equation

$$e^{i\pi} + 1 = 0 \qquad (12)$$

combines the five most important numbers in mathematics in a single equation.

```
Equation~\ref{eq:euler} in
Section~\ref{sec-early} below
...
\subsection{Early Results}
\label{sec-early}
Euler's equation
\begin{equation}
  e^{i\pi} + 1 = 0      \label{eq:euler}
\end{equation}
combines the five most important ...
```

A key can consist of any sequence of letters, digits, or punctuation characters (Section 2.1). Upper- and lowercase letters are different, so gnu and Gnu are distinct keys.

To assign the number of a sectional unit to a key, you can put the \label command anywhere within the unit except within an environment in which it would assign some other number, or you can put it in the argument of the sectioning command. The following environments generate numbers that can be assigned to keys with a \label comand: equation, eqnarray, enumerate (assigns the current item's number), `figure`, `table`, and any theorem-like environment defined with the `\newtheorem` command of Section 3.4.3. Since there can be several captions in a `figure` or `table` environment, `\caption` works like a sectioning command within the environment, with the `\label` command going either after the `\caption` command or in its argument.

The `\pageref` command is similar to the `\ref` command except it produces the page number of the place in the text where the corresponding `\label` command appears.

See page 42 for more details.

⋮

Text on page 42:
The meaning of life, the universe, and ...

```
See page~\pageref{'meaning'} for more
...
The \label{'meaning'} meaning of life, ...
```

See Section 2.2.1 for an explanation of why the ~ command is needed. A `\ref` or `\pageref` command generates only the number, so you have to type the "**page**" to produce "**page 42**".

The numbers generated by `\ref` and `\pageref` were assigned to the keys the previous time you ran LaTeX on your document. While section and equation numbers are changed only by adding or removing a section or equation, adding or deleting any text may change the page number assigned to a key.

The `\ref` and `\pageref` commands are fragile. A `\label` can appear in the argument of a sectioning or `\caption` command, but in no other moving argument. If you use a lot of keys (more than about forty), try to keep them reasonably short or you may cause LaTeX to run out of space.

Using keys for cross-referencing saves you from keeping track of the actual numbers, but it requires you to remember the keys. You can produce a list of the keys by running LaTeX on the input file `lablst`. (Your *Local Guide* tells exactly how to do this.) LaTeX will then ask you to type in the name of the input file whose keys you want listed, as well as the name of the document style specified by that file's `\documentstyle` command.

4.3   Bibliography and Citation

A citation is a cross-reference to another publication, such as a journal article, called the *source*. The modern method of citing a source is with a cross-reference to an entry in a list of sources at the end of the document. With LaTeX, you can either produce the list of sources yourself or else use a separate program called BibTeX to generate it from information contained in a bibliographic database.

4.3.1   Doing It Yourself

The source list is created with a `thebibliography` environment, which is like the `enumerate` environment described in Section 2.2.4 except that:

- List items are begun with the `\bibitem` command. Its argument is a key by which the source can be cited with a `\cite` command. (The `\bibitem` and `\cite` commands work much like the `\label` and `\ref` commands of Section 4.2.)

- The `thebibliography` environment has an argument that should be a piece of text the same width as or slightly wider than the widest item label in the source list.

See [67] for the hairy details.

⋮

References

⋮

[67] D. E. Knudson. *1966 World Gnus Almanac.* Permafrost Press, Novosibirsk.

```
See \cite{kn:gnus} for the hairy details.
...
\begin{thebibliography}{99}
...
\bibitem{kn:gnus} D. E. Knudson.
{\em 1966 World Gnus Almanac.}
...
\end{thebibliography}
```

Note that "99" is exactly as wide as all other two-digit numbers.

A key can be any sequence of letters, digits and punctuation characters, except that it may not contain a comma (,). As usual in LaTeX, upper- and lowercase letters are considered to be different.

You can cite multiple sources with a single `\cite`, separating the keys by commas. The `\cite` command has an optional argument that adds a note to the citation.

See [4,15,36] or [67, pages 222–333] for information on the care and feeding of gnus.

```
See \cite{tom-gnat,dick:gnu,harry-arm} or
\cite[pages 222--333]{kn:gnus} for ...
```

Instead of using numbers, you can choose your own labels for the sources by giving an optional argument to the `\bibitem` command.

See [Knud 66] for the hairy details.

⋮

References

⋮

[Knud 66] D. E. Knudson. *1966 World Gnus Almanac.* Permafrost Press, Novosibirsk.

```
See \cite{kn:gnus} for the hairy details.
...
\begin{thebibliography}{Dillo 83}
...
\bibitem[Knud 66]{kn:gnus} D. E. Knudson.
{\em 1966 World Gnus Almanac.}
...
\end{thebibliography}
```

In this example, "[Dillo 83]" should be the longest label. The optional argument of \bibitem is a moving argument.

As in any kind of cross-reference, citations are based upon the information gathered the previous time LaTeX was run on the file, so when you change the source list, the citations won't change until the second time you run LaTeX.

4.3.2   Using BibTeX

BibTeX is a separate program that produces the source list for a document, obtaining the information from a bibliographic database. With BibTeX, the \cite command is used as above for citations, but instead of typing the source list yourself, you type a \bibliography command whose argument specifies one or more files containing the bibliographic database. The names of the database files must have the extension bib. For example, the command

> \bibliography{insect,animal}

specifies that the source list is to be obtained from entries in the files insect.bib and animal.bib. See Appendix B to find out how to make bibliographic database files.

The \nocite command causes one or more entries to appear in the source list, but produces no output. For example, \nocite{g:nu,g:nat} causes BibTeX to put bibliography database entries having keys g:nu and g:nat in the source list. A \nocite command can go anywhere after the \begin{document} command, but it is fragile.

The \bibliographystyle command specifies the *bibliography style*, which determines the format of the source list—just as the document style determines the document's format. For example, the command

> \bibliographystyle{plain}

specifies that entries should be formatted as specified by the plain bibliography style. The \bibliographystyle command must go after the \begin{document} command.

The standard bibliography styles include the following.

plain Formatted more or less as suggested by van Leunen in *A Handbook for Scholars* [7]. Entries are sorted alphabetically and are labeled with numbers.

unsrt The same as plain except that entries appear in the order of their first citation.

alpha The same as plain except that entry labels like "Knu66", formed from the author's name and the year of publication, are used.

abbrv The same as `plain` except that entries are more compact because first
names, month names, and journal names are abbreviated.

BIBTEX's bibliography styles can be customized to handle most bibliography
formatting problems, but this requires sophisticated programming. The *Local
Guide* tells if any other bibliography styles are available and where to look for
information on creating your own styles.

To produce a source list with BIBTEX, you have to understand how LaTeX and
BIBTEX interact. When you ran LaTeX with the input file `sample.tex`, you may
have noticed that LaTeX created a file named `sample.aux`. This file, called an
auxiliary file, contains cross-referencing information. Since `sample.tex` contains
no cross-referencing commands, the auxiliary file it produces has no information.
However, suppose that LaTeX is run with an input file named `myfile.tex` that
has citations and bibliography-making commands. The auxiliary file `myfile.aux`
that it produces will contain all the citation keys and the arguments of the
`\bibliography` and `\bibliographystyle` commands. When BIBTEX is run,
it reads this information from the auxiliary file and produces a file named
`myfile.bbl` containing LaTeX commands to produce the source list. (Your
Local Guide explains how to run BIBTEX on your computer.) The next time
LaTeX is run on `myfile.tex`, the `\bibliography` command reads the `bbl` file
(`myfile.bbl`), which generates the source list.

This procedure has the disadvantage that adding or removing a citation
may require running BIBTEX again to produce a new source list. (Moreover,
remember that changes to the source list are not immediately reflected in the
citations.) It has the advantage that you can edit the `bbl` file yourself if you
don't like the source list BIBTEX produced. While BIBTEX gets most source-list
entries right, it is only a computer program, so you may occasionally encounter
a source that it does not handle properly. When this happens, you can correct
the entry on the `bbl` file.

4.4   Splitting Your Input

A large document requires a lot of input. Rather than putting the whole input
in a single large file, it's more efficient to split it into several smaller ones.
Regardless of how many separate files you use, there is one that is the *root* file;
it is the one whose name you type when you run LaTeX.

The `\input` command provides the simplest way to split your input into several files. The command `\input{gnu}` in the root file causes LaTeX to insert the
contents of the file `gnu.tex` right at the current spot in your manuscript—just
as if the `\input{gnu}` command were removed from the root file and replaced
by the contents of the file `gnu.tex`. (However, the input files are not changed.)
The file `gnu.tex` may also contain an `\input` command, calling another file that
may have its own `\input` commands, and so on.

Besides splitting your input into convenient-sized chunks, the \input command also makes it easy to use the same input in different documents. While text is seldom recycled in this way, you might want to reuse declarations. You can keep a file containing declarations that are used in all your documents, such as the definitions of commands and environments for your own logical structures (Section 3.4). You can even begin your root file with an \input command and put the \documentstyle command in your declarations file.

Another reason for splitting the input into separate files is to run LaTeX on only part of the document so, when you make changes, only the parts that have changed need to be processed. For this, you must use the \include command instead of \input. The two commands are similar in that \include{gnu} also specifies that the contents of the file gnu.tex should be inserted in its place. However, with the \include command, you can tell LaTeX either to insert the file or to omit it and process all succeeding text as if the file had been inserted, numbering pages, sections, equations, etc. as if the omitted file's text had been included.

To run LaTeX on only part of the document, the preamble must contain an \includeonly command whose argument is a list of files (first names only). The file specified by an \include command is processed only if it appears in the argument of the \includeonly command. Thus, if the preamble contains the command

\includeonly{gnu,gnat,gnash}

then an \include{gnat} command causes the file gnat.tex to be included, while the command \include{rmadlo} causes LaTeX *not* to include the file rmadlo.tex, but to process the text following it as if the file had been included. More precisely, it causes LaTeX to process the succeeding text under the assumption that the omitted file is exactly the same as it was the last time it was included. LaTeX does not read an omitted file and is unaware of any changes made to the file since it was last included.

The entire root file is always processed. If the preamble does not contain an \includeonly command, then every \include command inserts its file. The command \includeonly{} (with a null argument) instructs LaTeX to omit all \include'd files. An \include can appear only after the \begin{document} command.

The \include command has one feature that limits its usefulness: the included text always starts a new page, as does the text immediately following the \include command. It therefore works right only if the \include'd text and that following it should begin on a new page—for example, if it consists of one or more complete chapters. For a long document, the ability to process individual parts saves so much time that, while writing it, you may want to split the input into pieces smaller than a complete chapter with \include commands. The small files can be combined into chapter-sized ones when generating the final version.

   Another difficulty with the `\include` mechanism is that changing the document may require reprocessing some unchanged `\include`'d files in order to get the correct numbering of pages, sections, etc. When skipping an `\include`'d file, the numbering in the succeeding text is based upon the numbering in the file's text the last time it was processed. Suppose that the root file contains the commands

```
\include{gnu}
\chapter{Armadillo}
```

and an `\includeonly` in the preamble causes the `\include` command to omit file `gnu.tex`. If the text in `gnu.tex` ended in Chapter 5 on page 57 the last time it was processed, even if you've added seven more chapters and sixty pages of text before the `\include` command since then, the `\chapter` command will produce Chapter 6 starting on page 58. In general, to make sure everything is numbered correctly, you must reprocess an `\include`'d file if a change to the preceding text changes the numbering in the text produced by that file.

   When working on a large document, you should make each appropriately-sized sectional unit a separate `\include`'d file. (You may find it convenient to enter the `\includeonly` command from the terminal, using the `\typein` command described in Section 4.6.) Process each file separately as you write or revise it, and don't worry about numbers not matching properly. If the numbering gets too confusing, generate a coherent version by letting LATEX process all the files at once. Continue processing each file only when you change it, until you're ready to produce the final output. You can then replace each `\include` by an `\input`, so LATEX will process the whole document. However, if each file is a separate chapter that should begin a new page, you can leave the `\include` commands and either process the whole document at once by removing the `\includeonly` command, or else process it one or two files at a time, starting from the beginning and working towards the end.

4.5   Making an Index or Glossary

There are two steps in making an index or glossary: gathering the information and writing the LATEX input to produce it. These steps are discussed below in reverse order.

4.5.1   Producing an Index or Glossary

The `theindex` environment produces an index in two-column format. Each main index entry is begun by an `\item` command. A subentry is begun with `\subitem`, and a subsubentry is begun with `\subsubitem`. Blank lines between entries are ignored. An extra vertical space is produced by the `\indexspace` command, which is usually put before the first entry that starts with a new letter.

gnats 13, 97

gnus 24, 37, 233

    bad, 39, 236

      very, 235

    good, 38, 234

harmadillo 99, 144

```
\item gnats 13, 97
\item gnus 24, 37, 233
    \subitem bad, 39, 236
        \subsubitem very, 235
    \subitem good, 38, 234
\indexspace
\item harmadillo 99, 144
```

There is no environment expressly for glossaries. However, the `description` environment of Section 2.2.4 may be useful.

4.5.2   Compiling the Entries

Compiling an index or a glossary is not easy, but LATEX can help by writing the necessary information onto a special file. If the root file is named `myfile.tex`, index information is written on the file `myfile.idx`, the "idx" file. LATEX makes an `idx` file if the preamble contains a `\makeindex` command. The information on the file is written by `\index` commands, the command `\index{gnu}` appearing with the text for page 42 causing LATEX to write

> `\indexentry{gnu}{42}`

on the `idx` file. If there is no `\makeindex` command, the `\index` command does nothing. You can list the contents of an `idx` file by running LATEX on the file `idx.tex`; the *Local Guide* explains how.

The `\index` command produces no text, so you type

> `A gnat\index{gnat} with gnarled wings gnashed` ...

to index this instance of "gnat". It's best to put the `\index` command next to the word it references, with no space between them; this keeps the page number from being off by one if the word ends or begins a page.

As you write your document, you should type an `\index` command for every page reference you want in the index. When the document is complete except for the index, add the `\makeindex` command and run LATEX on the entire document to produce the `idx` file. You must then process the information in the `idx` file yourself to create a `theindex` environment that will generate the index; the *Local Guide* tells if there are any programs available on your computer to help. The `theindex` environment can either be inserted into your input file or made a separate file that is read by an `\input` or `\include` command (Section 4.4).

The procedure for making a glossary is completely analogous. In place of \index there is a \glossary command. The \makeglossary command produces a file with the extension glo that is similar to the idx file except with \glossaryentry entries instead of \indexentry entries.

The argument of \index or \glossary can contain any characters, including special characters like \ and $. However, curly braces must be properly balanced, each { having a matching }. The \index and \glossary commands are fragile. Moreover, an \index or \glossary command should not appear in the argument of any other command if its own argument contains any of LaTeX's ten special characters (Section 2.1).

4.6   Keyboard Input and Screen Output

When creating a large document, it's often helpful to leave a reminder to yourself in the input file—for example, to note a paragraph that needs rewriting. The use of the % character for putting comments into the text is described in Section 2.2.1. However, a passive comment is easy to overlook, so LaTeX provides the \typeout command for displaying messages on your screen. In the examples in this section, the left column shows what is produced on the screen by the input in the right column; the oval represents the screen.

```
   Don't forget to revise this!
```
\typeout{Don't forget to   revise this!}

Remember that everything LaTeX writes on your screen is also put in the log file.

It is sometimes useful to type input to LaTeX directly from your keyboard—for example, to enter an \includeonly command. This is done with a \typein command, such as the following:

```
   Enter 'includeonly', boss!

   \@typein=
```
\typein {Enter 'includeonly', boss!}

When this appears on your screen, LaTeX is waiting for you to enter a line of input, ended by pressing the return key. LaTeX then processes what you typed just as if it had appeared in the input file in place of the \typein command.

The \typein command has an optional first argument, which must be a command name. When this optional argument is given, instead of processing your typed input at that point, LaTeX defines the specified command to be equivalent to the text that you have typed.

```
Enter wife's name.                        \typein [\wife]{Enter wife's name.}
                                          I love \wife\ very much.
\wife=
```

Typing `Joan` and pressing the return key causes the `\typein` command to define the command `\wife` to be equivalent to `Joan`—just like the `\newcommand` or `\renewcommand` commands of Section 3.4. Thus, the input following this `\typein` command would produce

I love Joan very much.

The argument of the `\typeout` or `\typein` command is a moving argument. Both of these commands are fragile.

CHAPTER 5
Designing It Yourself

The preceding chapters describe LaTeX commands and environments for specifying a document's logical structure. This chapter explains how to specify its visual appearance. Before reading it, you should review the discussion in Section 1.4 of the dangers of visual design. Commands specifying the visual appearance of the document are usually confined to the preamble, either as style declarations or in the definitions of commands and environments for specifying logical structures. The notable exceptions are the line- and page-breaking commands of Section 5.2 and the picture-drawing commands of Section 5.5.

5.1   Document and Page Styles

5.1.1   Document Styles

The use of the `\documentstyle` command to specify the document style and the style options is explained in Section 2.2.2. Three standard LaTeX document styles and several style options are described there, and the `letter` document style for making letters is described in Section 3.8. The following are additional document-style options for these styles.

`titlepage` For use with the `article` style only. It causes the `\maketitle` command to generate a separate title page and the `abstract` environment to make a separate page for the abstract, just the way the `report` style does.

`leqno` Causes the formula numbers produced by the `equation` and `eqnarray` environments to appear on the left instead of the right.

`fleqn` Causes displayed formulas to be aligned on the left, a fixed distance from the left margin, instead of being centered.

Check the *Local Guide* to see what other style options are available on your computer.

Section 2.2.2 describes the `twocolumn` style option for making double-column pages. There is also a `\twocolumn` declaration that starts a new page and begins producing two-column output, and the inverse `\onecolumn` declaration that starts a new page and produces single-column output. The `twocolumn` style option makes appropriate changes to various style parameters, such as the amount of paragraph indentation, while the `\twocolumn` declaration does not. Therefore, the style option rather than the declaration should be used when all or most of the document is in two-column format.

In books, it is conventional for the height of the text to be the same on all full pages. The `\flushbottom` declaration makes all text pages the same height, adding extra vertical space when necessary to fill out the page. The `\raggedbottom` declaration has the opposite effect, letting the height of the text vary a bit from page to page. The default is \flushbottom for the book style and for the twoside option in the article and report styles, and \raggedbottom otherwise. You can change the default by putting the appropriate declaration in the preamble.

5.1.2   Page Styles

A page of output consists of three units: the *head*, the *body*, and the *foot*. In most pages of this book, the head contains a page number, a chapter or section title, and a horizontal line, while the foot is empty; but in the table of contents and the preface, the page head is empty and the foot contains the page number. The body consists of everything between the head and foot: the main text, footnotes, figures, and tables.

The information in the head and foot, which usually includes a page number, helps the reader find his way around the document. You can specify Arabic page numbers with a \pagenumbering{arabic} command and Roman numerals with a \pagenumbering{roman} command, the default being Arabic numbers. The \pagenumbering declaration resets the page number to one, starting with the current page. To begin a document with pages i, ii, etc. and have the first chapter start with page 1, put \pagenumbering{roman} anywhere before the beginning of the text and \pagenumbering{arabic} right after the first \chapter command.

Page headings may contain additional information to help the reader. They are most useful in two-sided printing, since headings on the two facing pages convey more information than the single heading visible with one-sided printing. Page headings are generally not used in a short document, where they tend to be distracting rather than helpful.

The *page style* determines what goes into the head and foot; it is specified with a \pagestyle declaration having the page style's name as its argument. There are four standard page styles:

plain   The page number is in the foot and the head is empty. It is the default
      page style for the article and report document styles.

empty   The head and foot are both empty. LaTeX still assigns each page a num-
      ber, but the number is not printed.

headings   The page number and other information, determined by the document
      style, is put in the head; the foot is empty.

myheadings   Similar to the headings page style, except you specify the "other
      information" that goes in the head, using the \markboth and \markright
      commands described below.

The \pagestyle declaration obeys the normal scoping rules. What goes into a page's head and foot is determined by the page style in effect at the end of the page, so the `\pagestyle` command usually comes after a command like `\chapter` that begins a new page.

The contents of the page headings in the `headings` and `myheadings` styles are set by the following commands:

> `\markboth{`*left_head*`}{`*right_head*`}`
> `\markright{`*right_head*`}`

The *left_head* and *right_head* arguments specify the information to go in the page heads of left-hand and right-hand pages, respectively. In two-sided printing, specified with the `twoside` document-style option, the even-numbered pages are the left-hand ones and the odd-numbered pages are the right-hand ones. In one-sided printing, all pages are considered to be right-hand ones.

In the `headings` page style, the sectioning commands choose the headings for you; Section C.4.2 explains how to use `\markboth` and `\markright` to override their choices. In the `myheadings` style, you must use these commands to set the headings yourself. The arguments of `\markboth` and `\markright` are processed in LR mode; they are moving arguments.

5.1.3   The Title Page and Abstract

The `\maketitle` command, which produces a title page in some document styles, is described in Sections 2.2.2 and C.4.3. You can also create your own title page with the `titlepage` environment. This environment creates a page with the `empty` page style, so it has no printed page number or heading, and causes the following page to be numbered one.

You are completely responsible for what appears on a title page made with the `titlepage` environment. The following commands and environments are useful in formatting a title page: the size-changing commands of Section 5.8.1, the style-changing commands of Section 3.1, and the `center` environment of Section 5.6. Recall also that the `\today` command, described in Section 2.2.1, generates the date. You will probably produce several versions of your document, so it's important to include a date on the title page.

An abstract is made with the `abstract` environment.

Abstract	`\begin{abstract}`
The mating habits of insects are quite different from those of large mammals.	`The mating habits of insects are quite different from those of large mammals`. `\end{abstract}`

The abstract is placed on a separate page in the `report` document style and when the `titlepage` style option is used with the `article` style; it acts like an ordinary displayed-paragraph environment with the plain `article` style. There is no `abstract` environment in the `book` document style, since books normally do not have abstracts.

5.1.4   Customizing the Document Style

If you don't like the standard LaTeX document styles, you can create your own. Changing the document style means changing the way the standard structures such as paragraphs and itemized lists are formatted, not creating new structures. Section 3.4 describes how to define new logical structures.

Before customizing the document style, remember that many authors make elementary errors when they try to design their own documents. The only way to avoid these errors is by consulting a trained typographic designer or reading about typographic design. All I can do here is warn you against the very common mistake of making lines that are too wide to read easily—a mistake you won't make if you follow this suggestion: *use lines that contain no more than 75 characters, including punctuation and spaces.*

The style of a particular document can be customized by adding declarations to its preamble. If the same style modifications are used in several documents, it is more convenient to make a new style option. A document-style option is created by writing the appropriate declarations on a `sty` file—a file whose first name is the option name and whose extension is `sty`, so the declarations defining the `bauhaus` style option are on the file named `bauhaus.sty`. Typing `bauhaus` as the optional argument of the `\documentstyle` command causes LaTeX to read the file `bauhaus.sty` after processing the declarations made by the main document style. If multiple style options are specified, their `sty` files are read in the indicated order.

When reading the `sty` file that defines a document-style option, TeX regards an `@` character as a letter, so it can be part of a command name like `\@listi`. Such a command name cannot be used in your document, since TeX would interpret it as the command `\@` followed by the text characters `listi`. Many of LaTeX's internal commands have an `@` in their name to prevent their accidental use within the document; these include some parameters described in Appendix C that are set by the document style.

The simplest way to modify the document style is by changing parameters such as the ones that control the height and width of the text on the page. LaTeX document-style parameters are described in this chapter and in Appendix C. Other modifications require redefining LaTeX commands. As an example of such a modification, let's suppose that you want chapters to be numbered like "Capítulo 3" instead of "Chapter 3". This requires changing the definition of the `\chapter` command. Defining a whole new `\chapter` command is a job for an expert in both TeX and the inner workings of LaTeX. Fortunately, all you have to do here is make a small modification to the existing `\chapter` command. The first step is finding that definition.

The `\chapter` command is defined by the document style. The declarations made by a main document style, like those of a style option, are contained in a `sty` file; a `\documentstyle{report}` command causes TeX to read the file `report.sty`. A `sty` file is designed for efficiency rather than human readability.

Each standard LaTeX `sty` file has a corresponding `doc` file that contains informative comments and is formatted for easier reading—`report.doc` being the
readable version of `report.sty`. The *Local Guide* describes where to find the
`doc` files.

For efficiency, most LaTeX commands are defined with TeX's `\def` command,
described in *The TeXbook*, rather than with the LaTeX commands of Section 3.4.
(Do not use `\def` yourself except when creating a whole new document style;
the LaTeX commands are safer, and the extra time required to process them is
negligible for a small number of definitions.) Therefore, to find the definition
of `\chapter`, you should start by examining the file `report.doc` with a text
editor and searching for "`\def\chapter`". However, you will quickly discover
that it's not there. As the comments at the beginning of the file explain, the
`report` document style reads additional declarations from the file `rep10.sty`,
`rep11.sty`, or `rep12.sty`, depending upon whether the default ten-point size
or the `11pt` or `12pt` style option is chosen. The `\chapter` command is defined
in these files.

Let's suppose that you want to change the ten-point version. Search the
file `rep10.doc` for "`\def\chapter`" to find the definition of `\chapter`. Unfor-
tunately, there is nothing in that definition to indicate where the "Chapter" is
generated. You could now look up the definitions of the commands contained in
`\chapter`'s definition, the definitions of the commands in those definitions, and
so on until you find what you are looking for. However, since the "Chapter"
must be generated by the input text `Chapter`, it is easier to search for all in-
stances of these seven characters. This quickly leads you to comments indicating
that the command `\@chapapp` is initially defined to be `Chapter`, and is redefined
to `Appendix` by the `\appendix` command. So, you just have to create a style
option with the command

$$\renewcommand{\@chapapp}{Cap\'{\i}tulo}$$

(Remember that commands with an `@` in their names can be defined only in a
`sty` file.) You might also want to redefine the `\appendix` command, replacing
`Appendix` by `Ap\'{e}ndice`.

This example gives some idea of what you must do to modify a command.
The procedure for modifying an environment is similar. Most environments are
defined with the TeX `\def` command—for example, the `quote` environment is
defined by defining `\quote`, which is executed by the `\begin{quote}` command,
and `\endquote`, which is executed by `\end{quote}`.

If you can't find a LaTeX command's definition in the `doc` files, it is probably
a built-in command that is defined in the file `latex.tex`. If the command is not
there either, it is most likely a TeX command whose definition can be found in
The TeXbook.

Not all modifications are as easy as the sample change to `\chapter`. Some
require understanding advanced TeX commands and knowing more about how

LATEX works. You can learn all about TEX by reading *The TEXbook*; most of what you need to know about LATEX is described in the comments in `latex.tex`, except that the font-selecting commands are explained in the file `lfonts.tex`. Consult the *Local Guide* to find out where these files are on your computer and to see if there is any other available information about document-style design.

5.2 Line and Page Breaking

TEX usually does a good job of breaking text into lines and pages, but it some-times needs help. Don't worry about line and page breaking until you're ready to prepare the final version. Most of the bad breaks that appear in early drafts will disappear as you change the text.

5.2.1 Line Breaking

Let's return to the line-breaking problem that we inserted into the `sample` input file in Section 2.3. Recall that it produced the following warning message:

```
Overfull \hbox (10.58649pt too wide) in paragraph at lines 172--175
[]\tenrm Mathematical for-mu-las may also be dis-played. A dis-played for-mula
is gnomonly
```

TEX could not find a good place to break the line and left the word "gnomonly" extending about 1/8 inch past the right margin.

The first line of this warning message states that the output line actually extends 10.58649 points past the right margin—a point being about $1/72^{nd}$ of an inch—and is in the paragraph generated by lines 172 through 175 of the input file. The next part of the message shows the input that produced the offending line, except TEX has inserted a "-" character every place that it's willing to hyphenate a word.

TEX is quite good at hyphenating words; it never[1] incorrectly hyphenates an English word and usually finds all correct possibilities. However, it does miss some. For example, it does not know how to hyphenate the word *gnomonly* (which isn't a very gnomonly used word), nor can it hyphenate *gnomon*.

A `\-` command tells TEX that it is allowed to hyphenate at that point. We could correct our sample hyphenation problem by changing `gnomonly` to `gno\-monly`, so TEX could break the line after *gno*. However, it's better to change it to `gno\-mon\-ly`, which also allows TEX to break right before the *ly*. While TEX will still break this particular sample line after *gno*, further changes to the text might make *gnomon-ly* better.

TEX will not hyphenate a word with a nonletter in the middle, where it treats any sequence of nonspace characters as a single word. While it hyphenates *ra-di-a-tion* properly, it does not hyphenate *x-radiation*—though it will break

---

[1] Well, hardly ever.

a line after the *x*-. You must type x-ra\-di\-a\-tion for TEX to consider all possible hyphenation points. However, it is generally considered a bad idea to hyphenate a hyphenated compound; you should do so only when there is no better alternative.

When writing a paper about sundials, in which the word *gnomon* appears frequently, it would be a nuisance to type it as gno\-mon everywhere it is used. You can teach TEX how to hyphenate words by putting one or more \hyphenation commands in the preamble. The command

```
\hyphenation{gno-mon gno-mons gno-mon-ly}
```

tells TEX how to hyphenate *gnomon*, *gnomons* and *gnomonly*—but it still won't know how to hyphenate *gnomonic*.

While it's very good at hyphenating English, an English-language version of LATEX will not hyphenate foreign words properly. Without a version explicitly made for a foreign language, you'll have to correct hyphenation errors as they occur by using \hyphenation or \- commands to tell TEX where it can hyphenate a word. See the *Local Guide* to find out if any foreign-language versions of LATEX are available for your computer.

Not all line-breaking problems can be solved by hyphenation. Sometimes there is just no good way to break a paragraph into lines. TEX is normally very fussy about line breaking; it lets you solve the problem rather than producing a paragraph that doesn't meet its high standards. There are three things you can do when this happens. The first is to rewrite the paragraph. However, having carefully polished your prose, you probably don't want to change it just to produce perfect line breaks.

The second way to handle a line breaking problem is to use a sloppypar environment or \sloppy declaration, which direct TEX not to be so fussy about where it breaks lines. Most of the time, you just enclose the entire paragraph that contains the bad line break between \begin{sloppypar} and \end{sloppypar} commands. However, sometimes its easier to use a \sloppy declaration. To explain how to use this declaration, it helps to introduce the concept of a *paragraph unit*. A paragraph unit is a portion of text that is treated as a single string of words to be broken into lines at any convenient point. For example, a paragraph containing a displayed equation would consist of two paragraph units—the parts of the paragraph that come before and after the equation. (Since the equation itself can't be broken across lines, it is not a paragraph unit.) Similarly, each item in a list-making environment begins a new paragraph unit.

TEX does its line breaking for a paragraph unit when it encounters the command or blank line that ends the unit, based upon the declarations in effect at that time. So, the scope of the \sloppy declaration should include the command or blank line that ends the paragraph unit with the bad line break. You can either delimit the scope of the \sloppy declaration with braces, or else use a countermanding \fussy declaration that restores TEX to its ordinary compulsive self. The \begin{sloppypar} command is equivalent to a blank line followed by {\sloppy, and \end{sloppypar} is equivalent to a blank line followed by a }.

The third way to fix a bad line break is with a \linebreak command, which forces TeX to break the line at that spot. The \linebreak is usually inserted right before the word that doesn't fit. An optional argument converts the \linebreak command from a demand to a request. The argument must be a digit from 0 through 4, a higher number denoting a stronger request. The command \linebreak[0] allows TeX to break the line there, but neither encourages nor discourages its doing so, while \linebreak[4] forces the line break just like an ordinary \linebreak command. The arguments 1, 2 and 3 provide intermediate degrees of insistence, and may succeed in coaxing TeX to overcome a bad line break. They can also be used to help TeX find the most aesthetically pleasing line breaks. The \linebreak[0] command allows a line break where it would normally be forbidden, such as within a word.

Both of these methods handle line-breaking problems by sweeping them under the rug. The "lump in the carpet" that they may leave is one or more lines with too much blank space between the words. Such a line will produce an "Underfull \hbox" warning message.

Although unwanted line breaks are usually prevented with the ˜ and \mbox commands described in Section 2.2.1, LaTeX also provides a \nolinebreak command that forbids TeX from breaking the line at that point. Like the \linebreak command, \nolinebreak takes a digit from 0 through 4 as an optional argument to convert the prohibition into a suggestion that this isn't a good place for a line break—the higher the number, the stronger the suggestion. A \nolinebreak[0] command is equivalent to \linebreak[0], and \nolinebreak[4] is equivalent to \nolinebreak.

A \linebreak command causes TeX to justify the line, stretching the space between words so the line extends to the right margin. The \newline command ends a line without justifying it.

I can think of no good reason why you would want to make a short line like this in the middle of a paragraph, but perhaps you can think of one.

```
I can think of no good reason why you would
want to make a short line like this
\newline in the middle of a paragraph,
but perhaps you can think of one.
```

You can type \\, which is the usual LaTeX command for ending a line, in place of \newline. In fact, LaTeX provides the \newline command only to maintain a complete correspondence between the line-breaking commands and the page-breaking commands described below.

The \linebreak, \nolinebreak, and \newline commands can be used only in paragraph mode. They are fragile commands. See Section C.1.1 if a [follows a \linebreak or \nolinebreak command that has no optional argument.

5.2.2   Page Breaking

TEX is as fussy about page breaks as it is about line breaks. As with line breaking, sometimes TEX can find no good place to start a new page. A bad page break usually causes TEX to put too little rather than too much text onto the page. When the \flushbottom declaration (Section 5.1.1) is in effect, this produces a page with too much extra vertical space; with the \raggedbottom declaration, it produces a page that is too short. In the first case, TEX warns you about the extra space by generating an "Underfull \vbox" message. With \raggedbottom in effect, TEX does not warn you about bad page breaks, so you you should check your final output for pages that are too short.

The LATEX page-breaking commands are analogous to the line-breaking commands described in Section 5.2.1 above. As with line breaking, LATEX provides commands to demand or prohibit a page break, with an optional argument transforming the commands to suggestions. The \pagebreak and \nopagebreak commands are the analogs of \linebreak and \nolinebreak. When used between paragraphs, they apply to that point; when used in the middle of a paragraph, they apply immediately after the current line. Thus, a \pagebreak command within a paragraph insists that TEX start a new page after the line in which the command appears, and \nopagebreak[3] suggests rather strongly that TEX *not* start a new page there.

Sometimes TEX is adamant about breaking a page at a certain point, and will not be deterred by a \nopagebreak command. When this happens, use a \samepage declaration to inhibit all page breaks and explicit \pagebreak commands where you wish to allow page breaking. A precise description of the \samepage command is given in Appendix C, but you can use it as follows to correct bad page breaks without understanding exactly how it works:

- Enclose a portion of text containing the bad page break in the scope of a \samepage declaration. The scope should include the blank line or command ending the paragraph unit that contains the bad break.

- Put a \nopagebreak command immediately after any blank line in the scope of the samepage declaration where you don't want a page break to occur.

- Put a \pagebreak command (with or without an optional argument) everywhere you wish to allow a page break.

The \samepage declaration also inhibits page breaking in the footnote generated by a \footnote command within its scope.

You can't put more text on a page than will fit. To squeeze extra text on a page, you must usually make room for it by removing some vertical space. This can be done with the commands of Section 5.4.2.

The \newpage command is the analog of \newline, creating a page that ends prematurely right at that point. Even when a \flushbottom declaration is in effect, a shortened page is produced. The \clearpage command is similar to \newpage, except that any left-over figures or tables are put on one or more separate pages with no text. The \chapter and \include commands (Section 4.4) use \clearpage to begin a new page. Adding an extra \newpage or \clearpage command will not produce a blank page; two such commands in a row are equivalent to a single one. To generate a blank page, you must put some invisible text on it, such as an empty \mbox.

When using the twoside style option for two-sided printing, you may want to start a sectional unit on a right-hand page. The \cleardoublepage command is the same as \clearpage except that it produces a blank page if necessary so that the next page will be a right-hand (odd-numbered) one.

When used in two-column format, the \newpage and \pagebreak commands start a new column rather than a new page. However, the \clearpage and \cleardoublepage commands start a new page.

The page-breaking commands can be used only where it is possible to start a new page—that is, in paragraph mode and not inside a box (Section 5.4.3). They are all fragile.

5.3   Numbering

Every number that LaTeX generates has a *counter* associated with it. The name of the counter is the same as the name of the environment or command that produces the number, except with no \. Below is a list of the counters used by LaTeX's standard document styles to control numbering.

part	paragraph	figure	enumi
chapter	subparagraph	table	enumii
section	page	footnote	enumiii
subsection	equation	mpfootnote	enumiv
subsubsection			

The counters enumi ... enumiv control different levels of enumerate environments, enumi for the outermost level, enumii for the next level, and so on. The mpfootnote counter numbers footnotes inside a minipage environment (Section 5.4.3). In addition to these, an environment created with the \newtheorem command (Section 3.4.3) has a counter of the same name unless an optional argument specifies that it is to be numbered the same as another environment. There are also some other counters used for document-style parameters; they are described in Appendix C.

The value of a counter is a single integer—usually nonnegative. Multiple numbers are generated with separate counters, the "2" and "4" of "Subsection 2.4" coming from the `section` and `subsection` counters, respectively. The value of a counter is initialized to zero and is incremented by the appropriate command or environment. For example, the `subsection` counter is incremented by the `\subsection` command before the subsection number is generated, and it is reset to zero when the `section` counter is incremented, so subsection numbers start from one in a new section.

The `\setcounter` command sets the value of a counter, and `\addtocounter` increments it by a specified amount.

Because[18] counters[17] are stepped before being used, you set them to one less than the number you want.

```
\setcounter{footnote}{17}
Because\footnote{...}
\addtocounter{footnote}{-2}%
counters\footnote{...} are stepped ...
```

When used in the middle of a paragraph, these commands should be attached to a word to avoid adding extra space.

The `\setcounter` and `\addtocounter` commands affect only the specified counter; for example, changing the `section` counter with these commands does not affect the `subsection` counter. The commands to change counter values are global declarations (Section C.1.4); their effects are not limited by the normal scope rules for declarations.

The `page` counter is used to generate the page number. It differs from other counters in that it is incremented *after* the page number is generated, so its value is the number of the current page rather than the next one. A `\setcounter{page}{27}` command in the middle of the document therefore causes the current page to be numbered 27. For this reason, the `page` counter is initialized to one instead of zero.

LaTeX provides the following commands for printing counter values; the list shows what they produce when the `page` counter has the value four.

4	`\arabic{page}`	iv	`\roman{page}`	d	`\alph{page}`
		IV	`\Roman{page}`	D	`\Alph{page}`

To generate a printed number, LaTeX executes a command whose name is formed by adding `\the` to the beginning of the appropriate counter's name; redefining this command changes the way the number is printed. For example, a subsection number is made by the `\thesubsection` command. To change the numbering of sections and subsections so the fourth subsection of the second section is numbered "II-D", you type the following (see Section 3.4 for an explanation of `\renewcommand`):

```
\renewcommand{\thesection}{\Roman{section}}
\renewcommand{\thesubsection}{\thesection-\Alph{subsection}}
```

Since sections are usually numbered the same throughout the document (at least until the appendix), the obvious place for this command is in the preamble.

A new counter is created with a `\newcounter` command having the name of the counter as its argument. The new counter's initial value is zero, and its initial `\the...` command prints the value as an arabic numeral. See Section 5.7 for an example of how a new counter is used in defining an environment. The `\newcounter` declaration should be used only in the preamble.

5.4 Length, Spaces, and Boxes

In visual design, one specifies how much vertical space to leave above a chapter heading, how wide a line of text should be, and so on. This section describes the basic tools for making these specifications.

5.4.1 Length

A length is a measure of distance. An amount of space or a line width is specified by giving a length as an argument to the appropriate formatting command. A length of one inch is specified by typing `1in`; it can also be given in metric units as `2.54cm` or `25.4mm`, or as `72.27pt`, where `pt` denotes *point*—a unit of length common with printers. A length can also be negative (for example, `-2.54cm`).

Note that `0` is not a length. A length of zero is written `0in` or `0cm` or `0pt`, not `0`. Writing `0` as a length is a common mistake.

While inches, centimeters, and points are convenient units, they should be avoided because they specify fixed lengths. A .25-inch horizontal space that looks good in one-column output may be too wide in a two-column format. It's better to use units of length that depend upon the appropriate document-style parameters. The simplest such units are the `em` and the `ex`, which depend upon the font (the size and style of type). A `1em` length is about equal to the width of an "M", and `1ex` is about the height of an "x". The `em` is best used for horizontal lengths and the `ex` for vertical lengths. An `em` ruler for the current font is given below, and an `ex` ruler is in the margin.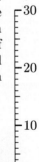

In addition to writing explicit lengths such as `1in` or `3.5em`, you can also express lengths with *length commands*. A length command has a *value* that is a length. For example, `\parindent` is a length command whose value specifies the width of the indentation at the beginning of a normal paragraph. Typing `\parindent` as the argument of a command is equivalent to typing the current value of `\parindent`. You can also type `2.5\parindent` for a length that is 2.5 times as large as `\parindent`, or `-2.5\parindent` for the negative of that length; `-\parindent` is the same as `-1.0\parindent`.

A length such as `1.5em` or `\parindent` is a *rigid* length. Specifying a space of width `1cm` always produces a one-centimeter-wide space. (It may not be exactly one centimeter wide because your output device might uniformly change all dimensions—for example, enlarging them by 5%.) However, there are also *rubber lengths* that can vary.[2] Space specified with a rubber length can stretch or shrink as required. For example, TEX justifies lines (produces an even right margin) by stretching or shrinking the space between words to make each line the same length.

A rubber length has a natural length and a degree of elasticity. Of particular interest is the special length command `\fill` that has a natural length of zero but is infinitely stretchable, so a space of width `\fill` tends to expand as far as it can. The use of such stretchable space is described in Section 5.4.2 below. Multiplying a length command by a number destroys its elasticity, producing a rigid length. Thus, `1\fill` and `.7\fill` are rigid lengths of value zero inches.

Most lengths used in LATEX are rigid. Unless a length is explicitly said to be rubber, you can assume it is rigid. All length commands are robust; a `\protect` command should never precede a length command.

Below are some of LATEX's *length parameters*—length commands that define document-style parameters; others are given in Appendix C. By expressing lengths in terms of these parameters, you can define formatting commands that work properly with different document styles.

`\parindent` The amount of indentation at the beginning of a normal paragraph.

`\textwidth` The width of the text on the page.

`\textheight` The height of the body of the page—that is, the normal height of everything on a page excluding the head and foot (Section 5.1.1).

`\parskip` The extra vertical space inserted between paragraphs. It is customary not to leave any extra space between paragraphs, so `\parskip` has a natural length of zero (except in the `letter` style). However, it is a rubber length, so it can stretch to add vertical space between paragraphs when the `\flushbottom` declaration (Section 5.1.1) is in effect.

`\baselineskip` The normal vertical distance from the bottom of one line to the bottom of the next line in the same paragraph. Thus, `\textheight` ÷ `\baselineskip` equals the number of lines of text that would appear on a page if it were all one paragraph.

LATEX provides the following declarations for changing the values of length commands and for creating new ones. These declarations obey the usual scoping rules.

---

[2]A rigid length is called a ⟨dimen⟩ and a rubber length is called a ⟨skip⟩ in *The TEXbook*.

\newlength Defines a new length command. You type \newlength{\gnat}
to make \gnat a length command with value 0in. An error occurs if a
\gnat command is already defined.

\setlength Sets the value of a length command. The value of \gnat is set to
1.01 inches by the command \setlength{\gnat}{1.01in}.

\addtolength Increments the value of a length command by a specified amount.
If the current value of \gnat is .01 inches, then executing the command
\addtolength{\gnat}{-.1\gnat} changes its value to .009 inches—the
original value plus −.1 times its original value.

\settowidth Sets the value of a length command equal to the width of a specified piece of text. The command \settowidth{\gnat}{\em small} sets
the value \gnat to the width of *small*—the text produced by typesetting
{\em small} in LR mode.

The value of a length command created with \newlength can be changed
at any time. This is also true for some of LaTeX's length parameters, while
others should be changed only in the preamble and still others should never be
changed. Consult Appendix C to find out when you can safely change the value
of a LaTeX parameter.

5.4.2   Spaces

A horizontal space is produced with the \hspace command. Think of \hspace
as making a blank "word", with spaces before or after it producing an interword
space.

├─ .5 in ─┤	
Here is a .5 inch space.	`Here\hspace{.5in}is a .5 inch space.`
Here is a .5 inch space.	`Here \hspace{.5in}is a .5 inch space.`
Here is a .5 inch space.	`Here \hspace{.5in} is a .5 inch space.`
Negative space is a backspace—like this.	`...---like this.\hspace{-.5in}/////`
├─ .5 in ─┤	

TeX removes space from the beginning or end of each line of output text, except
at the beginning and end of a paragraph—including space added with \hspace.
The \hspace* command is the same as \hspace except that the space it produces is never removed, even when it comes at the beginning or end of a line.
The \hspace and \hspace* commands are robust.

The \vspace command produces vertical space. It is most commonly used
between paragraphs; when used within a paragraph, the vertical space is added
after the line in which the \vspace appears.

You seldom add space like this between lines in

.25 in

a paragraph, but you sometimes remove space between them by adding some negative space.

7 mm

You more often add space between paragraphs—
especially before or after displayed material.

```
You\vspace{.25in} seldom add space like
this between lines in a paragraph, but you
... by adding some negative space.

\vspace{7 mm}

You more often add space between ...
```

Just as it removes horizontal space from the beginning and end of a line, TeX removes vertical space that comes at the beginning or end of a page. The \vspace* command creates vertical space that is never removed.

If the argument of an \hspace or \vspace command (or its *-form) is a rubber length, the space produced will be able to stretch and shrink. This is normally relevant only for the fine tuning of a document style. However, a space made with an infinitely stretchable length such as \fill is useful for positioning text because it stretches as much as it can, pushing everything else aside. The command \hfill is an abbreviation for \hspace{\fill}.

Here is a   stretched space.
Here are   two   equal ones.

```
Here is a \hfill stretched space.
Here are \hfill two \hfill equal ones.
```

Note that when two equally stretchable spaces push against each other, they stretch the same amount. You can use stretchable spaces to center objects or to move them flush against the right-hand margin. However, LaTeX provides more convenient methods of doing that, described in Section 5.6.

Infinitely stretchable space can be used in the analogous way for moving text vertically. The \vfill command is equivalent to a blank line followed by \vspace{\fill}. Remember that spaces produced by \hfill or \vfill at the beginning and end of a line or page disappear. You must use \hspace*{\fill} or \vspace*{\fill} for space that does not disappear.

The \dotfill command acts just like \hfill except it produces dots instead of spaces. The command \hrulefill works the same way, but it produces a horizontal line.

Gnats and gnus .... see pests.
This is _____ really _____ it.

```
Gnats and gnus \dotfill\  see pests.
This is \hrulefill\ really \hrulefill\ it.
```

5.4.3 Boxes

A *box* is a chunk of text that TeX treats as a unit, just as if it were a single letter. No matter how big it is, TeX will never split a box to fit onto a line or a page. The array and tabular environments (Section 3.6.2) both produce a single box that can be quite big, as does the picture environment described in Section 5.5.

LaTeX provides additional commands and environments for making three kinds of boxes: LR boxes, in which the contents of the box are processed in LR mode; parboxes, in which the contents of the box are processed in paragraph mode; and rule boxes, consisting of a rectangular blob of ink.

A box-making command or environment can be used in any mode. TeX uses the declarations in effect at that point when typesetting the box's contents, so the contents of a box appearing in the scope of an \em declaration will be emphasized—usually by being set in italic type. An exceptional case occurs if a box-making command appears in a mathematical formula, since the math-italic style in which formulas are normally typeset (Section 3.3.8) can be used only in math mode. Therefore, when a box-making command appears in math mode, its contents are set in the most recently declared type style other than math italic; this is usually the one in effect outside the math environment. Since the input that produces the box's contents is either the argument of a box-making command or the text of a box-making environment, any declarations made inside it are local to the box.

A box is often displayed on a line by itself. This can be done by treating the box as a formula and using the `displaymath` environment (\[... \]). The `center` environment described in Section 5.6 can also be used.

LR Boxes

The \mbox command introduced in Section 2.2.1 makes an LR box—a box whose contents are obtained by processing the command's argument in LR mode. It is an abbreviated version of the \makebox command; \makebox has optional arguments that \mbox doesn't. The box created by an \mbox command is just wide enough to hold its contents. You can specify the width of the box with a \makebox command that has an optional first argument. The default is to center the contents in the box, but this can be overridden by a second optional argument that consists of a single letter: l to move the contents to the left side of the box and r to move it to the right.

Good $\overset{\longleftarrow\ \text{1 in}\ \longrightarrow}{\quad gnus\quad}$ are here at last.	`Good \makebox[1in]{\em gnus}  are here ...`
Good *gnus* are here at last.	`Good \makebox[1in][l]{\em gnus} are ...`
Good *gnus* are here at last.	`Good \makebox[1in][r]{\em gnus} are ...`

A box is treated just like a word; space characters on either side produce an interword space.

The \framebox command is exactly the same as \makebox except it puts a frame around the outside of the box. There is also an \fbox command, the abbreviation for a \framebox command with no optional arguments.

There was not a ⟨$\overset{\longleftarrow\ \text{1 in}\ \longrightarrow}{\boxed{\text{gnu}\qquad\qquad}}$⟩ or ⟨$\boxed{\text{armadillo}}$⟩ in sight.	`There was not a \framebox[1in][l]{gnu}` `or \fbox{armadillo} in sight.`

When you specify a box of a fixed width, TEX acts as if the box has exactly that width. If the contents are too wide for the box, they will overflow into the surrounding text.

X Xwide armadillosX X   X X X\framebox[.5in]{wide armadillos}X X X

This can be used to control where TEX normally puts text. To understand how, first consider in what direction text overflows from a very narrow box.

gorilla gorilla   \framebox[2mm]{gorilla gorilla}
              gorilla gorilla   \framebox[2mm][l]{gorilla gorilla}
gorilla gorilla   \framebox[2mm][r]{gorilla gorilla}

Now imagine that instead of a 2 mm-wide \framebox we used a \makebox of width zero. Having no width, the box is a mathematically perfect vertical line. With no positioning argument, the contents of the box are centered with respect to that line. An l argument positions the contents so the left edge is on the line, and an r argument positions it so the right edge is on the line. Thus, if a \makebox[0in][r] is placed at the beginning of an output line, its contents appear in the left margin, with the right edge flush against the main text.

Zero-width boxes can be used in the tabular environment to align an item on some point other than its edge. For example, you can make TEX align "23.4" as if its right edge were between the "3" and the "." by typing it as 23\makebox[0pt][l]{.4}. (Remember that the width argument must be something like 0in or 0mm, not simply 0.)

Parboxes   p195

A *parbox* is a box whose contents are typeset in paragraph mode, with TEX producing a series of lines just as in ordinary text. The figure and table environments (Section 3.5.1) create parboxes. There are two ways to make a parbox at a given point in the text: with the \parbox command and the minipage environment. They can be used to put one or more paragraphs of text inside a picture or in a table item.

For TEX to break text into lines, it must know how wide the lines should be. Therefore, \parbox and the minipage environment have the width of the parbox as an argument. The second mandatory argument of the \parbox command is the text to be put in the parbox.

|← 1 in →|
Breaking lines in   expect to get a lot   \parbox{1in}{Breaking lines in a narrow
a narrow parbox YOU CAN of bad line breaks   parbox is hard.} \ YOU CAN \
is hard.   if you try this sort   \parbox{1in}{expect to get a lot of bad
                       of thing.   line breaks if you try ...}

There is no indentation at the beginning of a paragraph in these parboxes; LATEX sets the \parindent parameter, which specifies the amount of indentation, to zero in a parbox. You can set it to any other value with \setlength (Section 5.4.1).

In the above example, the parboxes are positioned vertically so the center of the box is aligned with the center of the text line. An optional first argument of t (for *top*) or b (for *bottom*) aligns the top or bottom line of the parbox with the text line.

<table>
<tr><td>

This is a parbox
aligned on its bot-
tom line.   AND THIS one is aligned on
its top line.

</td><td>

```
\parbox[b]{1in}{This is a parbox aligned
     on its bottom line.}
\ AND THIS \
\parbox[t]{1in}{one is aligned on its top
     line.}
```

</td></tr>
</table>

Finer control of the vertical positioning is obtained with the \raisebox command described below.

The \parbox command is generally used for a parbox containing a small amount of text. For a larger parbox or one containing a tabbing environment, a list-making environment, or any of the paragraph-making environments described in Section 5.6, you should use a minipage environment. The minipage environment has the same optional positioning argument and mandatory width argument as the \parbox command.

When used in a minipage environment, the \footnote command puts a footnote at the bottom of the parbox produced by the environment. This is particularly useful for footnotes inside figures or tables. Moreover, unlike in ordinary text, the \footnote command can be used anywhere within the environment—even inside another box or in an item of a tabular environment. To footnote something in a minipage environment with an ordinary footnote at the bottom of the page, use the \footnotemark and \footnotetext commands described in Section C.2.3.

<table>
<tr><td>

gnat: a tiny bug AND   *gnu*: a beast[a] that
that is very hard   is hard to miss.
to find.

                              ─────────
                      [a]See armadillo.

</td><td>

```
\begin{minipage}[t]{1in}
   {\em gnat\/}: a tiny bug that is very
   hard to find.
\end{minipage} \ AND \
\begin{minipage}[t]{1in}
   {\em gnu\/}: a beast\footnote{See
   armadillo.} that is hard to miss.
\end{minipage}
```

</td></tr>
</table>

If you have one minipage environment nested inside another, footnotes may appear at the bottom of the wrong one.

You may find yourself wishing that TEX would determine the width of a parbox by itself, making it just wide enough to hold the text inside. This is normally impossible because TeX must know the line width to do its line breaking. However, it doesn't have to know a line width when typesetting a `tabbing` environment because the input specifies where every line ends. Therefore, if a `minipage` environment consists of nothing but a `tabbing` environment, then TeX will set the width of the parbox to be either the width specified by the `minipage` environment's argument or the actual width of the longest line, choosing whichever is smaller.

Rule Boxes

A rule box is a rectangular blob of ink. It is made with the `\rule` command, whose arguments specify the width and height of the blob. There is also an optional first argument that specifies how high to raise the rule (a negative value lowers it).

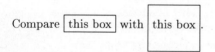

```
Rule 1: \rule{1mm}{5mm}
Rule 2: \rule[.1in]{.25in}{.02in}
```

A thin enough rule is just a line, so the `\rule` command can draw horizontal or vertical lines of arbitrary length and thickness.

A rule box of width zero is called a *strut*. Having no width, a strut is invisible; but it does have height, and TeX will adjust the vertical spacing to leave room for it.

Compare ⎡this box⎤ with ⎡this box⎤.

```
Compare \fbox{this box} with
\fbox{\rule[-.5cm]{0cm}{1cm}this box}.
```

Struts provide a convenient method of adding vertical space in places where `\vspace` can't be used, such as within a mathematical formula.

Raising and Lowering Boxes

The `\raisebox` command raises text by a specified length (a negative length lowers the text). It makes an LR box, just like the `\mbox` command.

You can *raise* or *lower* text.

```
You can \raisebox{.6ex}{\em raise} or
\raisebox{-.6ex}{\em lower} text.
```

It is sometimes useful to change how big TeX thinks a piece of text is without changing the text. The `\makebox` command tells TeX how wide the text is, while a strut can increase the text's apparent height but cannot decrease it. Optional arguments of `\raisebox` tell TeX how tall it should pretend that the text is. The command

```
\raisebox{.4ex}[1.5ex][.75ex]{\em text}
```

not only raises *text* by `.4ex`, but also makes TₑX think that it extends `1.5ex` above the bottom of the line and `.75ex` below the bottom of the line. (The bottom of the line is where most characters sit; a letter like *y* extends below it.) If you omit the second optional argument, TₑX will think the text extends as far below the line as it actually does. By changing the apparent height of text, you change how much space TₑX leaves for it. This is sometimes used to eliminate space above or below a formula or part of a formula.

Saving Boxes

If a single piece of text appears in several places, you can define a command with `\newcommand` (Section 3.4) to generate it. While this saves typing, TₑX doesn't save any time because it must do the work of typesetting the text whenever it encounters the command. If the text is complicated—especially if it contains a `picture` environment (Section 5.5)—TₑX will waste a lot of time typesetting it over and over again.

TₑX can typeset something once as a box and then save it in a named *storage bin*, from which it can be used repeatedly. The name of a storage bin is an ordinary command name; a new bin is created and named by the `\newsavebox` declaration. The `\savebox` command makes a box and saves it in a specified bin; it has the bin name as its first argument and the rest of its arguments are the same as for the `\makebox` command. The `\usebox` command prints the contents of a bin.

```
\newsavebox{\toy}
\savebox{\toy}[.65in]{gnats}
 . . .
```

|← .65 in →|

It's   gnats   and   gnats   and   gnats   ,   It's `\usebox{\toy}` and `\usebox{\toy}` and
wherever we go.   `\usebox{\toy}`, wherever we go.

The `\sbox` command is the short form of `\savebox`, with no optional arguments. The `\savebox` and `\sbox` commands are declarations that have the usual scope. However, the `\newsavebox` declaration is global (Section C.1.1) and does not obey the customary scoping rules.

5.5   Pictures   p196

The `picture` environment is used to draw pictures composed of text, straight lines, arrows, and circles. You position objects in the picture by specifying their x and y coordinates. So, before getting to the picture-making commands, let us first review a little bit of coordinate geometry.

A *coordinate* is a number such as 5, −7, 2.3, or −3.1416. Given an *origin* and a *unit length*, a pair of coordinates specifies a position. As shown in Figure 5.1,

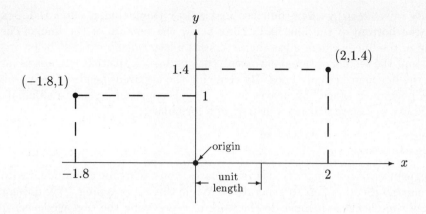

Figure 5.1: Points and their coordinates.

the coordinate pair $(-1.8, 1)$ specifies the position reached by starting at the origin and moving left 1.8 units and up 1 unit.

The unit length used in determining positions in a `picture` environment is the value of the length command `\unitlength`. Not just positions but all lengths in a `picture` environment are specified in terms of `\unitlength`. Its default value is 1 point (about 1/72nd of an inch), but it can be changed with the `\setlength` command described in Section 5.4.1. Changing the value of `\unitlength` magnifies or reduces a picture—halving the value halves the lengths of all lines and the diameters of all circles. This makes it easy to adjust the size of a picture. However, changing `\unitlength` does not change the widths of lines or the size of text characters, so it does not provide true magnification and reduction.

LaTeX provides two standard thicknesses for the lines in a picture—thin as in ☐ and thick as in ☐. They are specified by the declarations `\thinlines` and `\thicklines`, with `\thinlines` as the default. These commands are ordinary declarations and can be used at any time.

Many picture-drawing commands have a coordinate pair as an argument. Such an argument is not enclosed in braces, but is just typed with parentheses and a comma, as in `(-2,3.7)` or `(0,-17.2)`.

5.5.1 The `picture` Environment

The `picture` environment has a coordinate-pair argument that specifies the picture's size (in terms of `\unitlength`). The environment produces a box (Section 5.4.3) whose width and height are given by the two coordinates. The origin's default position is the lower-left corner of this box. However, the `picture` environment has an optional second coordinate-pair argument that specifies the coordinates of the box's lower-left corner, thereby determining the position of the origin. For example, the command

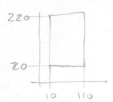

> \begin{picture}(100,200)(10,20)

produces a picture of width 100 units and height 200 units, whose lower-left corner has coordinates $(10, 20)$, so the upper-right corner has coordinates $(110, 220)$. Unlike ordinary optional arguments, the `picture` environment's optional argument is not enclosed in square brackets.

When first drawing a picture, you will usually omit the optional argument, leaving the origin at the lower-left corner. Later, if you want to modify the picture by shifting everything, you just add the appropriate optional argument.

The environment's first argument specifies the nominal size of the picture, which is used by TEX to determine how much room to leave for it. This need bear no relation to how large the picture really is; LATEX allows you to draw things outside the picture, or even off the page.

The `\begin{picture}` command puts LATEX in *picture mode*, a special mode that occurs nowhere else.[3] The only things that can appear in picture mode are `\put` and `\multiput` commands (described below) and declarations such as `\em`, `\thicklines`, and `\setlength`. You should not change `\unitlength` in `picture` mode.

The examples in this section all illustrate commands in picture mode, but the `\begin{picture}` and `\end{picture}` commands are not shown. To help you think in terms of arbitrary unit lengths, the examples assume different values of `\unitlength`. They are all drawn with the `\thicklines` declaration in effect. The pictures in the examples also contain lines and arrows, not produced by the commands being illustrated, that indicate positions and dimensions; these are drawn with `\thinlines` in effect, allowing you to compare the two line thicknesses.

Remember that the `picture` environment produces a box, which TEX treats just like a single (usually) large letter. See Section 5.6 for commands and environments to position the entire picture on the page. All the picture-drawing commands described in this section are fragile.

5.5.2   Picture Objects

Everything in a picture is drawn by the `\put` command. The command

> \put (11.3,-.3){*picture object*}

puts the *picture object* in the picture with its *reference point* having coordinates $(11.3, -.3)$. The various kinds of picture objects and their reference points are described below.

---

[3]LATEX's picture mode is really a restricted form of LR mode.

Text

The simplest kind of picture object is ordinary text, which is typeset in LR mode with the lower-left corner of the text as its reference point.

`\put(2.3,5){an armadillo}`

Boxes

A box picture object is made with the `\makebox` or `\framebox` command. These commands, and the related `\savebox` command, have a special form for use with pictures. The first argument is a coordinate pair that specifies the width and height of the box.

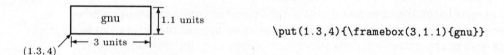

`\put(1.3,4){\framebox(3,1.1){gnu}}`

The reference point is the lower-left corner of the box. The default is to center the text both horizontally and vertically within the box, but an optional argument specifies other positioning. This argument consists of one or two of the following letters: `l` (left), `r` (right), `t` (top), and `b` (bottom). The letters in a two-letter argument can appear in either order.

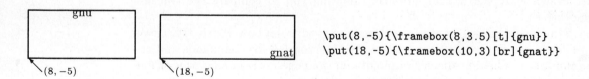

`\put(8,-5){\framebox(8,3.5)[t]{gnu}}`
`\put(18,-5){\framebox(10,3)[br]{gnat}}`

Unlike the ordinary `\framebox` command described in Section 5.4.3, the picture-making version adds no space between the frame and the text. There is a corresponding version of `\makebox` that works the same as `\framebox` except it does not draw the frame. These picture-making versions are used mainly as picture objects, although they can be used anywhere that an ordinary box-making command can.

The discussion of zero-width boxes in Section 5.4.3 should explain why a `\makebox(0,0)` command with no positioning argument puts the center of the text on the reference point, and with a positioning argument puts the indicated edge or corner of the text on the reference point.

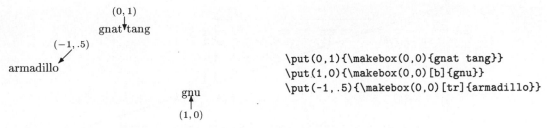

```
\put(0,1){\makebox(0,0){gnat tang}}
\put(1,0){\makebox(0,0)[b]{gnu}}
\put(-1,.5){\makebox(0,0)[tr]{armadillo}}
```

A \makebox(0,0) command is very useful for positioning text in a picture.

The \dashbox command is similar to \framebox but draws the frame with dashed lines. It has an additional first argument that specifies the width of each dash.

```
\put(4,2.2){\dashbox{.5}(5,2)[t]{gnat}}
```

A dashed box looks best when the width and the height are both multiples of the dash length—in this example, the width is ten times and the height four times the length of a dash.

Straight Lines

Straight lines can be drawn with only a fixed, though fairly large, choice of slopes. A line is not specified by giving its endpoints, since that might produce a slope not in LaTeX's repertoire. Instead, the slope and length of the line are specified. LaTeX's method of describing slope and length was chosen to make designing pictures easier, but it requires a bit of explanation.

The \line command produces a picture object that is a straight line, with one end of the line as its reference point. The command has the form

$$\texttt{\textbackslash line}(x,y)\{\mathit{len}\}$$

where the coordinate pair (x, y) specifies the slope and *len* specifies the length, in a manner I will now describe. (Figure 5.2 illustrates the following explanation with a particular example.) Let p_0 be the reference point, and suppose its coordinates are (x_0, y_0). Starting at p_0, move x units to the right and y units up to find the point p_1, so p_1 has coordinates $(x_0 + x, y_0 + y)$. (Negative distances have the expected meaning: moving right a distance of -2 units means moving 2 units to the left, and moving up -2 units means moving down 2 units.) The line drawn by this command lies along the straight line through p_0 and p_1. It starts at p_0 and goes in the direction of p_1 a distance determined as follows by *len*. If the line is not vertical ($x \neq 0$), it extends *len* units horizontally to the right or left of p_0 (depending upon whether x is positive or negative). If the line is vertical ($x = 0$), it extends *len* units above or below p_0 (depending upon whether y is positive or negative).

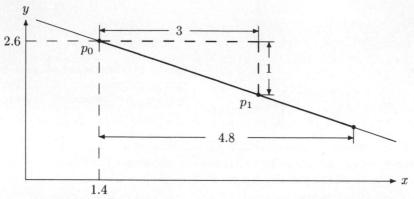

Figure 5.2: `\put (1.4,2.6){\line(3,-1){4.8}}`

The *len* argument therefore specifies the line's horizontal extent except for a vertical line, which has no horizontal extent, where it specifies the vertical distance. It equals the actual length of the line only for horizontal and vertical lines. The value of *len* must be nonnegative.

Since only a fixed number of slopes are available, there are only a limited number of values that x and y can assume. They must both be integers (numbers without decimal points) between -6 and $+6$, inclusive. Moreover, they can have no common divisor bigger than one. In other words, x/y must be a fraction in its simplest form, so you can't let $x = 2$ and $y = -4$; you must use $x = 1$ and $y = -2$ instead. The following are all *illegal* arguments of a `\line` command: `(1.4,3)`, `(3,6)`, `(0,2)`, and `(1,7)`.

LaTeX draws slanted (neither horizontal nor vertical) lines using a special font whose characters consist of small line segments. This means that there is a smallest slanted line that LaTeX can draw—its length is about 10 points, or 1/7-inch. If you try to draw a smaller slanted line, LaTeX will print nothing. It also means that LaTeX must print lots of line segments to make up a long slanted line, which can take a long time. However, LaTeX draws a horizontal or vertical line of any length reasonably quickly.

Arrows

An arrow—a straight line ending in an arrowhead—is made by the `\vector` command. It works exactly like the `\line` command.

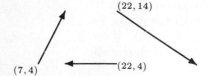

```
\put(7,4){\vector(1,2){5}}
\put(22,4){\vector(-1,0){10}}
\put(22,14){\vector(3,-2){15}}
```

The tip of the arrowhead lies on the endpoint of the line opposite the reference point. This makes any normal-length arrow point away from the reference point. However, for an arrow of length zero, both endpoints lie on the reference point, so the tip of the arrow is at the reference point.

LATEX can't draw arrows with as many different slopes as it can draw lines. The pair of integers specifying the slope in a \vector command must lie between −4 and +4, inclusive; as with the \line command, they must have no common divisor.

Stacks

The \shortstack command produces a box containing a single column of text with reference point at its lower-left corner. Its argument contains the text, rows being separated by a \\ command. The \shortstack command is much like a one-column tabular environment (Section 3.6.2), but the space between rows is designed for a vertical column of text in a picture. The default alignment is to center each row in the column, but an optional positioning argument of l (left) or r (right) aligns the text on the indicated edge.

```
\put(1,7){\shortstack{Gnats\\ and \\ gnus}}
\put(3,7){\shortstack[r]{May\\ break \\my}}
\put(5,7){\shortstack[l]{Sh\\o\\e\\s}}
```

Unlike an ordinary tabular environment, rows are not evenly spaced. You can change the inter-row spacing by using either the \\ command's optional argument (Section C.1.6) or a strut (Section 5.4.3). The \shortstack command is an ordinary box-making command that can be used anywhere, but it seldom appears outside a picture environment.

Circles

The \circle command draws a circle of the indicated diameter, with the center of the circle as reference point, and the \circle* command draws a disk (a circle with the center filled in). LATEX has only a fixed collection of circles and disks; the \circle and \circle* commands choose the one whose diameter is closest to the specified diameter.

```
\put(20,0){\circle{20}}
\put(20,0){\vector(0,1){10}}
\put(50,0){\circle*{5}}
```

On my computer, the largest circle that LATEX can draw has a diameter of 40 points (a little more than 1/2 inch) and the largest disk has a diameter of 15 points (about .2 inch). Consult the *Local Guide* to find out what size circles and disks are available on your computer.

Ovals and Rounded Corners

An oval is a rectangle with rounded corners—that is, a rectangle whose corners are replaced by quarter circles. It is generated with the \oval command, whose argument specifies the width and height, the reference point being the center of the oval. LaTeX draws the oval with corners as round as possible, using quarter circles with the largest possible radius.

`\put(1.1,-4){\oval(8,3.1)}`

Giving an optional argument to the \oval command causes LaTeX to draw only half or a quarter of the complete oval. The argument is one or two of the letters l (left), r (right), t (top), and b (bottom), a one-letter argument specifying a half oval and a two-letter argument specifying a quarter oval. The size and reference point are determined as if the complete oval were being drawn; the optional argument serves only to suppress the unwanted part.

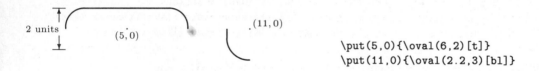

`\put(5,0){\oval(6,2)[t]}`
`\put(11,0){\oval(2.2,3)[bl]}`

Joining a quarter oval to straight lines produces a rounded corner. It takes a bit of calculating to figure out where to \put the quarter oval.

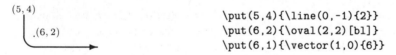

`\put(5,4){\line(0,-1){2}}`
`\put(6,2){\oval(2,2)[bl]}`
`\put(6,1){\vector(1,0){6}}`

Framing

The \framebox command puts a frame of a specified size around an object. It is often convenient to let the size of the object determine the size of the frame. The \fbox command described in Section 5.4.3 does this, but it puts extra space around the object that you may not want in a picture. The \frame command works very much like \fbox except it doesn't add any extra space.

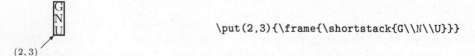

`\put(2,3){\frame{\shortstack{G\\N\\U}}}`

5.5.3 Reusing Objects

The \savebox command described in Section 5.4.3 is similar to \makebox except that, instead of being drawn, the box is saved in the indicated storage bin. Like \makebox, the \savebox command has a form in which the size of the box is indicated by a coordinate pair, with positioning determined by an optional argument.

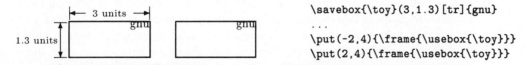

```
\savebox{\toy}(3,1.3)[tr]{gnu}
...
\put(-2,4){\frame{\usebox{\toy}}}
\put(2,4){\frame{\usebox{\toy}}}
```

The storage bin \toy in this example must be defined with \newsavebox. A \savebox command can be used inside a `picture` environment to save an object that appears several times in that picture, or outside to save an object that appears in more than one picture. Remember that \savebox is a declaration with the normal scoping rules.

It takes LaTeX a long time to draw a picture, especially if it contains slanted lines, so it's a good idea to use \savebox whenever an object appears in different pictures or in different places within the same picture. However, a saved box also uses TeX's valuable memory space, so a picture should be saved no longer than necessary. The space used by a saved box is reclaimed upon leaving the scope of the \savebox declaration. You can also use a command like \sbox{\toy}{}, which destroys the contents of storage bin \toy and reclaims its space.

5.5.4 Repeated Patterns

Pictures often contain repeated patterns formed by regularly spaced copies of the same object. Instead of using a sequence of \put commands, such a pattern can be drawn with a \multiput command. For any coordinate pairs (x, y) and $(\Delta x, \Delta y)$, the command

$$\multiput(x,y)(\Delta x,\Delta y)\{17\}\{object\}$$

puts 17 copies of *object* in the picture, starting at position (x, y) and stepping the position by $(\Delta x, \Delta y)$ units each time. It is equivalent to the 17 commands

```
\put(x,y){object}
\put(x + Δx,y + Δy){object}
\put(x + 2Δx,y + 2Δy){object}
...
\put(x + 16Δx,y + 16Δy){object}
```

as illustrated by the following example:

$(3,2.4)$ • |← 5.2 units →|

1.3 units

•

•

`\multiput(3,2.4)(5.2,-1.3){4}{\circle*{.3}}`

You can make a two-dimensional pattern by using a `picture` environment containing another `\multiput` in the argument of a `\multiput` command. However, `\multiput` typesets the object anew for each copy it makes, so it is much more efficient to make a two-dimensional pattern by saving a one-dimensional pattern made with `\multiput` in a storage bin, then repeating it with another `\multiput`. Saving the object in a bin can also save processing time for a one-dimensional pattern. However, any pattern with more than about 100 repetitions in all may cause TeX to run out of room.

5.5.5   Some Hints on Drawing Pictures

A small mistake in a picture-drawing command can produce strange results. It's usually simple to track down such an error, so don't panic when a picture turns out all wrong. If you find that some part of the picture is incorrectly positioned by a small amount, and you're sure that you haven't made a mistake in calculating its coordinates, check for stray spaces in the argument of the `\put` command. Remember that this argument is typeset in LR mode, so spaces before or after an object in that argument produce space in the output.

As you gain experience with the `picture` environment, you'll develop your own techniques for designing pictures. Here, I will describe some methods that I find useful. I like to use a small unit length, such as the default value of 1 point, so I seldom need decimals. I lay out the complete picture on graph paper before writing any LaTeX commands, using special graph paper made with LaTeX's `picture` environment. Designing your own graph paper is a nice exercise in using `\multiput`; print only one copy with LaTeX and then make xerographic copies of it. A copy made on a transparency provides a useful tool.

If a picture contains no slanted lines, I can just draw it on the graph paper and determine the coordinates directly from the drawing. However, this doesn't work well when using slanted lines because of LaTeX's limited choice of slopes. In that case, I first pick the slopes of all lines, then I *calculate* the position of each object before drawing it on the graph paper.

It's a good idea to break a complicated picture into "subpictures". The subpicture is drawn in a separate `picture` environment inside a `\put` argument, as in

`\put(13,14.2){\begin{picture}(10,7) ... \end{picture}}`

This permits easy repositioning of the subpicture and allows you to work in terms of "local" coordinates relative to the subpicture's origin instead of calculating

the position of every picture component with respect to a single origin. You can
also magnify or reduce just the subpicture by changing the value of \unitlength
with a \setlength command in the \put command's argument—but don't leave
any space after the \setlength command.

5.6   Centering and "Flushing"

The center environment is used to produce one or more lines of centered text,
a \\ command starting a new line.

This is the last line of text in the preceding paragraph.

Here are three
centered
lines of text.

This is the text immediately following the environment. It begins a new paragraph only if you leave
a blank line after the \end{center}.

```
... of text in the preceding paragraph.
\begin{center}
  Here are three\\  centered \\
  lines of text.
\end{center}
This is the text immediately ...
```

LaTeX is in paragraph mode inside the center environment, so it breaks lines
where necessary to keep them from extending past the margins.

The flushleft and flushright environments are similar, except instead
of each line of text being centered, it is moved to the left or right margin,
respectively.

These are the last lines of text from the preceding
paragraph.

These are two
flushed right lines.

```
... of text from the preceding paragraph.
\begin{flushright}
  These are two \\ flushed right lines.
\end{flushright}
```

The center and flushright environments are most commonly used with the
\\ command indicating line breaking. There is little purpose to using the
flushleft environment in this way, since the \\ command in ordinary text
produces a flushed-left line. By letting TeX do the line breaking, flushleft
produces ragged-right text.

Notice how TeX leaves these lines uneven,
without stretching them out to reach the right
margin. This is known as "ragged-right" text.

```
\begin{flushleft}
  Notice how \TeX\ leaves these lines
  uneven, withtout stretching them out ...
\end{flushleft}
```

The centering and flushing environments work by using certain declarations
that change how TeX makes paragraphs. These declarations are available as

LATEX commands, the declaration that corresponds to each environment is shown below:

environment: center   flushleft   flushright
declaration: `\centering`   `\raggedright`   `\raggedleft`

These declarations can be used inside an environment such as `quote` or in a parbox (Section 5.4.3).

This is text that comes at the end of the preceding paragraph.

<blockquote>
Here is a quote environment
whose lines are
flushed right.
</blockquote>

```
... at the end of the preceding paragraph.
\begin{quote}
  \raggedleft Here is a quote environment\\
  whose lines are \\  flushed right.
\end{quote}
```

The text of a figure or table can be centered on the page by putting a `\centering` declaration at the beginning of the `figure` or `table` environment.

Unlike the environments, the centering and flushing declarations do not start a new paragraph; they simply change how TEX formats paragraph units (Section 5.2.1). To affect a paragraph unit's format, the scope of the declaration must contain the blank line or `\end` command (of an environment like `quote`) that ends the paragraph unit.

5.7   List-Making Environments

A *list* is a sequence of items typeset in paragraph mode with indented left and right margins, each item begun with a label. A label can be empty and an indentation can be of length zero, so an environment not normally thought of as a list can be regarded as one. In fact, almost every one of LATEX's environments that begins on a new line is defined as a list. The list-making environments are: `quote`, `quotation`, `verse`, `itemize`, `enumerate`, `description`, `thebibliography`, `center`, `flushleft`, and `flushright`, as well as the theorem-like environments declared by `\newtheorem`.

LATEX provides two primitive list-making environments: `list` and `trivlist`, the latter being a restricted version of `list`. They are flexible enough to produce most lists and are used to define the environments listed above.

5.7.1   The `list` Environment

The `list` environment has two arguments. The first specifies how items should be labeled when no argument is given to the `\item` command; the second contains declarations to set the formatting parameters. The general form of a list and the meaning of most of its formatting parameters are shown in Figure 5.3. The vertical-space parameters are rubber lengths; the horizontal-space parame-

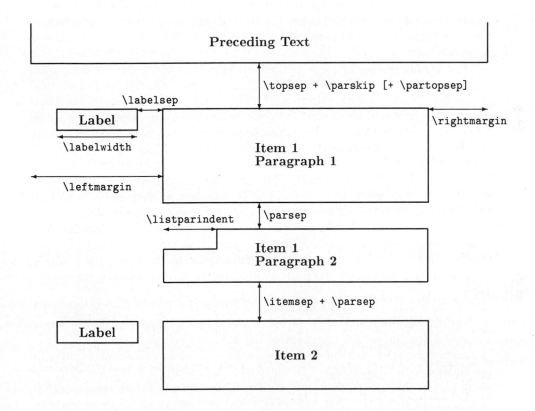

Figure 5.3: The format of a list.

ters are rigid ones. The extra \partopsep space is added at the top of the list only if the input file has a blank line before the environment. The vertical space following the environment is the same as the one preceding it.

Inside the list, the values of \parskip and \parindent are set to the values of \parsep and \listparindent, respectively. When one list is nested inside another, the \leftmargin and \rightmargin distances of the inner list are measured from the margins of the outer list.

There is one spacing parameter not shown in Figure 5.3: an extra space of length \itemindent is added before the label of each item, causing the label and first line of the item to be indented by that amount. The value of \itemindent is usually zero.

The default values of these parameters are determined by the document style, as described in Section C.5.3, and will depend upon the level of nesting of the list. These default values can be changed by declarations in the list environment's second argument. It is best to maintain the same spacing in all lists, so the default values of the vertical spacing and margin parameters should be used. However, the width and placement of the label may differ in different kinds of lists.

The label is typeset in LR mode. If it fits within a box of width \labelwidth, it is placed flush with the right-hand edge of a box of that width, which is positioned as shown in Figure 5.3. (It can be moved to a different position with the \hfill command of Section 5.4.2.) If the label is wider than \labelwidth, it is put into a box of its own width that extends to the right of the position shown in Figure 5.3. There is still a \labsep space to the right of the label's box, so the first line of the item will be indented to accomodate the extra-wide label.

The first argument of the environment is the text to be used as the label for any \item command with no optional argument. To number the items automatically, the second argument of the list environment should contain a \usecounter{*ctr*} command whose argument is the name of a counter—usually one defined with \newcounter (Section 5.6). This counter is reset to zero at the beginning of the environment and is incremented by one before the execution of any \item command that has no optional argument, so it can be used to generate a label number.

This sentence represents the end of the text that precedes the list.

B–I This is the first item of the list. Observe how the left and right margins are indented by the same amount.

B–II This is the second item.

As usual, the following text starts a new paragraph only if the list environment is followed by a blank line.

```
\newcounter{bean}
... the text that precedes the list.
\begin{list}%
{B--\Roman{bean}}{\usecounter{bean}
      \setlength{\rightmargin}{\leftmargin}}
 \item This is the first item of the list.
      Observe how the left and ...
 \item This is the second item.
\end{list}
As usual, the following text starts a ...
```

A `list` environment like this would be used to produce a one-of-a-kind list. The `list` environment is more commonly used with the `\newenvironment` command (Section 3.4) to define a new environment. Having many different list formats tends to confuse the reader. Instead of formatting each list individually, you should define a small number of list-making environments.

5.7.2   The `trivlist` Environment

The `trivlist` environment is a restricted form of the `list` environment in which margins are not indented and each `\item` command must have an optional argument. The environment has no arguments and is very much like a `list` environment whose second argument sets `\leftmargin`, `\rightmargin`, `\labelwidth`, and `\itemindent` to a length of zero.

The `trivlist` environment is used to define other environments that create a one-item list, usually with an empty label. For example, the `center` environment (Section 5.6) is equivalent to

```
\begin{trivlist} \centering \item[]  ...  \end{trivlist}
```

which is how it is defined.

5.8   Fonts

A *font* is a particular size and style of type from a *font family*. All the fonts used in this book are from the Computer Modern font family designed by Donald Knuth. The font used for most of this book is ten-point roman—its size is ten-point and its style is roman. LaTeX's fonts are now all chosen from the Computer Modern family, but versions of LaTeX that use other font families should be available in the future; see your *Local Guide* to find out if there are such versions on your computer. (Other popular font families are Times Roman and Helvetica.)

5.8.1   Changing Type Size

LaTeX's default type style is roman and its default type size is ten-point, but the `11pt` style option makes the default size eleven-point and the `12pt` option makes it twelve-point. Section 3.1 describes declarations to change the type style. LaTeX also has declarations for changing the type size; they are illustrated below:

Gnu	`\tiny`	Gnu	`\normalsize`	Gnu	`\LARGE`
Gnu	`\scriptsize`	Gnu	`\large`	Gnu	`\huge`
Gnu	`\footnotesize`	Gnu	`\Large`	Gnu	`\Huge`
Gnu	`\small`				

The point size of type produced by these declarations depends upon the default type size; the examples above are for a ten-point default size. The \normalsize declaration specifies the default size, \footnotesize specifies the size used for footnotes, and \scriptsize specifies the size used for subscripts and superscripts in \normalsize formulas. These size-changing declarations specify the roman style, regardless of the style currently in effect. For \large bold letters, you must type \large\bf, *not* \bf\large.

When you typeset an entire paragraph unit (Section 5.2.1) in a certain size, the scope of the size-changing declaration should include the blank line or \end command that ends the paragraph unit. A size-changing command may not be used in math mode. To set part of a formula in a different size of type, you can put it in an \mbox containing the size-changing command. All size-changing commands are fragile.

5.8.2   Loading Fonts

Not every type style is available in every size. If you try to use a font that is not available, LaTeX will type a warning and substitute a font of the same size that is as close as possible in style to the one you wanted.

There may be fonts available on your computer that LaTeX does not know about. Your *Local Guide* will tell you how to find out what fonts are available and what their names are. Suppose there is a twelve-point Plus Roman boldface font named "prbf10 scaled\magstep1". You choose a command name by which to call that font—let's call it \inhead—and type the declaration

\newfont{\inhead}{prbf10 scaled\magstep1}

which defines \inhead to be a declaration that causes TeX to use this font. The \inhead declaration does nothing else; in particular, it does not change the value of \baselineskip (Section 5.4.1), so it should be used within the scope of an appropriate size-changing declaration if you're setting an entire paragraph in this font. The \inhead command cannot be used in math mode. To use characters from that font in a formula, put them in an \mbox. The \inhead command is robust.

Some fonts contain special symbols in addition to or instead of ordinary letters. To produce a symbol from a font, you must know the *character-code* number of that symbol, which is a number from 0 to 255. The *Local Guide* tells you where to find tables of character codes for different fonts. To produce the symbol in the currently chosen font that has character code 26, you type \symbol{26}. Tables often list character codes in octal (base 8) or hexadecimal (base 16). An octal character code is prefaced by ' and a hexadecimal one by ", so \symbol{'32} and \symbol{"1A} produce the same symbol as \symbol{26}, since 32 is the octal and $1A$ the hexadecimal representation of 26.

CHAPTER 6
Errors

Section 2.3 describes first aid for handling errors; it explains how to deal with simple errors. This chapter is for use when you encounter an error or warning message that you don't understand. The following section tells how to locate the error; the remaining sections explain the meaning of specific error and warning messages.

As you saw in Section 2.3, an error can confuse LaTeX and cause it to produce spurious error messages when processing subsequent text that is perfectly all right. Such spurious errors are not discussed here. When TeX writes a page of output, it has usually recovered from the effects of any previous errors, so the next error message probably indicates a real error. The following section explains how to tell when TeX has written an output page.

6.1   Finding the Error

As described in Section 2.3, an error message includes an error indicator stating what TeX thinks the problem is, and an error locator that shows how much of your input file TeX had read when it found the error. Most of the time, the line printed in the error locator displays an obvious error in the input. If not, you should look up the error message in the following sections to find its probable cause. If you still don't see what's wrong, the first thing to do is locate exactly where the error occurred.

The error locator starts with a line number such as 1.14, meaning that the error was found while LaTeX was processing the fourteenth line from the beginning of the file. If your text editor allows you to break a file into pages, then the line number might be something like p.3,l.4, which indicates the fourteenth line of the third page of the input file.

If your input is all on a single file, then the error locator unambiguously identifies where TeX thinks the problem is. However, if you're using the commands of Section 4.4 to split your input into several files, then you also must know what file the error is in. Whenever TeX starts processing a file, it prints on your terminal (and on the log file) a "(" followed by the file name, and it prints a ")" when it finishes processing the file. For example, the terminal output

```
... (myfile.tex [1] [2] [3] (part1.tex [4]   [5]) (part2.tex [6] [7]
! Undefined control sequence.
l.249 \todzy
?
```

tells you that the error (a misspelled \today command) is on line 249 of the file part2.tex, which was included by an \input or \include command contained in the file myfile.tex. TeX had completely processed the file part1.tex, which was also read by a command in myfile.tex.

The error locator tells you how much of the input file TeX had processed before it discovered the error; the last command that TeX processed is usually the source of the problem. There is one important exception; but before discussing it, a digression is in order.

Logically, typesetting can be viewed as a two-step process: first the document is typeset on one continuous scroll that unrolls vertically, then the scroll is cut into individual pages to which headings and page numbers are added. (Since a 50-yard scroll of metal type is somewhat unwieldy, printers partition the logical scroll into convenient lengths called galleys.) Instead of first producing the entire scroll and then cutting it into pages, TEX does both steps together, alternately putting output on the scroll with one hand and cutting off a page with the other. It usually puts text on the scroll one paragraph unit (Section 5.2.1) at a time. After each paragraph unit, it checks whether there's enough for a page. If so, it cuts off the page, adds the heading and page number, and writes it out on a file. This way, TEX doesn't have to keep much more than one page of text in the computer's memory at a time.

Whenever TEX writes a page on its output file, it prints the page number on the terminal, enclosed in square brackets. Thus, any message that appears on the terminal after TEX prints [27] and before it prints [28] is generated between the time TEX wrote output pages 27 and 28. Whatever generated the message probably appeared in the text printed on page 28. However, it might also be in the text that was left on the scroll when TEX cut off page 28, putting it in the first paragraph of page 29. LATEX's warning messages are generated by TEX's scroll-making hand. It reports that a problem is on page 28 if it's detected between the time TEX writes pages 27 and 28, so the problem could actually appear at the top of page 29.

Now, let's get back to locating an error. Most errors are discovered while TEX is producing the scroll, but some errors, which (with apologies for abusing the English language) I will call *outputting* errors, are detected while it is cutting off a page. TEX identifies an outputting error by printing <output> on the terminal at the beginning of a line somewhere above the error locator. For an outputting error, the error locator shows how far TEX got when it was producing the scroll; the actual error occurred at or before that point. An outputting error is usually caused by a fragile command in a moving argument.

There is one other time when an error can occur: when LATEX has reached the end of your input file and is processing the \end{document} command. One of the things it does then is read auxiliary files that it has written. An error in the document can cause LATEX to write bad information on an auxiliary file, producing an error when the file is read at the end. You can tell that this has happened because the error locator will indicate that the problem is in the \end{document} command, and the messages on your terminal will show that TEX is now reading a file with the extension aux.

When the terminal output doesn't quickly lead you to the source of the error, look at the output. If LATEX reaches the end of your input or is stopped with a \stop command, the printed output will contain everything it has put on the scroll, and the location of the error will probably be obvious. If you stopped LaTeX by typing an X, then it will not print what was left on the scroll after the last full page was written out. Since the error probably occurred in this leftover text, the output will just narrow the possible location of the error.

If you still can't find the error, your next step is to find the smallest piece of your input file that produces the error. Start by eliminating everything between the \begin{document} and the last page or so of output. Then keep cutting the input in half, throwing away the part that does not cause the error. This should quickly lead to the source of the problem.

When all else fails, consult your *Local Guide* to find a LaTeX expert near you.

6.2   LaTeX's Error Messages

Here is a complete alphabetical list of LaTeX's error indicators, together with their causes.

! Bad \line or \vector argument.
The first argument of a \line or \vector command, which specifies the slope, is illegal. Look up the constraints on this argument in Section 5.5.

! Bad math environment delimiter.
TeX has found either a math-mode-starting command such as \[or \(when it is already in math mode, or else a math-mode-ending command such as \) or \] while in LR or paragraph mode. The problem is caused by either unmatched math mode delimiters or unbalanced braces.

! Bad use of \\.
A \\ command appears between paragraphs, where it makes no sense. This error message occurs when the \\ is used in a centering or flushing environment or else in the scope of a centering or flushing declaration (Section 5.6).

! \begin{...} ended by \end{...}.
LaTeX has found an \end command that doesn't match the corresponding \begin command. You probably misspelled the environment name in the \end command, have an extra \begin, or else forgot an \end.

! Can be used only in preamble.
LaTeX has encountered, after the \begin{document}, one of the following commands that should appear only in the preamble: \documentstyle, \nofiles, \includeonly, \makeindex, or \makeglossary. The error is also caused by an extra \begin{document} command.

! Command name ... already used.
You are using \newcommand, \newenvironment, \newlength, \newsavebox, or \newtheorem to define a command or environment name that is already defined, or \newcounter to define a counter that already exists. (Defining an environment named **gnu** automatically defines the command \gnu.) You'll have to choose a new name or, in the case of \newcommand or \newenvironment, switch to the \renew... command.

! Counter too large.
Some object that is numbered with letters, probably an item in an enumerated list, has received a number greater than 26. Either you're making a very long list or you've been resetting counter values.

! Environment ... undefined.
LATEX has encountered a \begin command for a nonexistent environment. You probably misspelled the environment name. This error can be corrected on the spot by typing an I followed by the correct command, ending with a *return*. (This does not change the input file.)

! Float(s) lost.
You put a **figure** or **table** environment or a \marginpar command inside a parbox—either one made with a **minipage** environment or \parbox command, or one constructed by LATEX in making a footnote, figure, etc. This is an outputting error, and the offending environment or command may be quite a way back from the point where LATEX discovered the problem. One or more figures, tables, and/or marginal notes have been lost, but not necessarily the one that caused the error.

! Illegal character in array arg.
There is an illegal character in the argument of an **array** or **tabular** environment, or in the second argument of a \multicolumn command.

! Missing \begin{document}.
LATEX produced printed output before encountering a \begin{document} command. Either you forgot the \begin{document} command or there is something wrong in the preamble. The problem may be a stray character or an error in a declaration—for example, omitting the braces around an argument or forgetting the \ in a command name.

! Missing p-arg in array arg.
There is a **p** that is not followed by an expression in braces in the argument of an **array** or **tabular** environment, or in the second argument of a \multicolumn command.

`! Missing @-exp in array arg.`

There is an @ character not followed by an @-expression in the argument of an `array` or `tabular` environment, or in the second argument of a `\multicolumn` command.

`! No such counter.`

You have specified a nonexistent counter in a `\setcounter` or `\addtocounter` command. This is probably caused by a simple typing error. However, if the error occurred while a file with the extension `aux` is being read, then you probably used a `\newcounter` command outside the preamble.

`! Not in outer par mode.`

You had a `figure` or `table` environment or a `\marginpar` command in math mode or inside a parbox.

`! \pushtabs and \poptabs don't match.`

LaTeX found a `\poptabs` with no matching `\pushtabs`, or has come to the `\end{tabbing}` command with one or more unmatched `\pushtabs` commands.

`! Something's wrong--perhaps a missing \item.`

The most probable cause is an omitted `\item` command in a list-making environment. It is also caused by forgetting the argument of a `thebibliography` environment.

`! Tab overflow.`

A `\=` command has exceeded the maximum number of tab stops that LaTeX permits.

`! There's no line here to end.`

A `\newline` or `\\` command appears between paragraphs, where it makes no sense. If you're trying to "leave a blank line", use a `\vspace` command (Section 5.4.2).

`! This may be a LaTeX bug.`

LaTeX has become thoroughly confused. This is probably due to a previously detected error, but it is possible that you have found an error in LaTeX itself. If this is the first error message produced by the input file and you can't find anything wrong, save the file and contact the person listed in your *Local Guide*.

`! Too deeply nested.`

There are too many list-making environments nested within one another. How many levels of nesting are permitted may depend upon what computer you are using, but at least four levels are provided, which should be enough.

`!  Too many unprocessed floats.`
While this error can result from having too many `\marginpar` commands on a page, a more likely cause is forcing LaTeX to save more figures and tables than it has room for. When typesetting its continuous scroll, LaTeX saves figures and tables separately and inserts them as it cuts off pages. This error occurs when LaTeX finds too many `figure` and/or `table` environments before it is time to cut off a page, a problem that is solved by moving some of the environments farther towards the end of the input file. The error can also be caused by a "logjam"—a figure or table that cannot be printed causing others to pile up behind it, since LaTeX will not print figures or tables out of order. The jam can be started by a figure or table that either is too large to fit on a page or won't fit where its optional placement argument (Section C.8.1) says it must go. This is likely to happen if the argument does not contain a `p` option.

`!  Undefined tab position.`
A `\>`, `\+`, `\-`, or `\<` command is trying to go to a nonexistent tab position—one not defined by a `\=` command.

`!  \< in mid line.`
A `\<` command appears in the middle of a line in a `tabbing` environment. This command should come only at the beginning of a line.

6.3 TₑX's Error Messages

Here is an alphabetical list of some of TₑX's error messages and what may have caused them.

`!  Counter too large.`
Footnotes are being "numbered" with letters or footnote symbols ($*$, $\dagger$, etc.) and LaTeX has run out of letters or symbols. This is probably caused by too many `\thanks` commands.

`!  Double subscript.`
There are two subscripts in a row in a mathematical formula—something like `x_{2}_{3}`, which makes no sense. To produce x_{2_3}, type `x_{2_{3}}`.

`!  Double superscript.`
There are two superscripts in a row in a mathematical formula—something like `x^{2}^{3}`, which makes no sense. To produce x^{2^3}, type `x^{2^{3}}`.

`!  Extra alignment tab has been changed to \cr.`
There are too many separate items (column entries) in a single row of an `array` or `tabular` environment. In other words, there were too many `&`'s before the end of the row. You probably forgot the `\\` at the end of the preceding row.

`! Extra }, or forgotten $.`
The braces or math mode delimiters don't match properly. You probably forgot a `{`, `\[`, `\(`, or `$`.

`! Font ... not loaded: Not enough room left.`
The document uses more fonts than TeX has room for. If different parts of the document use different fonts, then you can get around the problem by processing it in parts (Section 4.4).

`! I can't find file '...'.`
TeX can't find a file that it needs. If the name of the missing file has the extension `tex`, then it is looking for an input file that you specified—either your main file or another file inserted with an `\input` or `\include` command. If the missing file has the extension `sty`, then you have specified a nonexistent document style or style option. After printing this error message, TeX prints:

> `Please type another input file name:`

and waits for you to type the correct file name, followed by *return*.

`! Illegal parameter number in definition of ... .`
This is probably caused by a `\newcommand`, `\renewcommand`, `\newenvironment`, or `\renewenvironment` command in which a `#` is used incorrectly. A `#` character, except as part of the command name `\#`, can be used only to indicate an argument parameter, as in `#2`, which denotes the second argument. This error is also caused by nesting one of the above four commands inside another, or by putting a parameter like `#2` in the last argument of a `\newenvironment` or `\renewenvironment` command.

`! Illegal unit of measure (pt inserted).`
If you just got a

> `! Missing number, treated as zero.`

error, then this is part of the same problem. If not, it means that LaTeX was expecting a length as an argument and found a number instead. The most common cause of this error is writing 0 instead of something like 0in for a length of zero, in which case typing *return* should result in correct output. However, the error can also be caused by omitting a command argument.

`! Misplaced alignment tab character &.`
The special character `&`, which should be used only to separate items in an `array` or `tabular` environment, appeared in ordinary text. You probably meant to type `\&`, in which case typing `I\&` followed by *return* in response to the error message should produce the correct output.

! Missing control sequence inserted.

This is probably caused by a \newcommand, \renewcommand, \newlength, or \newsavebox command whose first argument is not a command name.

! Missing number, treated as zero.

This is usually caused by a LATEX command expecting but not finding either a number or a length as an argument. You may have omitted an argument, or a square bracket in the text may have been mistaken for the beginning of an optional argument. This error is also caused by putting \protect in front of either a length command or a command such as \value that produces a number.

! Missing { inserted.
! Missing } inserted.

TEX has become confused. The position indicated by the error locator is probably beyond the point where the incorrect input is.

! Missing $ inserted.

TEX probably found a command that can be used only in math mode when it wasn't in math mode. Remember that unless stated otherwise, all the commands of Section 3.3 can be used only in math mode. TEX is not in math mode when it begins processing the argument of a box-making command, even if that command is inside a math environment. This error also occurs if TEX encounters a blank line when it is in math mode.

! Not a letter.

Something appears in the argument of a \hyphenation command that doesn't belong there.

! Paragraph ended before ... was complete.

A blank line occurred in a command argument that shouldn't contain one. You probably forgot the right brace at the end of an argument.

! \scriptfont ... is undefined (character ...).
! \scriptscriptfont ... is undefined (character ...).
! \textfont ... is undefined (character ...).

These errors occur when an uncommon font is used in math mode—for example, if you use a \sc command in a formula inside a footnote, calling for a footnote-sized small caps font. This problem is solved by using a \load command, as explained in Section C.14.4.

! TeX capacity exceeded, sorry [...].

TEX has just run out of space and aborted its execution. Before you panic, remember that the least likely cause of this error is TEX not having the capacity to process your document. It was probably an error in your input file that caused TEX to run out of room. The following discussion explains how to decide whether you've really exceeded TEX's capacity and, if so, what to do. If the problem is an error in the input, you may have to use the divide and conquer method described previously to locate it. LATEX seldom runs out of space on a short input file, so if running it on the last few pages before the error indicator's position still produces the error, then there's almost certainly something wrong in the input file.

The end of the error indicator tells what kind of space TEX ran out of. The more common ones are listed below, with an explanation of their probable causes.

buffer size Can be caused by too long a piece of text as the argument of a sectioning, `\caption`, `\addcontentsline`, or `\addtocontents` command. This error will probably occur when the `\end{document}` is being processed, but it could happen when a `\tableofcontents`, `\listoffigures`, or `\listoftables` command is executed. To solve this problem, use a shorter optional argument. Even if you're producing a table of contents or a list of figures or tables, such a long entry won't help the reader.

exception dictionary You have used `\hyphenation` commands to give TEX more hyphenation information than it has room for. Remove some of the less frequently used words from the `\hyphenation` commands and insert `\-` commands instead.

hash size Your input file defines too many command names and/or uses too many cross-referencing labels.

input stack size This is probably caused by an error in a command definition. For example, the following command makes a circular definition, defining `\gnu` in terms of itself:

```
\newcommand{\gnu}{a \gnu} % This is wrong!
```

When TEX encounters this `\gnu` command, it will keep chasing its tail trying to figure out what `\gnu` should produce, and eventually run out of "input stack".

main memory size This is one kind of space that TEX can run out of when processing a short file. There are three ways you can run TEX out of main memory space: (1) defining a lot of very long, complicated commands, (2) making an index or glossary and having too many `\index` or `\glossary` commands on a single page, and (3) creating so complicated a page of output that TEX can't hold all the information needed to generate it.

The solution to the first two problems is obvious: define fewer commands or use fewer \index and \glossary commands. The third problem is nastier. It can be caused by large tabbing, tabular, array, and picture environments. TEX's space may also be filled up with figures and tables waiting for a place to go.

To find out if you've really exceeded TEX's capacity in this way, put a \clearpage command in your input file right before the place where TEX ran out of room and try running it again. If it doesn't run out of room with the \clearpage command there, then you did exceed TEX's capacity. If it still runs out of room, then there's probably an error in your file.

If TEX is really out of room, you must give it some help. Remember that TEX processes a complete paragraph before deciding whether to cut the page. Inserting a \newpage command in the middle of the paragraph, where TEX should break the page, may save the day by letting TEX write out the current page before processing the rest of the paragraph. (A \pagebreak command won't help.) If the problem is caused by accumulated figures and tables, you can try to prevent them from accumulating—either by moving them further towards the end of the document or by trying to get them to come out sooner. (See Section C.8.1 for more details.) If you are still writing the document, simply add a \clearpage command and forget about the problem until you're ready to produce the final version. Changes to the input file are likely to make the problem go away.

pool size You probably used too many cross-referencing labels and/or defined too many new command names. More precisely, the labels and command names that you define have too many characters, so this problem can be solved by using shorter names. However, the error can also be caused by omitting the right brace that ends the argument of either a counter command such as \setcounter, or a \newenvironment or \newtheorem command.

save size This occurs when commands, environments, and the scopes of declarations are nested too deeply—for example, by having the argument of a \multiput command contain a picture environment that in turn has a \footnotesize declaration whose scope contains a \multiput command containing a ....

! Text line contains an invalid character.
The input contains some strange character that it shouldn't. A mistake when creating the file probably caused your text editor to insert this character. Exactly what could have happened depends upon what text editor you used. If

examining the input file doesn't reveal the offending character, consult the *Local Guide* for suggestions.

`! Undefined control sequence.`

TeX encountered an unknown command name. You probably misspelled the name, in which case typing I followed by the desired command and a *return* will produce correct output. However, you still must change the input file later. If this message occurs when a LaTeX command is being processed, the command is probably in the wrong place—for example, the error can be produced by an `\item` command that's not inside a list-making environment. The error can also be caused by a missing `\documentstyle` command.

`! Use of ... doesn't match its definition.`

If the "..." is a LaTeX command, then it's probably one of the picture-drawing commands described in Section 5.5, and you have used the wrong syntax for specifying an argument. If it's `\@array` that doesn't match its definition, then there is something wrong in an @-expression in the argument of an `array` or `tabular` environment—perhaps a fragile command that is not `\protect`'ed.

`! You can't use 'macro parameter character #' in ... mode.`

The special character `#` has appeared in ordinary text. You probably meant to type `\#`, in which case you can respond to the error message by typing `I\#` followed by *return* to produce the correct output.

6.4   LaTeX Warnings

LaTeX's warning messages all begin with "LaTeX Warning:". The meanings of these messages are described below.

`Citation '...' on page ... undefined.`

The citation key in a `\cite` command was not defined by a `\bibitem` command. See Section 4.3.

`Label '...' multiply defined.`

Two `\label` or `\bibitem` commands have the same arguments. More precisely, they had the same arguments the preceding time that LaTeX processed the input.

`Label(s) may have changed.   Rerun to get cross-references right.`

The numbers printed by `\ref`, `\pageref`, and `\cite` commands may be wrong because the correct values have changed since the last time LaTeX processed the input.

`Marginpar on page ... moved.`
A marginal note was moved down on the page to avoid printing on top of a previous marginal note. It will therefore not be aligned with the line of text where the `\marginpar` command appeared.

`No ... typeface in this size, using ...`
A type style declaration specified a type style and size combination that is not available, so LATEX is substituting another one.

`Oval too small.`
An `\oval` command specified an oval so small that LATEX couldn't draw small enough quarter-circles to put in its corners. What LATEX did draw does not look very good.

`Reference '...' on page ... undefined.`
The argument of a `\ref` or `\pageref` command was not defined by a `\label` command. See Section 4.2.

`... in math mode.`
The indicated command is not permitted in math mode but was used there. Remember that `\boldmath`, `\unboldmath`, and size-changing commands may not be used in math mode.

6.5 TEX Warnings

You can identify a TEX warning message because it is not an error message, so no ? is printed, and it does not begin with "`LaTeX Warning:`". Below is a list of some of TEX's warnings.

`Overfull \hbox ...`
See Section 5.2.1.

`Overfull \vbox ...`
Because it couldn't find a good place for a page break, TEX put more on the page than it should. See Section 5.2.2 for how to deal with page-breaking problems.

`Underfull \hbox ...`
Check your output for extra vertical space. If you find some, it was probably caused by a problem with a `\\` or `\newline` command—for example, two `\\` commands in succession. This warning can also be caused by using the `sloppypar` environment or `\sloppy` declaration, or by inserting a `\linebreak` command.

`Underfull \vbox ...`

TEX could not find a good place to break the page, so it produced a page without enough text on it. See Section 5.2.2 for how to handle page-breaking problems.

APPENDIX A

SLIT_EX

SLITEX is a version of LATEX for making black-and-white or color slides. Consult your *Local Guide* for instructions on how to run SLITEX, and for any differences between the version described here and the one on your computer. The fonts used by SLITEX are different from the LATEX fonts with which this book is printed, so slides shown here are not accurate representations of SLITEX's output.

A.1   How SLITEX Makes Colors

No special printer is needed for color slides; they are made by copying ordinary black-and-white output onto colored transparencies. To make the slide

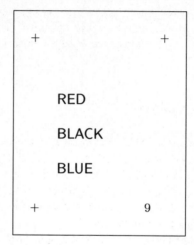

where "RED" is colored red, "BLACK" is colored black, and "BLUE" is colored blue, SLITEX would generate the following three separate pages of output:

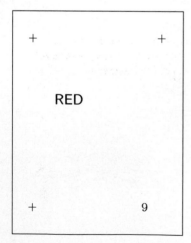 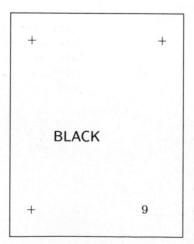 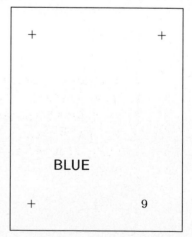

These pages are called *color layers*. Copying each of them onto a special sheet that produces a transparency of the appropriate color (such sheets are commercially available in an assortment of colors) and laying the three transparencies atop one another produces the desired three-color slide.

Text that is meant to be colored red on the slide, and is therefore printed by SLITEX on the red color layer, is called "red text". The color of a piece of text therefore refers only to the color layer on which it appears; SLITEX does not print anything in red ink.

It's hard to tell what a slide will look like from the separate color layers, so SLITEX can produce a black-and-white version of the slide that contains all the color layers properly superimposed. When creating a set of slides, you should first generate only the black-and-white versions, making the color layers after you've fixed all the problems that are visible in black and white. If you don't want color slides, you can just copy the black-and-white versions onto transparencies.

A.2 The Root File

The input to SLITEX consists of a *root file* and a separate *slide file*. The root file is the one whose name you type when running SLITEX. It begins with the usual \documentstyle command. The slides document style is the standard one for producing slides; there are no standard options. Consult your *Local Guide* to see if any other styles or options are available on your computer. The \documentstyle command is followed by the preamble, which may contain only declarations, followed in turn by the \begin{document} command.

Any text that comes after the \begin{document} is treated as "front matter" and not as slide material. You can use it for notes to identify the slides.

This is an example of front matter. Note the different type style, and how the text is vertically centered on the page.

```
\begin{document}
This is an example of front matter.
Note the different type style, and how
the text is vertically centered on the
page.
```

To produce color slides, there must be a `\colors` command to tell SLITₑX what colors will be used. The command

> `\colors{red,black,blue}`

states that there will be three colors named `red`, `black`, and `blue`. SLITₑX knows nothing about real colors, so the three colors could just as well be named `puce`, `mauve`, and `fred`. No `\colors` command is needed if only black-and-white slides are being made.

The text of the slides is contained in a separate slide file whose contents are discussed in the next section. The slide file may have any first name, but must have the extension `tex`. Suppose that it is called `myslid.tex`. Black-and-white slides are generated by placing the command `\blackandwhite{myslid}` in the root file. Color slides are generated by the command `\colorslides{myslid}`. The latter command generates a set of color-layer pages for each color specified by the `\colors` command. For example, the command

> `\colors{red,black,blue}`

causes a subsequent `\colorslides` command to generate first all the red color-layer pages, then the black ones, and then the blue ones.

As usual, the root file ends with an `\end{document}` command.

A.3   The Slide File

The main purpose of the root file is to tell SLITₑX what colors to use and where to find the slide file, so the root file is usually short. The slide file makes the individual slides; it may be split into parts with the `\input` command of Section 4.4, but this is seldom necessary because SLITₑX provides commands, described below, for selecting which slides to process. The `\includeonly` command may not be used with SLITₑX.

A.3.1   Slides

Each slide is produced by a `slide` environment with a single argument that is a list of all the colors contained on the slide. A slide that has the colors `red` and `blue` is created by an environment

> `\begin{slide}{red,blue}`
> `...`
> `\end{slide}`

The colors in the argument must be declared by a `\colors` command in the root file. They tell SLITₑX which color layers to produce for this particular slide. If there is green text in the slide, that text will appear in the black-and-white version, but no green color layer will be generated unless `green` is included in the `slide` environment's argument. If only black-and-white slides are to be made, then you can just type:

```
\begin{slide}{}
    ...
\end{slide}
```

The text appearing on a slide is produced with ordinary LaTeX commands. Any commands that make sense for slides can be used. Commands that *don't* make sense include sectioning commands, `figure` and `table` environments, indexing commands, commands for generating a bibliography, and page-breaking commands. The latter make no sense in a slide because each slide must fit on a single page.

Output generated by SLITeX differs from ordinary LaTeX output in two ways: text is automatically centered vertically on a slide and SLITeX uses type fonts especially chosen for slides. The characters in these fonts are much larger than the ones in the corresponding LaTeX fonts; SLITeX's `\normalsize` produces roughly the same size characters as LaTeX's `\LARGE` (Section 5.8.1). Moreover, SLITeX's ordinary roman type style is similar to LaTeX's sans serif style. The only type styles generally available are roman (`\rm`), italic (`\it`), bold (`\bf`), and typewriter (`\tt`). The `\em` command works as usual.

The only special SLITeX commands needed inside a slide are ones to specify color. The `\colors` command in the root file defines the color declarations; if the root file contains the command `\colors{red,black,blue}`, then `\red`, `\black`, and `\blue` are declarations that specify the color. They have the same scope rules as other declarations, as illustrated by the following example in which only the red color layer is shown:

```
\red
\begin{slide}{red,blue}
    This is red text with two
    {\blue blue words} here.

    This is more red text.
\end{slide}
```

A color declaration does not affect the type style. For example, the following input produces a slide whose red color layer contains only the words *RED ITALIC* in italic.

```
\begin{slide}{red,blue}
  \begin{blue} This is blue roman text.
      {\it This is blue italic and this is
            {\red  RED ITALIC}
      text.}
  \end{blue}
\end{slide}
```

A color declaration cannot be used in math mode. A multicolored formula is made with \mbox commands that contain the color declarations.

The command \invisible is a special color declaration for invisible text. Invisible text is not only colorless, appearing in no color layer, but does not appear in the black-and-white version either. The use of invisible text is explained below. Like other color declarations, \invisible cannot be used in math mode.

A.3.2   Overlays

The overlay environment is for making an *overlay*—a slide meant to be placed on top of another one. It is exactly the same as the slide environment except for how the page is numbered. The first overlay following slide number 9 is numbered "9-a", the second one is numbered "9-b", and so forth. To make an overlay that perfectly overlays a slide, the slide and the overlay should be identical except that text visible in one is invisible in the other.

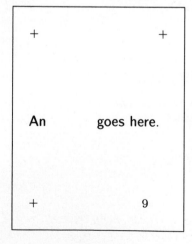

```
\begin{slide}{red}

\red
An {\invisible overlay}
goes here.

\end{slide}
```

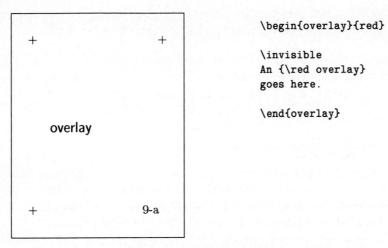

```
\begin{overlay}{red}

\invisible
An {\red overlay}
goes here.

\end{overlay}
```

When the slide and the overlay are placed on top of one another, they read:

An overlay goes here.

A.3.3   Notes

It is sometimes convenient to put notes to yourself in with the slides. The **note** environment produces a one-page note that appears only in the black-and-white version of the slides.

This is a note to myself, perhaps reminding me of what I wanted to say here.

9-1

```
\begin{note}
  This is a note to myself, perhaps
  reminding me of what I wanted to say
  here.

\end{note}
```

Notes that follow slide number 9 are numbered "9-1", "9-2", etc.

A.3.4   Page Styles for Slides

Slides and overlays normally have + symbols in the corners to help align the separate color layers. The presence or absence of these symbols and of the slide or overlay number is controlled by the page style (Section 5.1.2). The `slides` document style provides the following page styles.

`headings` Alignment marks and numbers are as shown in the examples. This is the default. The `\markboth` and `\markright` commands have no effect.

`plain` There are no alignment marks, but slides, overlays, and notes are numbered as shown.

`empty` No alignment marks or numbers are printed.

The page style can be changed with the `\pagestyle` declaration described in Section 5.1.2. It should not be used in a `slide`, `overlay`, or `note` environment. The `\thispagestyle` command should *not* be used in SLITEX.

A.4   Making Only Some Slides

For making corrections, it's convenient to generate only some of the slides from your input file. The command

   `\onlyslides{4,7-13,23}`

in the root file will cause the following `\blackandwhite` and `\colorslides` commands to generate only slides numbered 4, 7–13 (inclusive) and 23, plus all of their overlays. The slide numbers in the argument must be in ascending order, and can include nonexistent slides—for example, you can type

   `\onlyslides{10-9999}`

to produce all but the first nine slides. The argument of the `\onlyslides` command must be nonempty.

   There is also an analogous `\onlynotes` command to generate a subset of the notes. Notes numbered 11-1, 11-2, etc. will all be generated by specifying page 11 in the argument of the `\onlynotes` command. If the root file has an `\onlyslides` command but no `\onlynotes` command, then notes are produced for the specified slides. If there is an `\onlynotes` but no `\onlyslides`, then no slides are generated. Including both an `\onlyslides` and an `\onlynotes` command has the expected effect of producing only the specified slides and notes.

APPENDIX B
The Bibliography Database

Section 4.3.2 explains how the \bibliography command specifies one or more bib files—bibliographic database files whose names have the extension bib. BIBTEX uses the bib file(s) to generate a bbl file that is read by \bibliography to make the bibliography. This appendix explains how to create bib files.

The bibliography database files for use with BIBTEX are reasonably compatible with the ones used by the *Scribe* text formatting system [6]. While a bib file prepared according to the directions in this appendix will work with *Scribe*, it is better to prepare separate files for BIBTEX and *Scribe*. The compatibility makes it easy to convert from one to the other, or to maintain two copies of the database.

For any single document, it's easier to make the bibliography yourself than to create the bib file needed by BIBTEX. However, when you've made a bib file entry for a reference, it can be used for other documents as well. Once you start using BIBTEX, you will soon compile a bibliographic database that eliminates almost all the work of making a bibliography. Moreover, other people may have bib files that you can copy, or there may be a common database that you can use. Ask your friends or check the *Local Guide* to find out what facilities are available to ease the task of making bib files.

B.1 The Format of the bib File

B.1.1 The Entry Format

A bib file contains a series of reference entries like the following:

```
@BOOK{kn:gnus,
    AUTHOR = "Donald E. Knudson",
    TITLE  = "1966 World Gnus Almanac",
    PUBLISHER = {Permafrost Press},
    ADDRESS = {Novosibirsk}                    }
```

The @BOOK states that this is an entry of type *book*. Various entry types are described below. The kn:gnus is the *key*, as it appears in the argument of a \cite command referring to the entry.

This entry has four *fields*, named AUTHOR, TITLE, PUBLISHER, and ADDRESS. The meanings of these and other fields are described below. A field consists of the name, an = character with optional space around it, followed by its text. The text of a field is a string of characters, with no unmatched braces, surrounded by either a pair of braces or a pair of " characters. (Unlike in TEX input, \{ and \} are considered to be braces with respect to brace matching.) Entry fields are separated from one another, and from the key, by commas. A comma may have optional space around it.

The outermost braces that surround the entire entry may be replaced by parentheses. As in TEX input files, an end-of-line character counts as a space and one space is equivalent to one hundred. Unlike TeX, BibTeX ignores the case of letters in the entry type, key, and field names, so the above entry could have been typed as follows:

```
@Book(KN:Gnus, author={Donald E. Knudson} ,
        TiTlE  =       "1966 World
                       Gnus  Almanac",   ...     )
```

However, the case of letters does matter to LaTeX, so the key should appear exactly the same in all \cite commands in the LaTeX input file.

The quotes or braces can be omitted around text consisting entirely of numerals. The following two fields are equivalent:

```
Volume = "27"        Volume = 27
```

B.1.2   The Text of a Field

The text of the field is enclosed in braces or double quote characters ("). A part of the text is said to be *enclosed in braces* if it lies inside a matching pair of braces other than the ones enclosing the entire entry.

Names

The text of an **author** or **editor** field represents a list of names. The bibliography style determines the format in which the name is printed: whether the first name or last name appears first, if the full first name or just the first initial is used, etc. The bib file entry simply tells BibTeX what the name is. You should type an author's complete name and let the bibliography style decide what to abbreviate. van Leunen [7] recommends typing an author's name exactly as it appears in the cited work, but this could produce a confusing reference list if his name appears in a slightly different form in two different works—for example, with and without a middle initial. In this case, I recommend typing the name the way the author would like it, as indicated by how it appears in the majority of his publications.

Most names can be entered in the obvious way, either with or without a comma, as in the following examples.

```
"John Paul Jones"        "Jones, John Paul"
"Ludwig von Beethoven"   "von Beethoven, Ludwig"
```

Only the second form, with a comma, should be used for people who have multiple last names that are capitalized. For example, Per Brinch Hansen's last name is Brinch Hansen, so his name should be typed with a comma:

```
"Brinch Hansen, Per"
```

If you type `"Per Brinch Hansen"`, BIBTEX will think that "Brinch" is his middle name. "von Beethoven" or "de la Madrid" pose no problem because "von" and "de la" are not capitalized.

BIBTEX regards the text enclosed in braces as a single name, so braces should be used in cases where BIBTEX would otherwise get confused. For example, braces should surround a comma that is part of a name. The braces in

> `"{Barnes and Noble, Inc.}"`

prevent "Inc." from being interpreted as a first name, this particular author having no first name. Note that the two names

> `"von Beethoven, Ludwig"`   `"{von Beethoven}, Ludwig"`

are considered by BIBTEX to be different names. In the first, "Beethoven" is the last name, with "von" an auxiliary word; in the second, which in this case happens to be incorrect, the last name is "von Beethoven". The bibliography style will probably print both the same, but it may alphabetize them differently.

"Juniors" pose a special problem. Most people with "Jr." in their name precede it with a comma. Such a name should be entered as follows:

> `"Ford, Jr., Henry"`

However, some people do not use a comma; they are handled by considering the "Jr." to be part of the last name:

> `"{Steele Jr.}, Guy L."`   `"Guy L. {Steele Jr.}"`

If there are multiple authors or editors, their names are separated by the word "and". A paper written by Alpher, Bethe, and Gamow has the following entry:

> `AUTHOR = "Ralph Alpher and Bethe, Hans and George Gamow"`

An "and" separates author's names only if it is not enclosed in braces. Therefore, if the word "and" appears as part of a name, it is enclosed in braces, as in the example of "Barnes and Noble, Inc." given above. If an **author** or **editor** field has more names than you want to type, just end the list of names with **and others**; the standard styles convert this to the conventional *et al.*

Titles

The bibliography style determines whether or not a title is capitalized; the titles of books usually are, the titles of articles usually are not. You type a title the way it should appear if it is capitalized.

> `TITLE  =  "The Agony and the Ecstasy"`

You should capitalize the first word of the title, the first word after a colon, and all other words except articles and unstressed conjunctions and prepositions. BIBTEX will change uppercase letters to lowercase if appropriate. Uppercase letters that should not be changed are enclosed in braces. The following two titles are equivalent; the *A* of *Africa* will not be made lowercase.

```
"The Gnats and Gnus of {Africa}"
"The Gnats and Gnus of {A}frica"
```

B.1.3   Abbreviations

Instead of an ordinary text string, the text of a field can be replaced by an *abbreviation* for it. An abbreviation is a string of characters that starts with a letter and does not contain a space or any of the following ten characters:

```
"  #  %  '  (  )  ,  =  {  }
```

The abbreviation is typed in place of the text field, with no braces or quotation marks. If `jgg1` is an abbreviation for

```
Journal of Gnats and Gnus, Series~1
```

then the following are equivalent:

```
Journal = jgg1
Journal = "Journal of Gnats and Gnus, Series~1"
```

Some abbreviations are predefined by the bibliography style. These always include the usual three-letter abbreviations for the month: `jan`, `feb`, `mar`, etc. Bibliography styles usually contain abbreviations for the names of commonly referenced journals. Consult your *Local Guide* for a list of the predefined abbreviations for the bibliography styles available on your computer.

You can define your own abbreviations by putting a `@string` command in the `bib` file. The command

```
@string{jgg1 = "Journal of Gnats and Gnus, Series~1"}
```

defines `jgg1` to be the abbreviation assumed in the previous example. Parentheses can be used in place of the outermost braces in the `@string` command, and braces can be used instead of the quotation marks. The text must have matching braces.

The case of letters is ignored in an abbreviation as well as in the command name `@string`, so the above command is equivalent to

```
@STRING{JgG1 = "Journal of Gnats and Gnus, Series~1"}
```

A @string command can appear anywhere before or between entries in a bib file. However, it must come before any use of the abbreviation, so a sensible place for @string commands is at the beginning of the file. A @string command in the bib file takes precedence over a definition made by the bibliography style, so it can be used to change the definition of an abbreviation such as Feb.

B.2   The Entries

B.2.1   Entry Types

When entering a reference in the database, the first thing to decide is what type of entry it is. No fixed classification scheme can be complete, but BIBTEX provides enough entry types to handle almost any reference reasonably well.

References to different types of publications contain different information; a reference to a journal article might include the volume and number of the journal, which is usually not meaningful for a book. Therefore, database entries of different types have different fields. For each entry type, the fields are divided into three classes:

required Omitting the field will produce an error message and may result in a badly formatted bibliography entry. If the required information is not meaningful, you are using the wrong entry type.

optional The field's information will be used if present, but can be omitted without causing any formatting problems. A reference should contain any available information that might help the reader, so you should include the optional field if it is applicable.

ignored The field is ignored. BIBTEX ignores any field that is not required or optional, so you can include any fields you want in a bib file entry. It's a good idea to put all relevant information about a reference in its bib file entry—even information that may never appear in the bibliography. For example, if you want to keep an abstract of a paper in a computer file, put it in an abstract field in the paper's bib file entry. The bib file is likely to be as good a place as any for the abstract, and it is possible to design a bibliography style for printing selected abstracts.

The following are all the entry types, along with their required and optional fields, that are used by the standard bibliography styles. They are similar to those adapted by Brian Reid from the classification scheme of van Leunen [7] for use in the *Scribe* system. The meanings of the individual fields are explained in the next section. A particular bibliography style may ignore some optional fields in creating the reference. Remember that, when used in the bib file, the entry-type name is preceded by an @ character.

article An article from a journal or magazine. Required fields: `author`, `title`, `journal`, `year`. Optional fields: `volume`, `number`, `pages`, `month`, `note`.

book A book with an explicit publisher. Required fields: `author` or `editor`, `title`, `publisher`, `year`. Optional fields: `volume`, `series`, `address`, `edition`, `month`, `note`.

booklet A work that is printed and bound, but without a named publisher or sponsoring institution. Required field: `title`. Optional fields: `author`, `howpublished`, `address`, `month`, `year`, `note`.

conference The same as **inproceedings**, included for *Scribe* compatibility.

inbook A part of a book, which may be a chapter and/or a range of pages. Required fields: `author` or `editor`, `title`, `chapter` and/or `pages`, `publisher`, `year`. Optional fields: `volume`, `series`, `address`, `edition`, `month`, `note`.

incollection A part of a book with its own title. Required fields: `author`, `title`, `booktitle`, `publisher`, `year`. Optional fields: `editor`, `chapter`, `pages`, `address`, `month`, `note`.

inproceedings An article in a conference proceedings. Required fields: `author`, `title`, `booktitle`, `year`. Optional fields: `editor`, `pages`, `organization`, `publisher`, `address`, `month`, `note`.

manual Technical documentation. Required field: `title`. Optional fields: `author`, `organization`, `address`, `edition`, `month`, `year`, `note`.

mastersthesis A Master's thesis. Required fields: `author`, `title`, `school`, `year`. Optional fields: `address`, `month`, `note`.

misc Use this type when nothing else fits. Required fields: none. Optional fields: `author`, `title`, `howpublished`, `month`, `year`, `note`.

phdthesis A Ph.D. thesis. Required fields: `author`, `title`, `school`, `year`. Optional fields: `address`, `month`, `note`.

proceedings The proceedings of a conference. Required fields: `title`, `year`. Optional fields: `editor`, `publisher`, `organization`, `address`, `month`, `note`.

techreport A report published by a school or other institution, usually numbered within a series. Required fields: `author`, `title`, `institution`, `year`. Optional fields: `type`, `number`, `address`, `month`, `note`.

unpublished A document with an author and title, but not formally published. Required fields: `author`, `title`, `note`. Optional fields: `month`, `year`.

In addition to the fields listed above, each entry type also has an optional `key` field, used in some styles for alphabetizing and forming a `\bibitem` label. You should include a `key` field for any entry whose `author` and `editor` fields are both missing. Do not confuse the `key` field with the key that appears in the `\cite` command and at the beginning of the whole entry, after the entry type; this field is named "key" only for compatibility with *Scribe*.

B.2.2 Fields

Below is a description of all the fields recognized by the standard bibliography styles. An entry can also contain other fields that are ignored by those styles.

address Publisher's address. For major publishing houses, just the city is given. For small publishers, you can help the reader by giving the complete address.

annote An annotation. It is not used by the standard bibliography styles, but may be used by others that produce an annotated bibliography.

author The name(s) of the author(s), in the format described above.

booktitle Title of a book, part of which is being cited. See above for how to type titles.

chapter A chapter number.

edition The edition of a book—for example, "second".

editor Name(s) of editor(s), typed as indicated above. If there is also an `author` field, then the `editor` field gives the editor of the book or collection in which the reference appears.

howpublished How something strange has been published.

institution The institution that published the work.

journal A journal name. Abbreviations are provided for many journals; see the *Local Guide*.

key Used for alphabetizing and creating a label when the `author` and `editor` fields are missing. This field should not be confused with the key that appears in the `\cite` command and at the beginning of the entry.

month The month in which the work was published or, for an unpublished work, in which it was written. See above for abbreviations.

note Any additional information that can help the reader.

number The number of a journal, magazine, or technical report. An issue of a journal or magazine is usually identified by its volume and number; the organization that issues a technical report usually gives it a number.

organization The organization sponsoring a conference.

pages One or more page numbers or ranges of numbers, such as 42--111 or 7,41,73--97. To make it easier to maintain *Scribe*-compatible databases, the standard styles convert a single dash (as in 7-33) to the double dash used in TEX to denote number ranges (as in 7--33).

publisher The publisher's name.

school The name of the school where a thesis was written.

series The name of a series or set of books. When citing an entire book, the title field gives its title and the optional series field gives the name of a series in which the book was published.

title The work's title, typed as explained above.

type The type of a technical report—for example, "Research Note".

volume The volume of a journal or multivolume book.

year The year of publication or, for an unpublished work, the year it was written. It should consist only of numerals, such as 1984.

APPENDIX C
A Reference Manual

This appendix describes all LaTeX commands and environments, including some features, anomalies and special cases not mentioned earlier. You should look here when a command or environment does something surprising, or when you encounter a formatting problem not discussed in earlier chapters.

Command and environment descriptions are concise; material explained in an earlier chapter is sketched very briefly. The syntax of commands and environments is indicated by a *command form* such as:

> \newcommand{*cmd*}[*args*]{*def*}

Everything in a typewriter font, such as the "\newcommand{", represents material that appears in the input file exactly as shown. The italicized parts *cmd*, *args*, and *def* represent items that vary; the command's description explains their function. Arguments enclosed in square brackets [ ] are optional; they (and the brackets) may be omitted, so \newcomand can also have the form

> \newcommand{*cmd*}{*def*}

The case in which an optional argument is missing is called the *default*. If a command form has two optional arguments, when only one is present it is assumed to be the first one.

A number of *style parameters* are listed in this appendix. Except where stated otherwise, these parameters are length commands. A length is rigid unless it is explicitly said to be a rubber length (Section 5.4.1).

C.1   Commands and Environments

C.1.1   Command Names and Arguments

The six commands # $ & ~ _ ^ are the only ones with single-character names. The character %, while not a command, causes TeX to ignore all characters following it on the input line—including the space character that ends the line. A % can be used to begin a comment and to start a new line without producing space in the output. However, a command name cannot be split across lines.

About two dozen commands have two-character names composed of \ followed by a single nonletter. All other command names consist of \ followed by one or more letters. Command names containing an @ character can be used only in document-style (sty) files (Section 5.1.4). Upper- and lowercase letters are considered to be different, so \gamma and \Gamma are different commands. Spaces are ignored after a command name of this form, except that a blank line following the command still denotes the end of a paragraph.

Commands may have mandatory and/or optional arguments. A mandatory argument is enclosed by curly braces { and } and an optional argument is enclosed by square brackets [and]. There should be no space between the arguments.

The following commands take an optional last argument:

```
\\        \linebreak   \nolinebreak   \newcounter   \twocolumn
\item   \pagebreak    \nopagebreak    \newtheorem
```

If that argument is missing and the next nonspace character in the text is a [, then LaTeX will mistake this [for the beginning of an optional argument. Enclosing the [in braces prevents this mistake.

Enclosing text in braces can seldom cause trouble.

- [This is an aside.] This is the rest of the item.

```
...  \begin{itemize}
     \item {[This is an aside.]} This is ...
```

A] within the optional argument of an \item command must be enclosed in braces to prevent its being mistaken for the] that marks the end of the argument.

[**gnu**] A large animal, found mainly in dictionaries.

[**gnat**] A small animal, found mainly in tents.

```
\begin{description}
    \item [{[gnu]}] A large animal...
    \item [{[gnat]}] A small animal...
\end{description}
```

Some commands, including \\, have a *-form that is obtained by typing a * right after the command name. If a * is the first nonspace character following a \\ command, then it should be enclosed in braces; otherwise, LaTeX will mistake the \\ and * for a * command.

C.1.2 Environments

An environment is begun with a \begin command having the environment's name as the first argument. Any arguments of the environment are typed as additional arguments to the \begin. The environment is ended with an \end command having the environment's name as its only argument. If an environment has a *-form, the * is part of the environment's name, appearing in the argument of the \begin and \end commands.

C.1.3 Fragile Commands

Commands are classified as either *robust* or *fragile*. Type-style-changing declarations such as \em are robust, as are most of the math-mode commands of Section 3.3. Any command with an optional argument is fragile.

   Certain command arguments are called *moving* arguments. A fragile command that appears in a moving argument must be preceded by a \protect command. A \protect applies only to the command it precedes; fragile commands appearing in its argument(s) require their own \protect commands. The following are all the commands and environments with moving arguments:

- Commands with an argument that may be put into a table of contents, list of figures, or list of tables: \addcontentsline, \addtocontents, \caption, and the sectioning commands. If an optional argument is used with a sectioning or \caption command, then it is this argument that is the moving one.

- Commands to print on the terminal: \typeout and \typein. The optional argument of \typein is not a moving argument.

- Commands to generate page headings: \markboth (both arguments) and \markright. (The sectioning commands, already listed, fall under this category too.)

- The letter environment.

- The \thanks command.

- The optional argument of \bibitem.

- An @ in an array or tabular environment. (Although @ is not a command, fragile commands in an @-expression must be \protect'ed as if they were in a moving argument.)

All length commands are robust and must not be preceded by \protect. A \protect command should not be used in an argument of a \setcounter or \addtocounter command.

C.1.4 Declarations

A declaration is a command that changes the value or meaning of some command or parameter. The *scope* of a declaration begins with the declaration itself and ends with the first } or \end whose matching { or \begin occurs before the declaration. The commands \], \), and $ that end a math-mode environment and the } or] that end the argument of a LaTeX command also delimit the scope of a declaration; but the } ending the argument of a command defined with \newcommand or \renewcommand does *not* delimit its scope. A declaration is in effect throughout its scope, except within the scope of a subsequent countermanding declaration.

The following declarations are *global*; their scope is not delimited by braces or environments.

\newcounter	\pagenumbering	\newlength
\setcounter	\thispagestyle	\newsavebox
\addtocounter	\hyphenation	\newtheorem

C.1.5 Invisible Commands and Environments

A number of commands and environments are "invisible", meaning that they do not produce any text at the point where they appear. TeX regards an invisible command or environment in the middle of a paragraph as an invisible "word". Putting spaces or an end-of-line character both before and after an invisible word can generate two separate interword spaces, one on either side of this "word", producing extra space in the output. This is seldom a problem for a command with no argument, since spaces are ignored when they follow a command name that ends in a letter. Also, the following invisible commands and environments usually eliminate this extra space:[1]

\pagebreak	\nolinebreak	\vspace	figure
\nopagebreak	\label	\glossary	table
\linebreak	\index	\marginpar	

Any other invisible command with an argument that appears inside a paragraph should be attached to an adjacent word, as should the above commands and environments in certain unusual situations where they can produce extra space in the output.

C.1.6   The \\ command

\\ [len]
*[len]

These commands start a new line and add an extra vertical space of length *len* above it. The default is to add no extra space. The *-form inhibits a page break before the new line. They may be used in paragraph mode and within the following commands and environments:

array	eqnarray	\shortstack
tabular	tabbing	\author

TeX is in paragraph mode, so a \\ can be used, in the following environments (among others):

verse	center	flushleft	flushright

and when processing the argument of a \title, \date, or sectioning command. Do not use two \\ commands in a row in paragraph mode; instead, use an optional argument to add extra vertical space.

In the **array** and **tabular** environments, the spacing between rows is obtained by putting a strut (Section 5.4.3) on each line; a positive value of *len* increases the depth of this strut. This can fail to add the expected amount of extra space if an object in the row extends further below the line than the default strut.

The \\ and * commands are fragile.

---

[1]More precisely, spaces that follow these commands and environments are ignored if there is space in the output before the invisible "word" that they generate.

C.2   Sentences and Paragraphs

C.2.1   Making Sentences

Except where otherwise indicated, the following commands and characters are for use in paragraph and LR mode only and are robust.

quotes
    ' Apostrophe.   `'text'` Single quotes.   `''text''` Double quotes.

dashes
    - Intra-word.   -- Number-range.   --- Punctuation.

spacing

    `\,` Produces a small space used between a double and a single quote.

    `\␣` Produces an interword space.

    `~` Produces an interword space where no line break can occur.

    `\@` Causes an "end-of-sentence" space after punctuation when typed before the punctuation character. Needed only if the character preceding the punctuation character is not a lowercase letter or a number.

    `\frenchspacing` Suppresses extra space after punctuation, even when `\@` is used. Fragile.

    `\nonfrenchspacing` Reverses the effect of `\frenchspacing`. Fragile.

special characters
    `$` `\$`   `%` `\%`   `{` `\{`   `-` `\_`
    `&` `\&`   `#` `\#`   `}` `\}`
    See Sections 3.2 and 3.3.2 for other symbols.

logos The following commands may be used in math mode as well as paragraph and LR modes:
    `\TeX` Produces TeX logo.   `\LaTeX` Produces LaTeX logo.

`\today` Generates the current date, in the following format: July 29, 1985.

`\em` A declaration that emphasizes text, usually by printing it in italic type.

`\mbox{text}` Typesets *text* in LR mode inside a box, which prevents it from being broken across lines. (See Section 5.4.3.)

C.2.2   Making Paragraphs

A paragraph is ended by one or more completely blank lines—lines not containing even a `%`. A blank line should not appear where a new paragraph cannot be started, such as in math mode or in the argument of a sectioning command.

\noindent When used at the beginning of the paragraph it suppresses the paragraph indentation. It has no effect when used in the middle of a paragraph. Robust.

\indent Produces a horizontal space whose width equals the width of the paragraph indentation. It is used to add a paragraph indentation where it would otherwise be suppressed. Robust.

\par Equivalent to a blank line; often used to make command and environment definitions easier to read. Robust.

Style Parameters

\textwidth Normal width of text on the page. Should be changed only in the preamble.

\linewidth Width of lines in the current environment; equals \textwidth except when inside a displayed-paragraph environment such as quote or itemize. Its value should not be changed with the length-setting commands.

\parindent Width of the indentation at the beginning of a paragraph. Its value is set to zero in a parbox. Its value may be changed anywhere.

\baselineskip The minimum space from the bottom of one line to the bottom of the next line in a paragraph. (The space between individual lines may be greater if they contain tall objects.) Its value is set by a type-size-changing command (Section 5.8.1). The value used for the entire paragraph unit (Section 5.2.1) is the one in effect at the blank line or command that ends the paragraph unit. Its value may be changed anywhere.

\baselinestretch A decimal number (such as 2 or 1.5). Its default value is 1 and is changed with \renewcommand. The value of \baselineskip is set by \begin{document} and by each type-size-changing command[2] to its default value times \baselinestretch. You can produce a "double-spaced" version of the document for copy editing by setting \baselinestretch to 2, but it will be ugly and hard to read. Any other changes to the interline spacing should be part of a complete document-style design, best done by a competent typographic designer.

\parskip The extra vertical space inserted before a paragraph. It is a rubber length that usually has a natural length of zero. Its value may be changed anywhere, but should be a stretchable length when a \flushbottom declaration (Section 5.1.2) is in effect.

---

[2]However, a \normalsize command does not change \baselineskip when a \normalsize declaration is in effect.

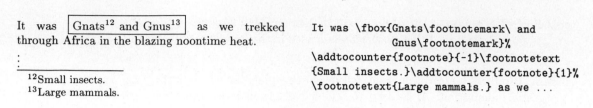

Figure C.1: Making footnotes without the \footnote command.

C.2.3   Footnotes

\footnote[*num*]{*text*}

Produces a footnote with *text* as its text and *num* as its number. The *num* argument is a positive integer, even when footnotes are "numbered" with letters or other symbols; if it is missing, then the footnote counter is stepped and its value used as the footnote number. This command may be used only in paragraph mode to produce ordinary footnotes. It should not be used inside a box except within a minipage environment, in which case it may be used in LR or math mode as well as paragraph mode and the footnote appears at the bottom of the box ended by the next \end{minipage}, which may be the wrong place for it if there are nested minipage environments. Fragile.

\footnotemark[*num*]

Used in conjunction with \footnotetext to footnote text where a \footnote command cannot be used. It produces a footnote mark (the footnote number that appears in the running text) just like \footnote, but it does not produce a footnote. See Figure C.1 for an example of its use. It steps the footnote counter if the optional argument is missing. It may be used in any mode. Fragile.

\footnotetext[*num*]{*text*}

Used in conjunction with \footnotemark to footnote text where the \footnote command cannot be used. See Figure C.1 for an example. It produces a footnote, just like the corresponding \footnote command, except that no footnote mark is generated and the footnote counter is not stepped. Fragile.

Style Parameters

\footnotesep The height of a strut placed at the beginning of every footnote to produce the vertical space between footnotes. It may be changed anywhere; the value used is the one in effect when the \footnote or \footnotetext command is processed.

\footnoterule A command that draws the line separating the footnotes from the main text. It is used by LaTeX in paragraph mode, between paragraphs (in TEX's inner vertical mode). The output it generates must take zero vertical space, so negative space should be used to compensate for the space occupied by the rule. It can be redefined anywhere with \renewcommand; the definition used is the one in effect when TEX produces the page of output.

C.2.4   Accents and Special Symbols

Commands for making accents in normal text are listed in Table 3.1 on page 40; commands for making accents in math formulas are listed in Table 3.11 on page 51. See Section C.9.1 for commands used in a tabbing environment to produce the accents normally made with \=, \', and \`.

Foreign-language symbols are made with commands listed in Table 3.2 on page 40. The following commands for making additional special symbols can also be used in any mode:

†	\dag	§	\S	©	\copyright
‡	\ddag	¶	\P	£	\pounds

Section 3.3.2 gives many commands for generating symbols in mathematical formulas.

C.3   Sectioning and Table of Contents

The use of the following commands for producing section headings and table of contents entries is illustrated in Figure C.2.

C.3.1   Sectioning Commands

sec_cmd [*toc_entry*] {*heading*}
sec_cmd *{*heading*}

Commands to begin a sectional unit. The *-form suppresses the section number, does not increment the counter, does not affect the running head, and produces no table of contents entry. The secnumdepth counter, described below, determines which sectional units are numbered.

sec_cmd One of the following:

\part	\section	\subsubsection	\subparagraph
\chapter	\subsection	\paragraph	

Each sectional unit should be contained in the next higher-level unit, except that \part is optional. The article document style does not have a \chapter command.

Gnats and Gnus Forever

From insects embedded in amber and fossils found in Africa, we find that ...

In table of contents:

In the text (on page 37):

2.3 Insects and Ungulates on Metamorphic Rock

```
\subsection*{Gnats and Gnus Forever}
From insects embedded in amber and ...


\addcontentsline{toc}{subsection}{Gnats}
\addtocontents{toc}{\protect\vspace
    {2ex}}
\addcontentsline{toc}{subsection}{\protect
    \numberline{2.2x}{Gnus}}
\subsection[Gnats and Gnus on
    Gneiss]{Insects and Ungulates on
    Metamorphic Rock}
```

Figure C.2: Sectioning and table of contents commands.

toc_entry Produces the table of contents entry and may be used for the running head (Section 5.1.2). It is a moving argument. If it is missing, the *heading* argument is used for these purposes.

heading Produces the section heading. If the *toc_entry* argument is missing, then it is a moving argument that provides the table of contents entry and may be used for the running head (Section 5.1.2).

C.3.2   The Appendix

`\appendix`

A declaration that changes the way sectional units are numbered. In the `article` document style, appendix sections are numbered "A", "B", etc. In the `report` and `book` styles, appendix chapters are numbered "A", "B", etc., and the chapter number is printed in the heading as "Appendix A", "Appendix B", etc. The `\appendix` command generates no text and does not affect the numbering of parts.

C.3.3   Table of Contents

```
\tableofcontents
\listoffigures
\listoftables
```

Generate a table of contents, list of figures, and list of tables, respectively. These commands cause LaTeX to write the necessary information on a file having the same first name as the root file and the following extension:

command:	`\tableofcontents`	`\listoffigures`	`\listoftables`
extension:	toc	lof	lot

A table of contents or a list of figures or tables compiled from the information on the current version of this file is printed at the point where the command appears.

Table of contents entries are produced by the sectioning commands, and list of figures or tables entries are produced by a \caption command in a figure or table environment (Section 3.5.1). The two commands described below also produce entries.

\addcontentsline{*file*}{*sec_unit*}{*entry*}

Adds an entry to the specified list or table.

file The extension of the file on which information is to be written: toc (table of contents), lof (list of figures), or lot (list of tables).

sec_unit Controls the formatting of the entry. It should be one of the following, depending upon the value of the *file* argument:

   toc: the name of the sectional unit, such as part or subsection.

   lof: figure

   lot: table

   There is no \ in the argument.

entry The text of the entry. It is a moving argument. To produce a line with a sectional unit or figure or table number, *entry* should be of the form

$$\protect\numberline{sec\_num}{heading}$$

where *sec_num* is the number and *heading* is the heading.

\addtocontents{*file*}{*text*}

Adds text (or formatting commands) directly to the file that generates the table of contents or list of figures or tables.

file The extension of the file on which information is to be written: toc (table of contents), lof (list of figures), or lot (list of tables).

text The information to be written. It is a moving argument.

C.3.4   Style Parameters

Document-style parameters control which sectional units are numbered and which are listed in the table of contents. Each sectional unit has a *level number*. In all document styles, sections have level number 1, subsections have level number 2, etc. In the article document style, parts have level number 0; in the report and book styles, chapters have level number 0 and parts have level number −1.

The following two counters (Section 5.3) are provided; they can be set in the preamble.

secnumdepth The level number of the least significant sectional unit with numbered headings. A value of 2 means that subsections are numbered but subsubsections are not.

tocdepth The level number of the least significant sectional unit listed in the table of contents.

C.4   Document and Page Styles

C.4.1   Document Styles

\documentstyle[*options*]{*style*}

Specifies the document style and options. It is usually the first command in the input file.

style The main document style; the standard ones are: article, report, book, and letter (for letters only). There is also a slides style for use only with SLITEX. The \documentstyle command reads the file *style*.sty.

options A list of one or more style options, separated by commas—with no spaces. The standard LATEX options are:

11pt Makes eleven-point type the normal (default) type size instead of ten-point type.

12pt Makes twelve-point type the normal (default) type size instead of ten-point type.

twoside Formats the output for printing on both sides of a page. (This is the default in the book style.)

twocolumn Produces two-column pages.

titlepage For article style only; causes the \maketitle command and the abstract environment each to make a separate page.

openbib Causes the bibliography (Section 4.3) to be formatted in open style. (See van Leunen [7].)

leqno Puts formula numbers on left side in equations and eqnarray environments.

fleqn Left-aligns displayed formulas.

Only leqno and fleqn can be used in SLITEX. LATEX implements style options by doing the following for each specified option *op*: if the command \ds@*op* is defined (usually by the main style), then it is executed, otherwise the file *op*.sty is read.

Style Parameters

\bibindent Width of the extra indentation of succeeding lines in a bibliography
  block with the openbib style option.

\columnsep The width of the space between columns of text in twocolumn style.

\columnseprule The width of a vertical line placed between columns of text in
  twocolumn style. Its default value is zero, producing an invisible line.

\mathindent The amount that formulas are indented from the left margin in
  the fleqn document-style option.

C.4.2 Page Styles

An output page consists of a *head*, a *body*, and a *foot*. Document-style parameters
determine their dimensions; the page style specifies the contents of the head and
foot. Left-hand and right-hand pages have different parameters. In two-sided
style, even-numbered pages are left-hand and odd-numbered pages are right-
hand; in one-sided style, all pages are right-hand. All commands described in
this section are fragile.

\pagestyle{*style*}

A declaration, with normal scoping rules, that specifies the current page style.
The style used for a page is the one in effect when TeX "cuts the scroll"
(page 119). Standard *style* options are:

plain The head is empty, the foot has only a page number. It is the default
  page style.

empty The head and foot are both empty.

headings The head contains information determined by the document style
  (usually a sectional-unit heading) and the page number; the foot is empty.

myheadings Same as headings, except head information specified by \markboth
  and \markright commands, described below.

\thispagestyle

Same as \pagestyle except it applies only to the current page (the next one to
be "cut from the scroll"). This is a global declaration (Section C.1.4).

\markright{*right_head*}
\markboth{*left_head*}{*right_head*}

These commands specify the following heading information for the headings
and myheadings page styles:

left-hand page Specified by *left_head* argument of the last \markboth before the end of the page.

right-hand page Specified by *right_head* argument of the first \markright or \markboth on the page, or if there is none, by the last one before the beginning of the page.

Both *right_head* and *left_head* are moving arguments. In the heading page style, sectioning commands set page headings with the \markboth and \markright commands as follows:

Printing Style	Command	Document Style	
		book, report	article
two-sided	\markboth[a]	\chapter	\section
	\markright	\section	\subsection
one-sided	\markright	\chapter	\section

[a]Specifies an empty right head.

These commands are overridden as follows:

\markboth Put a \markboth command right after the sectioning command.

\markright Put a \markright command immediately before and after the sectioning command, but omit the first one if the sectional unit starts a new page.

The right head information is always null for the first page of a document. If this is a problem, generate a blank first page with the titlepage environment.

\pagenumbering{*num_style*}

Specifies the style of page numbers. It is a global declaration (Section C.1.4). Possible values of *num_style* are:

arabic Arabic numerals.

roman Lowercase Roman numerals.

Roman Uppercase Roman numerals.

alph Lowercase letters.

Alph Uppercase letters.

The \pagenumbering command redefines \thepage to be *num_style*{page}.

\twocolumn[*text*]

Starts a new page by executing \clearpage (Section 5.2.2) and begins typesetting in two-column format. If the *text* argument is present, it is typeset in a double-column-wide parbox at the top of the new page. Fragile.

C.5 Displayed Paragraphs

The output produced by a displayed-paragraph environment starts on a new line, as does the output produced by the text following it. In addition to the environments described in this section, the `tabbing`, `center`, `flushleft`, and `flushright` environments and the environments defined by `\newtheorem` (Section 3.4.3) are also displayed-paragraph environments.

The text following a displayed-paragraph environment begins a new paragraph if there is a blank line after the `\end` command. However, even with no blank line, the following text may have a paragraph indentation if a right brace or `\end` command comes between it and the environment's `\end` command. This anomalous indentation is eliminated with a `\noindent` command (Section C.2.2).

Anomalous extra vertical space may be added after a displayed-paragraph environment that ends with a displayed equation (one made with the `displaymath`, `equation`, or `eqnarray` environment). This space can be removed by adding a negative vertical space with a `\vspace` command (Section 5.4.2).

All displayed-paragraph environments are implemented with the `list` or `trivlist` environment. These environments and the relevant formatting parameters are described in Section C.5.3 below.

C.5.1 Quotations and Verse

`\begin{quote}`   *text*   `\end{quote}`

Left and right margins are indented equally, there is no paragraph indentation, and extra vertical space is added between paragraphs.

`\begin{quotation}`   *text*   `\end{quotation}`

Left and right margins are indented equally; normal paragraph indentation and interparagraph vertical space is used.

`\begin{verse}`   *text*   `\end{verse}`

Left and right margins are indented equally. Lines within a stanza are separated by \\ commands and stanzas are separated by one or more blank lines.

C.5.2 List-Making Environments

`\begin{itemize}`   *item_list*   `\end{itemize}`
`\begin{enumerate}`   *item_list*   `\end{enumerate}`
`\begin{description}` *item_list*   `\end{description}`

The *item_list* consists of a sequence of items, each one begun with an `\item` command (see below). Numbering in an `enumerate` environment is controlled by the counter `enumi`, `enumii`, `enumiii`, or `enumiv`, depending upon its nesting level within other `enumerate` environments. The printed value of this counter is declared to be the current `\ref` value (Section C.10.2).

The default labels of an `itemize` environment are produced by the command `\labelitemi`, `\labelitemii`, `\labelitemiii`, or `\labelitemiv`, depending upon its nesting level within other `itemize` environments. The "tick marks" produced by the `itemize` environment may be changed by redefining these commands with `\renewcommand`.

If an item of a `description` environment begins with a displayed-paragraph environment, the item label may overprint the first line of that environment. If this happens, the item should begin with an `\mbox{}` command to cause the environment to start on a new line.

`\item[`*label*`]`

Starts a new item and produces its label. The item label is generated by the *label* argument if present, otherwise the default label is used. In `itemize` and `enumerate`, the label is typeset flush right a fixed distance from the item's left margin. In `enumerate`, the optional argument suppresses the incrementing of the enumeration counter. The default label is null in the `description` environment. The `\item` command is fragile.

C.5.3   The `list` and `trivlist` Environments   *p112*

`\begin{list}{`*default_label*`}{`*decls*`}`   *item_list*   `\end{list}`

Produces a list of labeled items.

item_list The text of the items. Each item is begun with an `\item` command (Section C.5.2).

default_label The label generated by an `\item` command with no optional argument.

decls A sequence of declarations for changing the default formatting parameters. Before executing the commands in *decls*, one of the commands `\@listi`, `\@listii` ... , `\@listvi` is executed, depending upon how many `list` environments the current one is nested within—the `\@listi` command being executed for the outermost `list` environment. These commands set the default values of some parameters.

The following are the parameters that control the formatting in a `list` environment.

`\topsep` The amount of extra vertical space (in addition to `\parskip`) inserted between the preceding text and the first list item, and between the last item and the following text. Its default value is set by `\@list...` . It is a rubber length.

\partopsep The extra vertical space (in addition to \topsep + \parskip)
inserted, if the environment is preceded by a blank line, between the
preceding text and the first list item and between the last item and
the following text. Its default value is set by \@list... . It is a
rubber length.

\itemsep The amount of extra vertical space (in addition to \parsep)
inserted between successive list items. Its default value is set by
\@list... . It is a rubber length.

\parsep The amount of vertical space between paragraphs within an item.
It is the value to which \parskip is set within the list. Its default is
set by \@list... . It is a rubber length.

\leftmargin The horizontal distance between the left margin of the enclosing environment and the left margin of the list. It must be nonnegative. In the standard document styles, it is set to \leftmargini
by \@listi, to \leftmarginii by \@listii, etc.

\rightmargin The horizontal distance between the right margin of the
enclosing environment and the right margin of the list. It must be
nonnegative. Its default value is zero unless set by \@list... .

\listparindent The amount of extra indentation added to the first line
of every paragraph except the first one of an item. Its default value
is zero unless set by \@list... . It may have a negative value.

\itemindent The amount of extra indentation added to each item before
the label. Its default value is zero unless set by \@list... . It may
have a negative value.

\labelsep The space between the end of the box containing the label and
the text of the item. In the standard document styles, it is not set
by \@list... , maintaining the same value for all nesting levels. It
may be set to a negative length.

\labelwidth The normal width of the box that contains the label. It
must be nonnegative. In the standard document styles, \@list...
sets it to \leftmargin... − \labelsep, so the left edge of the label
box is flush with the left margin of the enclosing environment. If
the natural width of the label is greater than \labelwidth, then the
label is typeset in a box with its natural width, so the label extends
further to the right than "normal".

\makelabel{*label*} A command that generates the label printed by the
\item command from the *label* argument. Unless it is redefined by
\@list... , its default definition positions the label flush right against
the right edge of its box. It may be redefined with \renewcommand.

In addition to declarations that set the above parameters, the following declaration may appear in *decls*:

\usecounter{*ctr*} Enables the counter *ctr* (Section 5.3) to be used for numbering list items. It causes *ctr* to be initialized to zero and incremented by \refstepcounter when executing an \item command that has no optional argument, causing its value to become the current \ref value (Section C.10.2). It is a fragile command.

\begin{trivlist}   *item_list*   \end{trivlist}

Acts like a list environment using the current values of the list-making parameters, except with \parsep set to the current value of \parskip and the following set to zero: \leftmargin, \labelwidth, \itemindent. It does not execute \@list..., so the values of the list-formatting parameters outside any list should be made the same as the ones set by \@listi.

Every \item command in *item_list* must have an optional argument. The trivlist environment is normally used to define an environment consisting of a single list item, with an \item[] command appearing as part of the environment's definition.

C.5.4   Verbatim

\begin{verbatim}   *literal_text*   \end{verbatim}
\begin{verbatim*}   *literal_text*   \end{verbatim*}

Typesets *literal_text* exactly as typed, including special characters, spaces and line breaks, using a typewriter (\tt) type style. The only text following the \begin command that is not treated literally is the \end command. The *-form differs only in that spaces are printed as ␣ symbols.

If there is no nonspace character on the line following the \begin command, then *literal_text* effectively begins on the next line. There can be no space between the \end and the {verbatim} or {verbatim*}.

A verbatim or verbatim* environment may not appear in the argument of any command.

\verb*char*   *literal_text*   *char*
\verb**char*   *literal_text*   *char*

Typesets *literal_text* exactly as typed, including special characters and spaces, using a typewriter (\tt) type style. There may be no space between \verb or \verb* and *char*. The *-form differs only in that spaces are printed as ␣ symbols.

char Any nonspace character, except it may not be a * for \verb.

literal_text Any sequence of characters not containing an end-of-line character or *char*.

A \verb or \verb* command may not appear in the argument of any other command.

C.6   Mathematical Formulas

Unless otherwise noted, all commands described in this section can be used only in math mode. See Section 3.3.8 for an explanation of the display and text math styles.

C.6.1   Math Mode Environments

```
$               formula   $
\(              formula   \)
\begin{math}    formula   \end{math}
```

These equivalent forms produce an in-text formula by typesetting *formula* in math mode using text style. They may be used in paragraph of LR mode. The \(and \) commands are fragile; $ is robust.

```
\[                    formula   \]
\begin{displaymath}   formula   \end{displaymath}
```

These equivalent forms produce a displayed formula by typesetting *formula* in math mode using display style. They may be used only in paragraph mode. The displayed formula is centered unless the fleqn document-style option is used (Section 5.1.1). The commands \[and \] are fragile.

```
\begin{equation}   formula   \end{equation}
```

The same as displaymath except that an equation number is generated using the equation counter. The equation number is positioned flush with the right margin, unless the leqno document-style option is used (Section 5.1.1).

```
\begin{eqnarray}    eqns   \end{eqnarray}
\begin{eqnarray*}   eqns   \end{eqnarray*}
```

Produces a sequence of displayed formulas aligned in three columns. The *eqns* text is like the body of an array environment (Section 3.3.3) with argument rcl; it consists of a sequence of rows separated by \\ commands, each row consisting of three columns separated by & characters. (However, a \multicolumn command may not be used.) The first and third columns are typeset in display style, the second in text style. These environments may be used only in paragraph mode.

The eqnarray environment produces an equation number for each row, generated from the equation counter and positioned as in the equation environment. A `\nonumber` command suppresses the equation number for the row in which it appears. The `eqnarray*` environment produces no equation numbers.

The command `\lefteqn{`*formula*`}` prints *formula* in display math style (Section 3.3.8), but pretends that it has zero width. It is used within an `eqnarray` or `eqnarray*` environment for splitting long formulas across lines.

An overfull `\hbox` warning occurs if a formula extends beyond the prevailing margins, but not if it only overprints the equation number.

Style Parameters

`\jot` The amount of extra vertical space added between rows in an `eqnarray` or `eqnarray*` environment.

`\mathindent` The indentation from the left margin of displayed formulas in the `fleqn` document-style option.

`\abovedisplayskip` The amount of extra space left above a long displayed formula—except in the `fleqn` document-style option, where `\topsep` is used. A long formula is one that lies closer to the left margin than does the end of the preceding line. It is a rubber length.

`\belowdisplayskip` The amount of extra space left below a long displayed formula—except in the `fleqn` document-style option, where `\topsep` is used. It is a rubber length.

`\abovedisplayshortskip` The amount of extra space left above a short displayed formula—except in the `fleqn` document-style option, which uses `\topsep`. A short formula is one that starts to the right of where the preceding line ends. It is a rubber length.

`\belowdisplayshortskip` The amount of extra space left below a short displayed formula—except in the `fleqn` document-style option, which uses `\topsep`. It is a rubber length.

C.6.2   Common Structures

`_{`*sub*`}` Typesets *sub* as a subscript. Robust.

`^{`*sup*`}` Typesets *sup* as a superscript. Robust.

`'` Produces a prime symbol ($'$). Robust.

`\frac{`*numer*`}{`*denom*`}` Generates a fraction with numerator *numer* and denominator *denom*. Robust.

`\sqrt[`*n*`]{`*arg*`}` Generates the notation for the nth root of *arg*. With no argument, it produces the square root (no indicated root). Fragile.

ellipsis The following commands produce an ellipsis (three dots) arranged as indicated. They are all robust.

\ldots Horizontally at the bottom of the line $(\ldots)$. It may be used in paragraph and LR mode as well as math mode.

\cdots Horizontally at the center of the line $(\cdots)$.

\vdots Vertically $(\vdots)$.

\ddots Diagonally $(\ddots)$.

C.6.3   Mathematical Symbols

See Tables 3.3 through 3.8 on pages 43–45. The ones in Table 3.8 are printed differently in display and text styles; in display style, subscripts and superscripts may be positioned directly above and below the symbol. All the commands listed in those tables are robust.

Log-like functions, which are set in roman type, are listed in Table 3.9 on page 46. Subscripts appear directly below the symbol in display style for \det, \gcd, \inf, \lim, \liminf, \limsup, \max, \min, \Pr, and \sup. All log-like commands are robust. The following commands also create symbols.

\bmod Produces a binary *mod* symbol. Robust.

\pmod{*arg*} Produces "(mod *arg*)". Robust.

\cal A type-style declaration to produce calligraphic letters. Only uppercase letters should appear in its scope. Robust.

C.6.4   Arrays

See Section C.9.2.

C.6.5   Delimiters

\left*delim*   *formula*   \right*delim*

Typesets *formula* and puts large delimiters around it, where *delim* is one of the delimiters in Table 3.10 on page 48 or a '.' character to signify an invisible delimiter. The \left and \right commands are robust.

C.6.6   Putting One Thing Above Another

\overline{*formula*}

Typesets *formula* with a horizontal line above it. Robust.

\underline{*formula*}

Typesets *formula* with a horizontal line below it. May be used in paragraph or LR mode as well as math mode. Fragile.

accents

Table 3.11 on page 51 lists math-mode accent-making commands. They are robust, as are the following additional accenting commands:

\widehat Wide version of \hat.

\widetilde Wide version of \tilde.

\imath Dotless i for use with accents.

\jmath Dotless j for use with accents.

\stackrel{*top*}{*bot*}

Typesets *top* immediately above *bot*, using the same math style for *top* as if it were a superscript.

C.6.7   Spacing

The following commands produce horizontal space in math mode. They are all robust. The \, command may also be used in paragraph and LR mode.

\,	thin space	\:	medium space
\!	negative thin space	\;	thick space

C.6.8   Changing Style

Type Style

The type-style declarations of Section 3.1 may be used in math mode. They affect only letters, not symbols, where uppercase Greek letters are treated as letters and lowercase ones as symbols. There are two additional type-style declarations that can be used only in math mode: \mit for math italic style and \cal for calligraphic style (uppercase letters only). Like all type-style declarations, they are robust.

See Section C.14 for an explanation of anomalous behavior by type-style-changing commands when used in math mode, and for a description of the \boldmath declaration that produces bold symbols.

Math Style

The following declarations can appear only in math mode. They choose the type size and certain formatting parameters, including ones that control the placement of subscripts and superscripts. All are robust commands.

\displaystyle Default style for displayed formulas.

\textstyle Default style for in-text formulas and for the items in an **array** environment.

`\scriptstyle` Default style for first-level subscripts and superscripts.

`\scriptscriptstyle` Default style for higher-level subscripts and superscripts.

C.7   Definitions

C.7.1   Defining Commands

`\newcommand   {`*cmd*`}[`*args*`]{`*def*`}`
`\renewcommand{`*cmd*`}[`*args*`]{`*def*`}`

These commands define (or redefine) a command. They are both fragile.

cmd A command name beginning with `\`. For `\newcommand` it must not be already defined and must not begin with "`\end`"; for `\renewcommand` it must already be defined.

args An integer from 1 to 9 denoting the number of arguments of the command being defined. The default is for the command to have no arguments.

def The text to be substituted for every occurrence of *cmd*; a parameter of the form `#n` in *cmd* is replaced by the text of the nth argument when this substitution takes place. It should contain no command- or environment-defining command.

The argument-enclosing braces of a command defined with `\newcommand` or redefined with `\renewcommand` do not delimit the scope of a declaration in that argument. (However, the scope may be delimited by braces that appear within *def*.) The defined command is fragile if *def* includes a fragile command, otherwise it is robust.

C.7.2   Defining Environments

`\newenvironment   {`*nam*`}[`*args*`]{`*begdef*`}{`*enddef*`}`
`\renewenvironment{`*nam*`}[`*args*`]{`*begdef*`}{`*enddef*`}`

These commands define or redefine an environment. They are both fragile.

nam The name of the environment. For `\newenvironment` there must be no currently defined environment by that name, and the command `\`*nam* must be undefined; for `\renewenvironment` the environment must already be defined.

args An integer from 1 to 9 denoting the number of arguments of the newly-defined environment. The default is no arguments.

begdef The text substituted for every occurrence of `\begin{`*nam*`}`; a parameter of the form `#n` in *cmd* is replaced by the text of the nth argument when this substitution takes place.

enddef The text substituted for every occurrence of \end{*nam*}. It may not
contain any argument parameters.

The *begdef* and *enddef* arguments should contain no command- or environment-
defining command. The argument-enclosing braces of an environment defined
with \newenvironment or \renewenvironment do not delimit the scope of a
declaration contained in the argument.

C.7.3   Theorem-like Environments

\newtheorem {*env_name*}{*caption*}[*within*]
\newtheorem {*env_name*}[*numbered_like*]{*caption*}

This command defines a theorem-like environment. It is a global declaration
(Section C.1.4) and is fragile.

env_name The name of the environment—a string of letters. Must not be the
name of an existing environment or counter.

caption The text printed at the beginning of the environment, right before the
number.

within The name of an already-defined counter, usually of a sectional unit. If
this argument is present, the command \the*env_name* is defined to be

$$\text{\the}\textit{within}.\text{\arabic\{}\textit{env\_name}\text{\}}$$

and the *env_name* counter will be reset by a \stepcounter{*within*} or
\refstepcounter{*within*} command (Section C.7.4). If the *within* argument is missing, \the*env_name* is defined to be \arabic{*env_name*}.

numbered_like The name of an already defined theorem-like environment. If this
argument is present, the *env_name* environment will be numbered in the
same sequence (using the same counter) as the *numbered_like* environment
and will declare the current \ref value (Section C.10.2) to be the text
generated by \the*numbered_like*.

Unless the *numbered_like* argument is present, this command creates a counter
named *env_name*, and the environment declares the current \ref value (Section C.10.2) to be the text generated by \the*env_name*.

The \newtheorem command may have at most one optional argument. See
Section C.1.1 if a \newcommand without a final optional argument is followed by
a [character.

C.7.4   Numbering   ♭ 91

\newcounter{*newctr*}[*within*]

Defines a new counter named *newctr* that is initialized to zero, with \the*newctr*
defined to be \arabic{*newctr*}. It is a global declaration. The \newcounter

command may not be used in an \include'd file (Section 4.4). Fragile.

newctr A string of letters that is not the name of an existing counter.

within The name of an already-defined counter. If this argument is present, the *newctr* counter is reset to zero whenever the *within* counter is stepped by \stepcounter or \refstepcounter (see below).

\setcounter{*ctr*}{*num*}

Sets the value of counter *ctr* to *num*. It is a global declaration (Section C.1.4). Fragile.

\addtocounter{*ctr*}{*num*}

Increments the value of counter *ctr* by *num*. It is a global declaration (Section C.1.4). Fragile.

\value{*ctr*}

Produces the value of counter *ctr*. It is used mainly in the *num* argument of a \setcounter or \addtocounter command—for example, the command \setcounter{bean}{\value{page}} sets counter bean equal to the current value of the page counter. However, it can be used anywhere that LaTeX expects a number. The \value command is robust, and must never be preceded by a \protect command.

numbering commands

The following commands print the value of counter *ctr* in the indicated format. They are all robust.

\arabic{*ctr*} Arabic numerals.

\roman{*ctr*} Lowercase Roman numerals.

\Roman{*ctr*} Uppercase Roman numerals.

\alph{*ctr*} Lowercase letters. Value of *ctr* must be less than 27.

\Alph{*ctr*} Uppercase letters. Value of *ctr* must be less than 27.

\fnsymbol{*ctr*} Produces one of the nine "footnote symbols" from the following sequence: $*$ † ‡ § ¶ ‖ $**$ †† ‡‡. It may be used only in math mode. The value of *ctr* must be less than 10.

\the*ctr*

A command used to print the value associated with counter *ctr*. Robust.

```
\stepcounter    {ctr}
\refstepcounter{ctr}
```

Increment the value of counter *ctr* by one and reset the value of any counter numbered "within" it. For example, the `subsection` counter is numbered within the `section` counter, which, in the `report` or `book` document style, is numbered within the `chapter` counter. The `\refstepcounter` command also declares the current `\ref` value (Section C.10.2) to be the text generated by `\the`*ctr*.

C.8 Figures and Other Floating Bodies

C.8.1 Figures and Tables

```
\begin{figure}[loc]     body    \end{figure}
\begin{figure*}[loc]    body    \end{figure*}
\begin{table}[loc]      body    \end{table}
\begin{table*}[loc]     body    \end{table*}
```

These environments produce floating figures and tables. In two-column format, the ordinary forms produce single-column figures and tables and the *-forms produce double-column ones. The two forms are equivalent in single-column format.

The *body* is typeset in a parbox of width `\textwidth`. It may contain one or more `\caption` commands (see below). The *loc* argument is a sequence of zero to four letters, each one specifying a location where the figure or table may be placed, as follows:

h *Here*: at the position in the text where the environment appears. (Not possible for double-column figures and tables in two-column format.)

t *Top*: at the top of a text page.

b *Bottom*: at the bottom of a text page. (Not possible for double-column figures or tables in two-column format.)

p *Page of floats*: on a separate page containing no text, only figures and tables.

If the *loc* argument is missing, the default specifier is `tbp`, so the figure or table may be placed at the top or bottom of a text page or on a separate page consisting only of figures and/or tables. The placement of the figure or table is determined by the following rules.

- It is printed at the earliest place that does not violate subsequent rules, except that an h (here) position takes precedence over a t (top) position.

- It will not be printed on an earlier page than the place in the text where the `figure` or `table` environment appears.

- A figure will not be printed before an earlier figure, and a table will not be printed before an earlier table.

- It may appear only at a position allowed by the *pos* argument, or, if that argument is missing, by the default `tbp` specifier.

- Placement of the figure cannot produce an overfull page.

- The page constraints determined by the formatting parameters described below are not violated.

The last three rules are suspended when a `\clearpage`, `\cleardoublepage`, or `\end{document}` command occurs, all unprocessed figures and tables being allowed a `p` option and printed at that point.

When giving an optional *loc* argument, include enough options so the above rules allow the figure or table to go somewhere, otherwise it and all subsequent figures or tables will be saved until the end of the chapter or document, probably causing TeX to run out of space.

`\caption[`*lst_entry*`]{`*heading*`}`

Produces a numbered caption.

lst_entry Generates the entry in the list of figures or tables. Such an entry should not contain more than about three hundred characters. If this argument is missing, the *heading* argument is used. It is a moving argument.

heading The text of the caption. It produces the list of figures or tables entry if the *lst_entry* argument is missing, in which case it is a moving argument. If this argument contains more than about three hundred characters, a shorter *lst_entry* argument should be used—even if no list of figures or tables is being produced.

A `\label` command that refers to the caption's number must go in *heading* or after the `\caption` command in the *body* of the `figure` or `table` environment. The `\caption` command can be used only in paragraph mode, but can be placed in a parbox made with a `\parbox` command or `minipage` environment (Section 5.4.3). It is fragile.

Style Parameters

Changes made to the following parameters in the preamble apply from the first page on. Changes made afterwards take effect on the next page, not the current one. A *float* denotes either a figure or a table, and a *float page* is a page containing only floats and no text. Parameters that apply to all floats in a one-column page style apply to single-column floats in a two-column style.

`topnumber` A counter whose value is the maximum number of floats allowed at the top of a page.

\topfraction The maximum fraction of the page that can be occupied by floats at the top of the page. Thus, the value .25 specifies that as much as the top quarter of the page may be devoted to floats. It is changed with \renewcommand.

bottomnumber Same as topnumber except for the bottom of the page.

\bottomfraction Same as \topfraction except for the bottom of the page.

totalnumber A counter whose value is the maximum number of floats that can appear on a single page, irrespective of their positions.

\textfraction The minimum fraction of a text page that must be devoted to text. The other $1 - $ \textfraction fraction may be occupied by floats. It is changed with \renewcommand.

\floatpagefraction The minimum fraction of a float page that must be occupied by floats, limiting the amount of blank space allowed on a float page. It is changed with \renewcommand.

dbltopnumber The analog of topnumber for double-column floats in two-column style.

\dbltopfraction The analog of \topfraction for double-column floats on a two-column page.

\dblfloatpagefraction The analog of \floatpagefraction for a float page of double-column floats.

\floatsep The vertical space added between floats that appear at the top or bottom of a text page. It is a rubber length.

\textfloatsep The vertical space added between the floats appearing at the top or bottom of a page and the text on that page. It is a rubber length.

\intextsep The vertical space placed above and below a float that is put in the middle of the text with the h location option. It is a rubber length.

\dblfloatsep The analog of \floatsep for double-width floats on a two-column page. It is a rubber length.

\dbltextfloatsep The analog of \textfloatsep for double-width floats on a two-column page. It is a rubber length.

C.8.2   Marginal Notes

\marginpar [*left_text*] {*right_text*}

Produces a marginal note using *right_text* if it goes in the right margin or there is no optional argument, otherwise using *left_text*. The text is typeset in a parbox.

For two-sided, single-column printing, the default placement of marginal notes is on the outside margin—left for even-numbered pages, right for odd-numbered ones. For one-sided, single-column printing, the default placement is in the right margin. These defaults may be changed by the following declarations:

\reversemarginpar Causes marginal notes to be placed in the opposite margin from the default one.

\normalmarginpar Causes marginal notes to be placed in the default margin.

When a marginal note appears within a paragraph, its placement is determined by the declaration in effect at the blank line ending the paragraph. For two-column format, marginal notes always appear in the margin next to the column containing the note, irrespective of these declarations.

A marginal note is normally positioned so its top line is level with the line of text containing the \marginpar command; if the command comes between paragraphs, the note is usually level with the last line of the preceding paragraph. However, the note is moved down and a warning message printed on the terminal if this would make it overlap a previous note. Switching back and forth between reverse and normal positioning with \reversemarginpar and \normalmarginpar may inhibit this movement of marginal notes, resulting in one being overprinted on top of another.

Style Parameters

\marginparwidth The width of the parbox containing a marginal note.

\marginparsep The horizontal space between the outer margin and a marginal note.

\marginparpush The minimum vertical space allowed between two successive marginal notes.

C.9   Lining It Up in Columns

C.9.1   The tabbing Environment   p 62

\begin{tabbing}   *rows*   \end{tabbing}

This environment may be used only in paragraph mode. It produces a sequence of lines, each processed in LR mode, with alignment in columns based upon a sequence of tab stops. Tab stops are numbered 0, 1, 2, etc. Tab stop number i is said to be *set* if it is assigned a horizontal position on the page. Tab stop 0 is always set to the prevailing left margin (the left margin in effect at the beginning of the environment). If tab stop i is set, then all tab stops numbered 0 through

```
Gnat:     swatted by: men              \begin{tabbing}
                    cows              Armadillo: \=                        \kill
              and  gnus              Gnat:        \> swatted by: \= men \+\+  \\
         not very filling                                      cows           \\
Armadillo: not edible                                  and \' gnus  \-        \\
(note also the: aardvark                         not very filling   \-        \\
          albatross          eton)   Armadillo: \> not edible                 \\
Gnu:      eaten by    gnats           \pushtabs
                                      (note also the: \= aardvark              \\
                                               \> albatross  \' eton) \\
                                      \poptabs
                                      Gnu:        \> eaten by   \> gnats
                                      \end{tabbing}
```

Figure C.4: A `tabbing` environment example.

$i - 1$ are also set. Tab stop number $i - 1$ is normally positioned to the left of tab stop number i.

The behavior of the tabbing commands is described in terms of the values of two quantities called *next_tab_stop* and *left_margin_tab*. Initially, the value of *next_tab_stop* is 1, the value of *left_margin_tab* is 0, and only tab number 0 is set. The value of *next_tab_stop* is incremented by the \> and \= commands, and it is reset to the value of *left_margin_tab* by the \\ and \kill commands. The following commands, all of which are fragile, may appear in *rows*; their use is illustrated in Figure C.4.

\= If the value of *next_tab_stop* is i, then this command sets tab stop number i's position to be the current position on the line and changes the value of *next_tab_stop* to $i + 1$.

\> If the value of *next_tab_stop* is i, then this command starts the following text at tab stop i's position and changes the value of *next_tab_stop* to $i + 1$.

\\ Starts a new line and sets the value of *next_tab_stop* equal to the value of *left_margin_tab*. See Section C.1.6 for more details.

\kill Throws away the current line, keeping the effects of any tab-stop-setting commands, starts a new line, and sets the value of *next_tab_stop* to the value of *left_margin_tab*.

\+ Increases the value of *left_margin_tab* by one. This causes the left margin of subsequent lines to be indented one tab stop to the right, just as if a \> command were added to the beginning of subsequent lines. Multiple \+ commands have the expected cumulative effect.

\- Decreases the value of *left_margin_tab*, which must be positive, by one. This has the effect of canceling one preceding \+ command, starting with the following line.

\< Decreases the value of *next_tab_stop* by one. This command can be used only at the beginning of a line, where it acts to cancel the effect, on that line, of one previous \+ command.

\' Used to put text flush right against the right edge of a column or against the left margin. If the value of *next_tab_stop* is i, then it causes everything in the current column—all text from the most recent \>, \=, \', \\ or \kill command—to be positioned flush right a distance of \tabbingsep (a style parameter) from the position of tab stop number $i-1$. Text following the \' command is placed starting at the position of tab stop number $i-1$.

\` Moves all following text on the line flush against the prevailing right margin. There must be no \>, \=, or \ command after the \` and before the command that ends the output line.

\pushtabs Saves the current positions of all tab stops, to be restored by a subsequent \poptabs command. You can nest \pushtabs commands, but \pushtabs and \poptabs commands must come in matching pairs within a tabbing environment.

\poptabs See \pushtabs.

\a... The commands \=, \', and \` usually produce accents, but are redefined to tabbing commands inside the tabbing environment. The commands \a=, \a', and \a` produce those accents in a tabbing environment.

The tabbing environment exhibits the following anomalies:

- The scope of a declaration appearing in *rows* is ended by any of the following commands:

\=	\>	\+	\'	\pushtabs	\kill
\\	\<	\-	\`	\poptabs	\end{tabbing}

  No environment contained within the tabbing environment can contain any of these tabbing commands.

- The commands \=, \', \`, and \- are redefined to have special meanings inside a tabbing environment. The ordinary \- command would be useless in this environment; the effects of the other three are obtained with the \a... command described above. These commands revert to their ordinary meanings inside a parbox contained within the tabbing environment.

- One tabbing environment cannot be nested within another, even if the inner one is inside a parbox.

Style Parameters

\tabbingsep See the description of the \' command above.

GG&A Hoofed Stock		
	Price	
Year	low	high	Comments
1971	97–245		Bad year for farmers in the west.
72	245–245		Light trading due to a heavy winter.
73	245–2001		No gnus was very good gnus this year.

```
\begin{tabular}{|r||r@{--}l|p{1.25in}|}
\hline
\multicolumn{4}{|c|}{GG\&A Hoofed Stock}
   \\ \hline\hline
&\multicolumn{2}{c|}{Price}& \\ \cline{2-3}
\multicolumn{1}{|c||}{Year}
& \multicolumn{1}{r@{\,\vline\,}}{low}
& high & \multicolumn{1}{c|}{Comments}
   \\ \hline
1971 & 97 & 245 & Bad year for
            farmers in the west.   \\ \hline
  72 & 245 & 245  & Light trading due to a
                  heavy winter.   \\ \hline
  73 &    245 & 2001 & No gnus was very
                good gnus this year. \\ \hline
\end{tabular}
```

Figure C.5: An example of the `tabular` environment.

C.9.2   The array and tabular Environments

tabular p63

\begin{array}[*pos*]{*cols*}   *rows*   \end{array}
\begin{tabular}[*pos*]{*cols*}   *rows*   \end{tabular}
\begin{tabular*}{*wdth*}[*pos*]{*cols*}   *rows*   \end{tabular*}

These environments produce a box (Section 5.4.3) consisting of a sequence of rows of items, aligned vertically in columns. The `array` environment can be used only in math mode, while `tabular` and `tabular*` can be used in any mode. A large example, illustrating most of the features of these environments, appears in Figure C.5.

wdth Specifies the width of the `tabular*` environment. There must be rubber space between columns that can stretch to fill out the specified width; see the `\extracolsep` command below.

pos Specifies the vertical positioning; the default is alignment on the center of the environment.

    t align on top row.

    b align on bottom row.

cols Specifies the column formatting. It consists of a sequence of the following specifiers, corresponding to the sequence of columns and intercolumn material.

    l A column of left-aligned items.

    r A column of right-aligned items.

c A column of centered items.

| A vertical line the full height and depth of the environment.

@{*text*} This specifier is called an @-*expression*. It inserts *text* in every
row, where *text* is processed in math mode in the `array` environment
and in LR mode in the `tabular` and `tabular*` environments. The
text is considered a moving argument, so any fragile command within
it must be `\protect`'ed.

An @-expression suppresses the intercolumn space normally inserted
between columns; any desired space between the inserted text and the
adjacent items must be included in *text*. To change the space between
two columns from the default to *wd*, put an @{\hspace{*wd*}} command (Section 5.4.1) between the corresponding column specifiers.

An `\extracolsep{`*wd*`}` command in an @-expression causes an extra
space of width *wd* to appear to the left of all subsequent columns,
until countermanded by another `\extracolsep` command. Unlike
ordinary intercolumn space, this extra space is not suppressed by an
@-expression. An `\extracolsep` command can be used only in an @-
expression in the *cols* argument. It is most commonly used to insert
a `\fill` space (Section 5.4.1) in a `tabular*` environment.

p{*wd*} Produces a column with each item typeset in a parbox of width
wd, as if it were the argument of a `\parbox[t]{`*wd*`}` command (Section 5.4.3). However, a `\\` may not appear in the item, except in the
following situations: (i) inside an environment like `minipage`, `array`
or `tabular`, (ii) inside an explicit `\parbox`, or (iii) in the scope of a
`\centering`, `\raggedright`, or `\raggedleft` declaration. The latter
declarations must appear inside braces or an environment when used
in a p-column element.

*{*num*}{*cols*} Equivalent to *num* copies of *cols*, where *num* is any positive
integer and *cols* is any list of column-specifiers, which may contain
another *-expression.

An extra space, equal to half the default intercolumn space, is put before
the first column unless *cols* begins with a | or @-expression, and after
the last column unless *cols* ends with a | or @-expression. This space
usually causes no problem, but is easily eliminated by putting an @{} at
the beginning and end of *cols*.

rows A sequence of rows separated by `\\` commands (Section C.1.6). Each row
is a sequence of items separated by & characters; it should contain the same
number of items as specified by the *cols* argument. The text comprising
each item is processed as if it were enclosed in braces, so the scope of any
declaration in an item lies within that item. The following commands may
appear in an item:

\multicolumn{*num*}{*col*}{*item*} Makes *item* the text of a single item spanning *num* columns, positioned as specified by *col*. If *num* = 1, then the command serves simply to override the item positioning specified by the environment argument. The *col* argument must contain exactly one l, r, or c and may contain one or more @-expressions and | characters. It replaces that part of the environment's *cols* argument corresponding to the *num* spanned columns, where the part corresponding to any column except the first begins with l, r, c, or p, so the *cols* argument |c|l@{:}lr has the four parts |c|, l@{:}, l, and r. A \multicolumn command must either begin the row or else immediately follow an &. It is fragile.

\vline When used within an l, r, or c item, it produces a vertical line extending the full height and depth of its row. An \hfill command (Section 5.4.2) can be used to move the line to the edge of the column. A \vline command can also be used in an @-expression. It is robust.

The following commands can go between rows to produce horizontal lines. They must appear either before the first row or immediately after a \\ command. A horizontal line after the last row is produced by ending the row with a \\ followed by one of these commands. (This is the only case in which a \\ command appears after the last row of an environment.) These commands are fragile.

\hline Draws a horizontal line extending the full width of the environment. Two \hline commands in succession leave a space between the lines; vertical rules produced by | characters in the *cols* argument do not appear in this space.

\cline{*col*$_1$-*col*$_2$} Draws a horizontal line across columns *col*$_1$ through *col*$_2$. Two or more successive \cline commands draw their lines in the same vertical position. See the \multicolumn command above for how to determine what constitutes a column.

The following properties of these environments, although mentioned above, are often forgotten:

- These environments make a box; see Section 5.6 for environments and commands that can be used to position this box.

- The box made by these commands may have blank space before the first column and after the last column; this space can be removed with an @-expression.

- Any declaration in *rows* is within an item; its scope is contained within the item.

- An @-expression in *cols* suppresses the default intercolumn space.

Style Parameters

The following style parameters can be changed anywhere outside an `array` or `tabular` environment. They can also be changed locally within an item, but the scope of the change should be explicitly delimited by braces or an environment.

`\arraycolsep` Half the width of the default horizontal space between columns in an `array` environment.

`\tabcolsep` Half the width of the default horizontal space between columns in a `tabular` or `tabular*` environment.

`\arrayrulewidth` The width of the line created by a | in the *cols* argument or by an `\hline`, `\cline`, or `\vline` command.

`\doublerulesep` The width of the space between lines created by two successive | characters in the *cols* argument, or by two successive `\hline` commands.

`\arraystretch` Controls the spacing between rows. The normal interrow space is multiplied by `\arraystretch`, so changing it from its default value of 1 to 1.5 makes the rows 1.5 times farther apart. Its value is changed with `\renewcommand` (Section 3.4).

C.10   Moving Information Around

C.10.1   Files

A number of different files may be created when LaTeX is run. They all have the same first name as the root file (Section 4.4). These files are referred to, and listed below, by their extension. A `\nofiles` command in the preamble prevents LaTeX from writing some of them. Knowing when and under what circumstances they are read and written can help in locating and recovering from errors.

aux Used for cross-referencing and in compiling the table of contents, list of figures and list of tables. In addition to the main `aux` file, a separate `aux` file is also written for each `\include`'d file (Section 4.4), having the same first name as that file. All `aux` files are read by the `\begin{document}` command. The `\begin{document}` command also starts writing the main `aux` file; writing of an `\include`'d file's `aux` file is begun by the `\include` command and is ended when the `\include`'d file has been completely processed. A `\nofiles` command suppresses the writing of all `aux` files.

The table of contents and cross-reference information in the `aux` files can be printed by running LaTeX on the file `lablst.tex`.

bbl This file is written by BibTeX, not by LaTeX, using information on the `aux` file. It is read by the `\bibliography` command.

dvi This file contains LaTeX's output, in a form that is independent of any particular printer. Another program must be run to print the information on the `dvi` file. The file is always written unless LaTeX has generated no printed output.

glo Contains the `\glossaryentry` commands generated by `\glossary` commands. The file is written only if there is a `\makeglossary` command and no `\nofiles` command.

idx Contains the `\indexentry` commands generated by `\index` commands. The file is written only if there is a `\makeindex` command and no `\nofiles` command.

lof Read by the `\listoffigures` command to generate a list of figures; it contains the entries generated by all `\caption` commands in `figure` environments. The `lof` file is generated by the `\end{document}` command. It is written only if there is a `\listoffigures` command and no `\nofiles` command.

log Contains everything printed on the terminal when LaTeX is executed, plus additional information and some extra blank lines. It is always written. In some systems, this file has an extension other than `log`.

lot Read by the `\listoftables` command to generate a list of tables; it contains the entries generated by all `\caption` commands in `table` environments. The `lot` file is generated by the `\end{document}` command. It is written only if there is a `\listoftables` command and no `\nofiles` command.

toc Read by the `\tableofcontents` command to generate a table of contents; it contains the entries generated by all sectioning commands (except the *-forms). The `toc` file is generated by the `\end{document}` command. It is written only if there is a `\tableofcontents` command and no `\nofiles` command.

C.10.2 Cross-References

```
\label    {key}
\ref      {key}
\pageref{key}
```

The *key* argument is any sequence of letters, digits, and punctuation symbols; upper- and lowercase letters are regarded as different. LaTeX maintains a *current* `\ref` *value*, which is set with the `\refstepcounter` declaration (Section C.7.4). (This declaration is issued by the sectioning commands, by numbered environments like `equation`, and by an `\item` command in an `enumerate` environment.) The `\label` command writes an entry on the `aux` file (Section C.10.1) containing *key*, the current `\ref` value, and the number of the current page. When this `aux` file entry is read by the \begin{document} command (the next time LaTeX is run on the same input file), the \ref value and page number are associated with *key*, causing a \ref{*key*} or \pageref{*key*} command to produce the associated \ref value or page number, respectively.

These three commands are fragile. However, \label can be used in the argument of a sectioning or \caption command.

C.10.3   Bibliography and Citation

\bibliography{*bib_files*}

Used in conjunction with the BIBTEX program (Section 4.3.2) to produce a bibliography. The *bib_files* argument is a list of first names of bibliographic database (bib) files, separated by commas; these files must have the extension bib. The \bibliography command does two things: (i) it creates an entry on the aux file (Section C.10.1) containing *bib_files* that is read by BIBTEX, and (ii) it reads the bbl file (Section C.10.1) generated by BIBTEX to produce the bibliography. (The bbl file will contain a thebibliography environment.) The database files are used by BIBTEX to create the bbl file.

\begin{thebibliography}{*widest_label*}   *entries*   \end{thebibliography}

Produces a bibliography or reference list. In the article document style, this reference list is labeled "References"; in the report and book style, it is labeled "Bibliography". See Section 5.1.4 for information on how to create a document-style option to change the reference list's label.

widest_label   Text that, when printed, is approximately as wide as the widest item label produced by the \bibitem commands in *entries*. It controls the formatting.

entries   A list of entries, each begun by the command

>   \bibitem[*label*]{*cite_key*}

which generates an entry labeled by *label*. If the *label* argument is missing, a number is generated as the label, using the enumi counter. The *cite_key* is any sequence of letters, numbers, and punctuation symbols not containing a comma. This command writes an entry on the aux file (Section C.10.1) containing *cite_key* and the item's label. When this aux file entry is read by the \begin{document} command (the next time LaTeX is run on the same input file), the item's label is associated with *cite_key*, causing reference to *cite_key* by a \cite command to produce the associated label.

`\cite[`*text*`]{`*key_list*`}`

The *key_list* argument is a list of citation keys (see `\bibitem` above). This command generates an in-text citation to the references associated with the keys in *key_list* by entries on the `aux` file read by the `\begin{document}` command. It also writes *key_list* on the `aux` file, causing BⅠBTEX to add the associated references to the bibliography(Section 4.3.2). If present, *text* is added as a remark to the citation. Fragile.

`\nocite{`*key_list*`}`

Produces no text, but writes *key_list*, which is a list of one or more citation keys, on the `aux` file. This causes BⅠBTEX to add the associated references to the bibliography (Section 4.3.2). The `\nocite` command must appear after the `\begin{document}`. It is fragile.

C.10.4   Splitting the Input

`\input{`*file_name*`}`

Causes the indicated file to be read and processed, exactly as if its contents had been inserted in the current file at that point. The *file_name* may be a complete file name with extension or just a first name, in which case the file *file_name*`.tex` is used. If the file cannot be found, an error occurs and TEX requests another file name.[3]

`\include{`*file*`}`
`\includeonly{`*file_list*`}`

Used for the selective inclusion of files. The *file* argument is the first name of a file, denoting the file *file*`.tex`, and *file_list* is a possibly empty list of first names of files separated by commas. If *file* is one of the file names in *file_list* or if there is no `\includeonly` command, then the `\include` command is equivalent to

   `\clearpage \input{`*file*`} \clearpage`

except that if file *file*`.tex` does not exist, then a warning message rather than an error is produced. If *file* is not in *file_list*, the `\include` command is equivalent to `\clearpage`.

The `\includeonly` command may appear only in the preamble; the `\include` command may not appear in the preamble or in a file read by another `\include` command. Both commands are fragile.

---

[3]To maintain compatibility with plain TEX, LATEX allows you to leave out the braces around the file name in an `\input` command.

C.10.5 Index and Glossary

Producing an Index

`\begin{theindex}` *text* `\end{theindex}`

Produces a double-column index. Each entry is begun with either an `\item` command, a `\subitem` command, or a `\subsubitem` command.

Compiling the Entries

`\makeindex` Causes the `\indexentry` entries produced by `\index` commands to be written on the `idx` file, unless a `\nofiles` declaration occurs. The `\makeindex` command may appear only in the preamble.

`\makeglossary` Causes the `\glossaryentry` entries produced by `\glossary` commands to be written on the `glo` file, unless a `\nofiles` declaration occurs. The `\makeglossary` command may appear only in the preamble.

`\index{`*str*`}` If an `idx` file is being written, then this command writes an `\indexentry{`*str*`}{`*pg*`}` entry on it, where *pg* is the page number. The *str* argument may contain any characters, including special characters, but it must have no unmatched braces, where the braces in `\{` and `\}` are included in the brace matching. The `\index` command may not appear inside another command's argument unless *str* contains only letters, digits, and punctuation characters. The command is fragile.

`\glossary{`*str*`}` If a `glo` file is being written, then this command writes a `\glossaryentry{`*str*`}{`*pg*`}` entry on it, where *str* and *pg* are the same as in the `\index` command, described above. The `\glossary` command may not appear inside another command's argument unless *str* contains only letters, digits, and punctuation characters. The command is fragile.

C.10.6 Terminal Input and Output

`\typeout{`*msg*`}`

Prints *msg* on the terminal and in the `log` file. Commands in *msg* that are defined with `\newcommand` or `\renewcommand` are replaced by their definitions before being printed. LaTeX commands in *msg* may produce strange results. Preceding a command name by `\protect` causes that command name to be printed.

TeX's usual rules for treating multiple spaces as a single space and ignoring spaces after a command name apply to *msg*. A `\space` command in *msg* causes a single space to be printed. The `\typeout` command is fragile; moreover, putting it in the argument of another LaTeX command may do strange things. The *msg* argument is a moving argument.

\typein[*cmd*]{*msg*}

Prints *msg* on the terminal, just like \typeout{*msg*}, and causes TEX to stop and wait for you to type a line of input, ending with *return*. If the *cmd* argument is missing, the typed input is processed as if it had been included in the input file in place of the \typein command. If the *cmd* argument is present, it must be a command name. This command name is then defined or redefined to be the typed input. Thus, if *cmd* is not already defined, then the command acts like

    \typeout{*msg*}
    \newcommand{*cmd*}{*typed input*}

The \typein command is fragile; moreover, it may produce an error if it appears in the argument of a LATEX command. The *msg* argument is a moving argument.

C.11   Line and Page Breaking

C.11.1   Line Breaking

\linebreak   [*num*]
\nolinebreak[*num*]

The \linebreak command encourages and \nolinebreak discourages a line break, by an amount depending upon *num*, which is a digit from 0 through 4. A larger value of *num* more strongly encourages or discourages the line break; the default is equivalent to a *num* argument of 4, which either forces or completely prevents a line break. An underfull \hbox message is produced if a \linebreak command results in too much space between words on the line. Both commands are fragile.

\\[*len*]
\newline

These commands start a new line without justifying the current one, producing a "ragged right" effect. The optional argument adds an extra vertical space of length *len* above the new line. The \newline command may be used only in paragraph mode, and should appear within a paragraph; it produces an underfull \hbox warning and extra vertical space if used at the end of a paragraph, and an error when used between paragraphs. The \\ command behaves the same way when used in paragraph mode. Both commands are fragile.

\-

Permits the line to be hyphenated (the line broken and a hyphen inserted) at that point. It inhibits hyphenation at any other point in the current word except where allowed by another \- command. Robust.

`\hyphenation{`*words*`}`

Declares allowed hyphenation points, where *words* is a list of words, separated by spaces, in which each hyphenation point is indicated by a - character. It is a global declaration (Section C.1.4) and is robust.

`\sloppy`
`\fussy`

Declarations that control line breaking. The `\fussy` declaration, which is the default, prevents too much space between words, but leaves words extending past the right-hand margin if no good line break is found. The `\sloppy` declaration almost always breaks lines at the right-hand margin, but may leave too much space between words, in which case TEX produces an underfull `\hbox` warning. Line breaking is controlled by the declaration in effect at the blank line ending the paragraph.

`\begin{sloppypar}` *pars* `\end{sloppypar}`

Typesets *pars*, which must consist of one or more complete paragraphs, with the `\sloppy` declaration in effect.

C.11.2 Page Breaking

`\pagebreak` `[`*num*`]`
`\nopagebreak[`*num*`]`

The `\pagebreak` command encourages and `\nopagebreak` discourages column breaking by an amount depending upon *num*, where the entire page is a single column in a one-column page style. The *num* argument is a digit from 0 through 4, a larger value more strongly encouraging or discouraging a break; the default is equivalent to *num* having the value 4, which forces or entirely prevents a break. When used within a paragraph, these commands apply to the point immediately following the line in which they appear. When `\flushbottom` is in effect (Section 5.1.1), an underfull `\vbox` message is produced if `\pagebreak` results in too little text on the page. A `\nopagebreak` command will have no effect if another LATEX command has explicitly allowed a page break to occur at that point. Both commands are fragile.

`\samepage`

A declaration that prevents page breaks in the following places: between lines of a paragraph unit that ends within its scope, before or after a displayed equation, displayed-paragraph environment or section heading lying within its scope, or before an item in a list environment, other than the first, whose `\item` command lies within its scope—except where explicitly allowed by `\pagebreak` or `\nopagebreak` (with optional argument). A paragraph unit is any portion of text that TEX treats as a single text stream for purposes of line-breaking, so a displayed equation within a paragraph separates the paragraph into two paragraph units. The \samepage command is fragile.

```
\newpage
\clearpage
\cleardoublepage
```

When one-column pages are being produced, these commands all end the current paragraph and the current page. Any unfilled space in the body of the page (Section 5.1.2) appears at the bottom, even with \flushbottom in effect (Section 5.1.1). The \clearpage and \cleardoublepage commands also cause all figures and tables that have so far appeared in the input to be printed, using one or more pages of only figures and/or tables if necessary. In a two-sided printing style, \cleardoublepage also makes the next page a right-hand (odd-numbered) page, producing a blank page if necessary.

When two-column text is being produced, \newpage ends the current column rather than the current page; \clearpage and \cleardoublepage end the page, producing a blank right-hand column if necessary. These commands should be used only in paragraph mode; they should not be used inside a parbox (Section 5.4.3). The \newpage and \clearpage commands are robust; \cleardoublepage is fragile.

C.12   Lengths, Spaces, and Boxes

C.12.1   Length

explicit lengths An explicit length is written as an optional sign (+ or -) followed by a decimal number (a string of digits with an optional decimal point) followed by a *dimensional unit*. The following dimensional units are recognized by TEX.

cm Centimeters.

em One em is about the width of the letter M in the current font.

ex One ex is about the height of the letter x in the current font.

in Inches.

pc Picas (1pc = 12pt).

pt Points (1in = 72.27pt).

mm Millimeters.

\fill A rubber length (Section 5.4.1) having a natural length of zero and the ability to stretch to any arbitrary (positive) length. Robust.

\stretch{*dec_num*} A rubber length having zero natural length and *dec_num* times the stretchability of \fill, where *dec_num* is a signed decimal number (an optional sign followed by a string of digits with an optional decimal point). Robust.

\newlength{*cmd*} Declares *cmd* to be a length command, where *cmd* is the name of a command not already defined. The value of *cmd* is initialized to zero inches. Fragile.

\setlength{*cmd*}{*len*} Sets the value of the length command *cmd* equal to *len*. Robust.

\addtolength{*cmd*}{*len*} Sets the value of the length command *cmd* equal to its current value plus *len*. Robust.

\settowidth{*cmd*}{*text*} Sets the value of the length command *cmd* equal to the natural width of the output generated when *text* is typeset in LR mode. Robust.

C.12.2   Space

\hspace {*len*}
\hspace*{*len*}

Produce a horizontal space of width *len*. The space produced by \hspace is removed if it falls at a line break; that produced by \hspace* is not. These commands are robust.

\vspace {*len*}
\vspace*{*len*}

Add a vertical space of height *len*. If the command appears in the middle of a paragraph, then the space is added after the line containing it. The space produced by \vspace is removed if it falls at a page break; that produced by \vspace* is not. These commands may be used only in paragraph mode; they are fragile.

\bigskip
\medskip
\smallskip

These commands are equivalent to the three commands

    \vspace{\bigskipamount}   \vspace{\smallskipamount}
    \vspace{\medskipamount}

where the three length parameters \bigskipamount, \medskipamount, and \smallskipamount are determined by the document style. These space-producing commands can be used in the definitions of environments to provide standard amounts of vertical space. They are fragile.

`\addvspace{`*len*`}`

This command normally adds a vertical space of height *len*. However, if vertical space has already been added to the same point in the output by a previous `\addvspace` command, then this command will not add more space than needed to make the natural length of the total vertical space equal to *len*. It is used to add the extra vertical space above and below most LaTeX environments that start a new paragraph. It may be used only in paragraph mode between paragraphs—that is, after a blank line or `\par` command (in TeX's vertical mode). Fragile.

C.12.3 Boxes

A *box* is an object that is treated by TeX as a single character, so it will not be broken across lines or pages.

`\mbox {`*text*`}`
`\makebox [`*wdth*`][`*pos*`]{`*text*`}`

Typesets *text* in LR mode in a box. The box has the width of the typeset text except for a `\makebox` command with a *wdth* argument, in which it has width *wdth*. In the latter case, the position of the text within the box is determined by the one-letter *pos* argument as follows:

l Flush against left edge of box.

r Flush against right edge of box.

The default positioning is centered in the box. The `\mbox` command is robust; `\makebox` is fragile.

`\fbox {`*text*`}`
`\framebox [`*wdth*`][`*pos*`]{`*text*`}`

Similar to `\mbox` and `\makebox`, except that a rectangular frame is drawn around the resulting box. The `\fbox` command is robust; `\framebox` is fragile.

`\newsavebox{`*cmd*`}`

Declares *cmd*, which must be a command name that is not already defined, to be a bin for saving boxes. Fragile.

`\sbox {`*cmd*`}{`*text*`}`
`\savebox {`*cmd*`}[`*wdth*`][`*pos*`]{`*text*`}`

These commands typeset *text* in a box just as for `\mbox` or `\makebox`, respectively. However, instead of printing the resulting box, they save it in bin *cmd*, which must have been declared with `\newsavebox`. The `\sbox` command is robust; `\savebox` is fragile.

`\usebox {cmd}`

Prints the box most recently saved in bin *cmd* by a `\savebox` command. Robust.

`\parbox          [pos]{wdth}{text}`
`\begin{minipage}[pos]{wdth}   text   \end{minipage}`

They produce a *parbox*—a box of width *wdth* formed by typesetting *text* in paragraph mode. The vertical positioning of the box is specified by the one-letter *pos* argument as follows:

b The bottom line of the box is aligned with the current line of text.

t The top line of the box is aligned with the current line of text.

The default vertical positioning is to align the center of the box with the center of the current line of text.

The list-making environments listed in Section 5.7 and the `tabular` environment may appear in *text* with the `minipage` environment, but not with the `\parbox` command. A `\footnote` or `\footnotetext` command appearing in *text* in a `minipage` environment produces a footnote at the bottom of the parbox ended by the next `\end{minipage}` command, which may be the wrong place for it when there are nested `minipage` environments. These footnote-making commands may not be used in the *text* argument of `\parbox`.

A `minipage` environment that begins with a displayed equation or with an `eqnarray` or `eqnarray*` environment will have extra vertical space at the top (except with the `fleqn` document-style option). This extra space can be removed by starting *text* with a `\vspace{-\abovedisplayskip}` command.

The `\parbox` command is fragile.

`\rule[raise_len]{wdth}{hght}`

Generates a solid rectangle of width *wdth* and height *hght*, raised a distance of *raise_len* above the bottom of the line. (A negative value of *raise_len* lowers it.) The default value of *raise_len* is zero inches. Fragile.

`\raisebox {raise_len}[hght][dpth]{text}`

Creates a box by typesetting *text* in LR mode, raising it by *raise_len*, and pretending that the resulting box extends a distance of *hght* above the bottom of the current line and a distance of *dpth* below it. If the *dpth* argument or both optional arguments are omitted, TeX uses the actual extent of the box. Fragile.

Style Parameters

`\fboxrule` The width of the lines comprising the box produced by `\fbox` and `\framebox`. However, the version of `\framebox` used in the `picture` environment (Section 5.5) employs the same width lines as other picture commands.

\fboxsep The amount of space left between the edge of the box and its contents by \fbox and \framebox. It does not apply to the version of \framebox used in the picture environment (Section 5.5).

C.13   The picture Environment   ▷ 101

A *coordinate* is a decimal number—an optional sign followed by a string of digits with an optional decimal point. It represents a length in multiples of \unitlength. All argument names in this section that begin with x or y are coordinates.

\begin{picture}(*x_dimen*,*y_dimen*)(*x_offset*,*y_offset*)
    pict_cmds
\end{picture}

Creates a box of width *x_dimen* and height *y_dimen*, both of which must be non-negative. The (*x_offset*,*y_offset*) argument is optional. If present, it specifies the coordinates of the lower-left corner of the picture; if absent, the lower-left corner has coordinates $(0, 0)$. (Like all dimensions in the picture environment, the lengths specified by the arguments of the picture environment are given in multiples of \unitlength.) The picture environment can be used anywhere that ordinary text can, including within another picture environment.

The *pict_cmds* are processed in picture mode—a special form of LR mode—and may contain only \put commands, \multiput commands, and declarations. Figure C.6 illustrates many of the picture-drawing commands described below.

C.13.1   Picture-Mode Commands

The following are the only commands, other than declarations, that can be used in picture mode.

\put(*x_coord*,*y_coord*){*picture_object*}

Places *picture_object* in the picture with its reference point at the position specified by coordinates (*x_coord*,*y_coord*). The *picture_object* can be arbitrary text, which is typeset in LR mode with its lower-left corner as the reference point, or else one of the special picture-object commands described below. The \put command is fragile.

\multiput(*x_coord*,*y_coord*)(*x_incr*,*y_incr*){*num*}{*picture_object*}

Places *num* copies of *picture_object*, the ith one positioned with its reference point having coordinates $(x\_coord + [i - 1]x\_incr, y\_coord + [i - 1]y\_incr)$. The

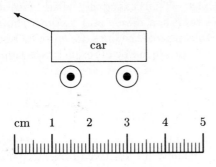

```
\newcounter{cms}
. . .
\setlength{\unitlength}{1mm}
\begin{picture}(50,39)
\put(0,7){\makebox(0,0)[bl]{cm}}
\multiput(10,7)(10,0){5}{\addtocounter
        {cms}{1}\makebox(0,0)[b]{\arabic{cms}}}
\put(15,20){\circle{6}}
\put(30,20){\circle{6}}
\put(15,20){\circle*{2}}
\put(30,20){\circle*{2}}
\put(10,24){\framebox(25,8){car}}
\put(10,32){\vector(-2,1){10}}
\multiput(1,0)(1,0){49}{\line(0,1){2.5}}
\multiput(5,0)(10,0){5}{\line(0,1){3.5}}
\thicklines
\put(0,0){\line(1,0){50}}
\multiput(0,0)(10,0){6}{\line(0,1){5}}
\end{picture}
```

Figure C.6: A sample picture environment.

picture_object is the same as for the \put command above. It is typeset *num* times, so the copies need not be identical if it includes declarations. (See Figure C.6.) Fragile.

C.13.2 Picture Objects

\makebox (*x_dimen*, *y_dimen*) [*pos*] {*text*}
\framebox(*x_dimen*, *y_dimen*) [*pos*] {*text*}
\dashbox {*dash_dimen*}(*x_dimen*, *y_dimen*) [*pos*] {*text*}

Produce a box having width *x_dimen* and height *y_dimen* (in multiples of \unitlength) with reference point at its lower-left corner. The *text* is typeset in LR mode, positioned in the box as specified by the one- or two-letter *pos* argument as follows:

l Horizontally positioned flush against the left edge of the box.

r Horizontally positioned flush against the right edge of the box.

t Vertically positioned flush against the top edge of the box.

b Vertically positioned flush against the bottom edge of the box.

The default horizontal and vertical positioning is to center *text* in the box. The \framebox command also draws a rectangle showing the edges of the box, and \dashbox draws the rectangle with dashed lines, composed of dashes and spaces of length *dash_dimen* (in multiples of \unitlength), where *dash_dimen* is a positive decimal number. For best results, *x_dimen* and *y_dimen* should be integral multiples of *dash_dimen*. The thickness of the lines drawn by \framebox and \dashbox equals the width of the lines produced by other picture commands; it is not determined by \fboxrule. All three commands are fragile.

\line   (*h_slope*, *v_slope*){*dimen*}
\vector(*h_slope*, *v_slope*){*dimen*}

Draw a line having its reference point at the beginning and its slope determined by (*h_slope*, *v_slope*), where *h_slope* and *v_slope* are positive or negative integers of magnitude at most 6 for \line and at most 4 for \vector, with no common divisors except ±1. In addition, \vector draws an arrowhead at the opposite end of the line from the reference point. The horizontal extent of the line is *dimen* (in multiples of \unitlength) unless *h_slope* is zero, in which case *dimen* is the (vertical) length of the line. However, a line that is neither horizontal nor vertical may not be drawn unless *dimen* times \unitlength is at least 10 points (1/7 inch). The \vector command always draws the arrowhead. Both commands are fragile.

\shortstack [*pos*]{*col*}

The *pos* argument must be either l, r, or c, the default being equivalent to c. This command produces the same result as

\begin{tabular}[b]{*pos*} *col* \end{tabular}

(Section 3.6.2) except that no space is left on either side of the resulting box and there is usually less interrow space. The reference point is the lower-left corner of the box. Fragile.

\circle {*diam*}
\circle*{*diam*}

Draw a (hollow) circle and a disk (filled circle), respectively, with diameter as close as possible to *diam* times \unitlength and reference point in the center of the circle. The largest circle LaTeX can draw has a diameter of 40 points (about 1/2 inch) and the largest disk has a diameter of 15 points (about .2 inch). Both commands are fragile.

\oval(*x_dimen*, *y_dimen*) [*part*]

Draws an oval inscribed in a rectangle of width *x_dimen* and height *y_dimen*, its corners made with quarter circles of the largest possible diameter. The reference point is the center of the (complete) oval. The *part* argument consists of one or two of the following letters to specify a half or quarter oval: l (left), r (right), t (top), b (bottom). The default is to draw the entire oval. Fragile.

`\frame{`*picture_object*`}`

Puts a rectangular frame around *picture_object*. The reference point is the bottom left corner of the frame. No extra space is put between the frame and *picture_object*. Fragile.

C.13.3 Picture Declarations

The following declarations can appear anywhere in the document, including in picture mode. They obey the normal scope rules.

`\savebox{`*cmd*`}(`*x_dimen*`,`*y_dimen*`)[`*pos*`]{`*text*`}`

Same as the corresponding `\makebox` command, except the resulting box is saved in the bin *cmd*, which must be defined with `\newsavebox` (Section 5.4.3). Fragile.

`\thinlines`
`\thicklines`

They select one of the two standard thicknesses of lines and circles in the `picture` environment. The default is `\thinlines`. Robust.

`\linethickness{`*len*`}`

Declares the thickness of horizontal and vertical lines in a `picture` environment to be *len*, which must be a positive length. It does not affect the thickness of slanted lines and circles, or of the quarter circles drawn by `\oval` to form the corners of an oval.

C.14 Font Selection

C.14.1 Changing the Type Style

The following declarations select the indicated type style.

`\rm`	Roman	`\it`	*Italic*	`\sc`	SMALL CAPS
`\em`	*Emphatic*	`\sl`	*Slanted*	`\tt`	Typewriter
`\bf`	**Bold**	`\sf`	Sans Serif		

If a type style is not available in the current size, the declaration chooses a substitute style and prints a warning message on the terminal. See Section C.14.4 below for restrictions on the use of these commands in math mode. These commands are all robust. Words typeset in `\tt` style or in two different styles are not hyphenated except where permitted by `\-` commands.

C.14.2   Changing the Type Size

The following declarations select a type size and also select the roman style of that size. They are listed in nondecreasing size; two of the declarations may have the same effect in some document styles.

```
\tiny              \small            \large          \huge
\scriptsize        \normalsize       \Large          \Huge
\footnotesize                        \LARGE
```

These commands may not be used in math mode; they are all fragile.

C.14.3   Loading Fonts   *p116*

\newfont{*cmd*}{*font_name*}

Defines the command name *cmd*, which must not be currently defined, to be a declaration that selects the font named *font_name* to be the current font. The newly-defined *cmd* command is robust, but it cannot be used in math mode. The \newfont command is fragile.

\symbol{*num*}

Chooses the symbol with number *num* from the current font. Octal (base 8) and hexadecimal (base 16) numbers are preceded by ' and ", respectively. Robust.

C.14.4   Fonts in Math Mode

LaTeX allows ten different sizes and eight different styles of type, including math italic (Section 3.3.8). To each of these eighty size/style combinations corresponds a separate font. These fonts are divided into three classes: *preloaded, loaded on demand*, and *unavailable*. The *Local Guide* tells you to which category each font belongs. When an unavailable font is requested, another one, which may be preloaded or loaded on demand, is substituted for it and a warning message printed on the terminal. Preloaded and loaded-on-demand fonts act the same when used in paragraph and LR mode, but differ in math mode.

A size/style combination that corresponds to a loaded-on-demand font may not work right when used in math mode, either printing the wrong size characters or not printing any characters and generating one of the following error messages:

```
! \textfont          ... is undefined (character ...).
! \scriptfont        ... is undefined (character ...).
! \scriptscriptfont ... is undefined (character ...).
```

The rules describing exactly when this problem will occur are complicated, but the solution is simple: use a command of the form

    \load{*size*}{*style*}

where *size* is a size-changing command and *style* is the type-style command that together specify the desired font. The `\load` command should come before the first use of the font in math mode, and should not be inside braces or an environment.

This proves that $\mathsf{xt} > 7$ in all cases.[5]

⋮

_____

[5] Remember that xyt^2 is odd.

```
This proves that ${\sf xt}>7$ in all
\load{\footnotesize}{\sf}
cases.\footnote{Remember that
${\sf xyt}^{2}$ is odd.}
```

In math mode, there are four math styles: *display*, *text*, *script*, and *scriptscript*. Display and text styles differ mainly in the size of the symbols in Table 3.8 (page 45) and in the placement of subscripts on some symbols and on the log-like functions in Table 3.9 (page 46). The script style is used for sub- and superscripts and the scriptscript style for further levels of sub- and superscripting.

Each type style/size combination requires three fonts in math mode: one for display and text style, one for script style, and one for scriptscript style. Ideally, these fonts should be of different size, except when this would result in a font too small to read. However, the choice of fonts is restricted in LaTeX by two rules: (i) only preloaded fonts can be used in script and scriptscript style, and (ii) a style/size combination corresponding to a loaded-on-demand font uses the same font for all math styles. This means that subscripts and superscripts may be typeset in too large a font for some style/size combinations.

```
\displaystyle
\textstyle
\scriptstyle
\scriptscriptstyle
```

These declarations choose the indicated math style. They are robust.

```
\boldmath
\unboldmath
```

The `\boldmath` declaration selects a bold math italic font and bold math symbol fonts. This causes letters, numbers and most symbols used in math mode to be set in bold type, including Greek letters, calligraphic letters (selected by `\cal`), and the symbols in Tables 3.4–3.7 (pages 44–45). However, symbols made by combining two other symbols, such as $\Longrightarrow$ (`\Longrightarrow`), which is made from $=$ and $\Rightarrow$, may produce incorrect results. The following are not emboldened by `\boldmath`.

- Text (usually subscripts and superscripts) typeset in script or scriptscript style.

- Text produced by the following input characters:

$$+ \quad : \quad ; \quad ! \quad ? \quad (\quad) \quad [\quad]$$

- The variable-sized symbols of Table 3.8 (page 45).

- Large delimiters produced with \left and \right. However, normal-sized delimiters other than parentheses and square brackets produced by \left and \right are made bold.

The \unboldmath declaration undoes the effect of \boldmath. Neither command may be used in math mode. They are both fragile.

APPENDIX D
Using Plain T_EX Commands

LATₑX is implemented as a TₑX "macro package"—a series of predefined TₑX commands. Plain TₑX is the standard version of TₑX, consisting of "raw" TₑX plus the `plain` macro package. Most Plain TₑX commands can be used in LATₑX, but only with care. LATₑX is designed so its commands fit together as a single system. Many compromises have been made to ensure that a command will work properly when used in any reasonable way with other LATₑX commands. A LATₑX command may not work properly when used with Plain TₑX commands not described in this book.

There is no easy way to tell whether a Plain TₑX command will cause trouble, other than by trying it. A general rule is not to combine a LATₑX command or environment with Plain TₑX commands that might modify parameters it uses. For example, don't use a Plain TₑX command such as `\hangindent` that modifies TₑX's paragraph-making parameters inside one of LATₑX's list-making environments.

You should not modify any parameters that are used by LATₑX's `\output` routine, except as specified in this book. In particular, you should forget about most of Chapter 15 of *The TₑXbook*. However, LATₑX does obey all of TₑX's conventions for the allocation of registers, so you can define your own counts, boxes, etc., with ordinary TₑX commands.

Below are listed all the Plain TₑX commands whose definitions have been eliminated or changed in LATₑX. Not listed are LATₑX commands that approximate the corresponding Plain TₑX versions, and some "internal" commands whose names contain @ characters.

Tabbing Commands

The following commands are made obsolete by LATₑX's `tabbing` environment.

| `\tabs` | `\tabsdone` | `\settabs` | `\+` |
| `\tabset` | `\cleartabs` | `\tabalign` | |

Output, Footnotes, and Figures

The following commands that require Plain TₑX's output routine are obsolete. They are replaced by LATₑX's footnote-making commands and its `figure` and `table` environments.

`\pageno`	`\nopagenumbers`	`\makeheadline`	`\footstrut`
`\headline`	`\advancepageno`	`\makefootline`	`\topins`
`\footline`	`\nopagenumbers`	`\dosupereject`	`\topinsert`
`\normalbottom`	`\plainoutput`	`\pagecontents`	`\midinsert`
`\folio`	`\pagebody`	`\vfootnote`	`\pageinsert`
			`\endinsert`

Font-Selecting Commands

The following Plain TEX commands are not defined in LATEX. See the file `lfonts.tex` to find the corresponding LATEX commands.

`\fivei`	`\fivebf`	`\sevensy`
`\fiverm`	`\seveni`	`\teni`
`\fivesy`	`\sevenbf`	`\oldstyle`

Consult the Plain TEX definition of `\oldstyle` to understand how to obtain its effects in LATEX.

Aligned Equations

The following Plain TEX commands are made obsolete by LATEX's `eqnarray` and `eqnarray*` environments.

`\eqalign` `\eqalignno` `\leqalignno`

Miscellaneous

Plain TEX's `\beginsection` command is replaced by LATEX's sectioning commands; its `\end` and `\bye` commands are replaced by `\end{document}`. The Plain TEX commands `\centering` and `\line` have had their names usurped by LATEX commands. Most functions performed by Plain TEX's `\line` command can be achieved by the `center`, `flushleft`, and `flushright` environments. The `\magnification` command of Plain TEX has no counterpart in LATEX. Magnification of the output can often be done by the program that prints the `dvi` file.

Bibliography

[1] Theodore M. Bernstein. *The Careful Writer: A Modern Guide to English Usage.* Atheneum, New York, 1965.

[2] *The Chicago Manual of Style.* University of Chicago Press, thirteenth edition 1982.

[3] Donald E. Knuth. *The TEXbook.* Addison-Wesley, Reading, Massachusetts, 1984.

[4] N. E. Steenrod, P. R. Halmos, M. M. Schiffer, and J. A. Dieudonné. *How to Write Mathematics.* American Mathematical Society, 1983.

[5] William Strunk, Jr. and E. B. White. *The Elements of Style.* The Macmillan Company, New York, 1979.

[6] Unilogic, Ltd. *Scribe Document Production System User Manual.* April 1984.

[7] Mary-Claire van Leunen. *A Handbook for Scholars.* Alfred A. Knopf, New York, 1979.

[8] *Words Into Type.* Prentice-Hall, Inc., Englewood Cliffs, New Jersey, third edition 1974.

Index

margins of nested lists, 114

mark, footnote, 156

mark, question (?), 34

mark, quotation, 13, 34

\markboth, 84, 161
   not used in slides document style, 138
   moving arguments of, 152

\markright, 84, 161
   in myheadings page style, 83, 161
   not used in slides style, 138
   moving argument of, 152

mastersthesis bibliography entry type, 145

matching, brace, 17

math
   accents, 51
   environment, 20, 41, 169
   formula, *see* formula
   italic, 53, 172, 200
   mode, 38, 41
      ' in, 170
      accents in, 51, 172
      bold letters in, 201
      changing type style in, 53
      environments, 169
      entering, 38
      leaving, 38
      loaded-on-demand font in, 200
      spaces ignored in, 38, 52
      unmatched delimiter, 124
   notation, 54
   style, 54, 172, 201
      display, 54, 169, 201
      for displayed formula, 54, 172
      for in-text formula, 172
      for sub- and superscripts, 54, 172
      of array items, 172
      scriptscript, 54, 201
      script, 54, 201
      text, 54, 169, 201
   symbols, 42ff
      bold, 53, 201
      variable-sized, 44

mathematical, *see* math

\mathindent, 161, 170

matrix, 47

matter, front, 133

\max (max), 46
   subscript of, 171

\mbox, 18, 34, 53, 97, 154, 194
   empty, 91
   for font selection and size changing in formula, 116
   for multicolored formula, 136
   how it works, 38
   in formula, 40, 41
   use in defining commands, 55

medium space, 52

\medskip, 193

\medskipamount, 193

memory size, 126

message
   generating, 79, 189
   LaTeX error, 120
   LaTeX warning, 128
   TeX error, 123
   TeX warning, 129
   warning, 31

\mho (℧), 45

\mid (|), 44

\midinsert (TeX command), 204

millimeter (mm), 93, 192

\min (min), 46
   subscript of, 171

minimum size of slanted line, 106

minipage environment, 98, 99, 195
   footnote counter for, 91
   footnote in, 156, 195
   \footnote in, 99, 195
   \footnotetext in, 195
   in p-column, 183
   nested, 99
   tabbing environment in, 100

minus sign, 14

misc bibliography entry type, 145

misplaced
   #, 128
   &, 124
   alignment tab error, 124
   \documentstyle, 120
   figure environment, 121, 122
   \includeonly, 120
   \makeglossary, 120